D0427348

I'm No Saint

I'm No Saint

A NASTY LITTLE MEMOIR OF LOVE AND LEAVING

Elizabeth Hayt

WARNER BOOKS

NEW YORK   BOSTON

Permission to reprint excerpts from the following original sources is gratefully acknowledged: "For Stylish Orthodox Women, Wigs That Aren't Wiggy," *The New York Times*, April 27, 1997 © 1997, by The New York Times Co. Reprinted with permission. "Sprucing Up for the Holidays: It's a Mitzvah," *The New York Times*, September 20, 1998 © 1998, by The New York Times Co. Reprinted with permission. "Fear of Fashion: An Art Historian's Battle with Repressed Desire," *The New York Times*, December 27, 1998 © 1998, by The New York Times Co. Reprinted with permission. "Pretty Poison," *Vogue*, February 1998. Reprinted with permission. "Lift Off," *Vogue*, December 1998. Reprinted with permission. "Merchant of Paris," *Vogue*, July 1997. Reprinted with permission.

The names and identifying characteristics of certain individuals portrayed in this book have been changed to protect their privacy and the privacy of their families.

Warner Books

Time Warner Book Group
1271 Avenue of the Americas, New York, NY 10020
Visit our Web site at www.twbookmark.com.

Printed in the United States of America

First Edition: October 2005
10 9 8 7 6 5 4 3 2 1

Library of Congress Cataloging-in-Publication Data
Hayt, Elizabeth.
   I'm no saint : a nasty little memoir of love and leaving / Elizabeth Hayt.— 1st ed.
     p. cm.
   ISBN 0-446-53194-4
   1. Women—Sexual behavior.   2. Man-woman relationships.   3. Self-actualization
(Psychology)   4. Women radicals—United States—Biography.   I. Title.
   HQ29.H395 2005
   306.81'0973—dc22   2005014833

Book design by Giorgetta Bell McRee

To my beloved Bobby and Hunter

Acknowledgments

My deepest thanks to:

My parents and brothers for their love, loyalty, tolerance, and fodder. In particular, my mother for teaching me that self-expression is *not* the same as self-indulgence. My father, a role model of perseverance, who instilled in me the value of a hard day's work. My brothers for always staying on my case and never letting me take myself too seriously.

Baree Fehrenbach for a lifetime of friendship and madcap memories. Peggy Schneider for keeping me real. My sister-in-law, Jacqueline, for being so much more—a best friend.

Susan Kandel for her compassion and advice.

Daniel Greenberg, my agent, a man with a vision who made the magic happen; Laurence Kirshbaum, Chairman of Time Warner Book Group, who rooted for me from the start and offered endless faith, encouragement, and guidance; Caryn Karmatz Rudy, my editor, whose good cheer is exceeded only by her keen mind; Diane Luger, executive art director, for putting up with me; and Linda Cowen for her legal—and literary—counsel.

My friends and acquaintances who acted as editors, contributors, sounding boards, consultants, therapists, publicists, assistants, and cheerleaders, including Helene Verin, Jackie Greenberg, Tiffany Dubin, Ellen Tien, Elizabeth Beier, Deborah Michel, Susanna Rubin, Robin Zendell, Regina Blackmon, Peter Lunenfeld, Mark Garrison, Stuart Bagus, Scott Carlson, Stanley Pottinger, Richard Bradley, Robert Rosenblum, Ryder Ripps, Jeffrey Kalinsky, Brad Katchen, and Don Purcell, not to mention Don at the Westside

Deli in East Quogue, all the salespeople on "my strip," and the staff of my apartment building, who kept at me to finish this book.

Diane Rudolph and Alan Manevitz for trying to keep my head screwed on straight during the process.

Trip Gabriel and Joni Evans for their early support.

Fabrizio Ferri and Industria for their glorious work.

Franci Rivera and Miriam Correa for minding the fort, as well as Larry Reznick, the most reliable computer guy ever.

Cadbury Adams, manufacturers of Chiclets peppermint gum, for alleviating my oral fixation.

My faithful, four-legged companions, Marilyn, Joe, and Jackie, for making my job a lot less lonely.

My son who is the most understanding, insightful, and decent human being I know—and not just because I'm his mother.

Bobby for his bottomless heart.

NAMELESS PAIN

I should be happy with my lot:
A wife and mother—is it not
Enough for me to be content?
What other blessing could be sent?

A quiet house, and homely ways,
That make each day like other days;
I only see Time's shadow now
Darken the hair on baby's brow!

No world's work ever comes to me,
No beggar brings his misery;
I have no power, no healing art
With bruisèd soul or broken heart.

I read the poets of an age,
'Tis lotus-eating in a cage;
I study Art, but Art is dead
To one who clamors to be fed

With milk from Nature's rugged breast,
Who longs for Labor's lusty rest.
O foolish wish! I still should pine
If any other lot were mine.

—*Elizabeth Drew Barstow Stoddard*
  (1823–1902)

CHAPTER 1

ON AN AUGUST MORNING IN 1986, I stepped down the aisle to "Here Comes the Bride" and walked the plank. Instead of a sword against my back, prodding me to take the plunge, it was my father at my side, gripping my elbow as I clutched a bouquet of white roses, rouged cheeks pulled taut, a perma-smile tacked across my face.

A few hours earlier, I had performed cunnilingus on one of my bridesmaids, Cathy. On the eve of my wedding, she and I had spent the night in Great Neck, in the house where I'd grown up, sharing my girlhood bedroom decorated with 1970s yellow plastic furniture, *A Chorus Line* posters, and hand-painted ceramic cats. While Cathy was in a sleeping bag on the cherry-red shag carpeting, I tossed and turned in my bed. At dawn, I stripped naked, slid beside her, and parted the strawberry-blond-haired lips of her vagina. Lifting her head from her pillow, she looked at me lynx-eyed. "Better get it out of your system now," she said, grinning.

That was my last gasp of freedom before taking my vows. I wasn't a lesbian or bisexual—I preferred cock to cooch. I was simply experimenting. I didn't know who I was, only that, as a twenty-five-year-old woman, I was just beginning to develop a taste for adventure. Trying out new opportunities and testing my limits. Now, with the arrival of The Big Day, I was supposed to gladly put that research and curiosity behind me. Instead, it felt like the start of a very long long prison sentence.

My mother stood at the end of the aisle under a white lattice canopy woven with pink gerberas and spider lilies. I could always count on her to save me, but not now. Today she was acting the Jewish ur-mother, eyes brimming, hand patting her fluttering heart. My two younger brothers, Warren, twenty-three, and Andrew, twenty-two, flanked her, looking uncomfortable, their rented black-and-gray morning suits stiff like plaster body casts. I had one more year of graduate school to go, not a bit too young to get married. My mother had told me the best time to find a man was in college. After that, a girl's chances dried up. It didn't matter that my mother also confessed she wished she hadn't married so young, at twenty-three. A greater loss would be to pass up a young man like Charlie.

"We're all smitten with him," she said. "He's real and he treats you well, better than all the others we've seen."

My friends were more understanding about my reluctance. Andee, my best friend from Great Neck, was a photographer's stylist who had gotten married two months before me and moved into a West Broadway loft with her new husband. All my life I envied her. We were the same age and had grown up a mile apart. While I had always been on the puny side, my grandmother called her "a tall drink of water." By the time Andee was thirteen, she had nearly reached her full height of five foot ten, with legs so long they came up to my waist and a rack to rival a Playmate of the Year's. After five minutes in the sun, her skin was as brown as a bottle of Hawaiian Tropic Oil. Honey blond and coy, she attracted a flock of boys who circled her like vultures. I, on the other hand— flat, freckled, and brunette—was told I talked too much.

Andee's husband, Paul, was now in business school. At her bridal shower, she and I had sneaked into the bathroom so she could smoke a Marlboro Light. She plunked down on the edge of the bathtub, her head in her hands.

"I don't want to get married," she confessed. "That's why I've been engaged for a year and a half. I'm, like, not ready. I was content with my life the way it was, working freelance, going from boyfriend to boyfriend, living in my own apartment on Grove Street. In my heart, I don't want to do this, but I think I'm supposed to. My mother is, like, encouraging it. Paul is the most substantial guy I've met, and he loves me."

Now I, too, was about to marry a decent Jewish guy with a promising future who also loved me. My mother was filled with pride, and, in anticipation of her day of glory as the mother-of-the-bride, had undergone a face-lift. She had also been on a starvation diet so she would fit into her new, size 6, Emanuel Ungaro raspberry silk dress, which revealed not only her nipped waistline but plenty of cleavage as well. I barely recognized her. Normally she dressed like a rumpled artist in a paint-splattered work shirt.

The groom's parents stood glumly on the opposite side of the canopy. Charlie's father was a Westchester accountant renowned for his ability to concoct tax shelters. He had socked away enough money to afford a new car every two years and provide his wife with a fur wardrobe—minks, foxes, and a spectacular chinchilla—as well as enough jewelry to make the windows of Fortunoff look as if they'd been looted. But the finery was just for show. At heart, Charlie's parents were budget-minded and simple. Nothing made them happier than receiving a greeting card on Groundhog Day.

I got the sense that Charlie's parents didn't like me. Perhaps they thought I would pressure their son to provide me with a lifestyle beyond his means. His mother would look me up and down and I would imagine her thinking: *Pretty fancy girl wearing Kenzo and not even out of grad school.* It felt like a dig every time they ticked off their other daughter-in-law's achievements: Law degree! Master's in international relations! In-house counsel at a national shipping company! Stock options!

A wedding was supposed to be the happiest moment of a girl's life, the day she dreams of since her first bridal Barbie. But that

August morning, nothing was turning out right. The sky was a noxious shade of gray-green, and the clouds rumbled with thunder as an electrical storm brewed. A makeup artist caked my face with alabaster foundation, painted my lips crimson, and applied a thick coat of black liquid liner to my lids. I looked like a geisha.

In preparation for taking my vows, I had taken a squirt of Binaca peppermint breath spray but, because my hand was jittery, missed my mouth and instead spritzed my eyeball. My eye felt as if it had been doused with lighter fluid and started watering uncontrollably. My geisha face was now running down my neck. A blushing bride I was not.

I was no longer on speaking terms with Andee. I had asked her to be my maid of honor and wear a Betsey Johnson pink lace dress, the color of Pepto-Bismol, like my other bridesmaids. She refused, or rather her mother did, convincing her daughter it was a waste to spend money—$350 to be exact, plus another $75 for a crinoline—on a shade she would never wear again. She was willing to buy the dress but only in white, which her mother insisted would be more versatile. I said no dice. Only the bride could be in white. If Andee didn't agree to wear pink, she couldn't be in the wedding party. Fine, she huffed. Then she went ahead, bought the dress in white, and wore it to my wedding out of spite.

I had been fantasizing about my gown since elementary school, when I would sketch in the margins of my composition books little tiara-topped brides in Cinderella skirts, Empire waists, high Victorian necks, or plunging décolletés. The version that I wound up with—a white silk taffeta confection with pouf sleeves, a bow-trimmed neckline, lace bodice, and six-foot train—was the dress of the moment, a knockoff of Lady Di's. The Princess of Wales and I were nearly the same age and, although her fairy-tale marriage was already fraying by the time mine came around, when I spotted a copy of her dress at Bergdorf's it conjured all kinds of romantic fantasies. Charlie was going to be my prince and we would live happily-ever-after in a manse trimmed and tasseled by a professional decorator where we would entertain and breed well. When my mother saw the two-thousand-dollar price tag of the dress, she vetoed it until we saw the design again for half the cost at Klein-feld, a discount bridal shop in Brooklyn.

The entire wedding was an exercise in cutting corners. I wanted to be married at a swank hotel in Manhattan, like the Plaza or Pierre, even if it meant settling for a bare-bones cocktail party with pigs-in-a-blanket and cheese puffs. My mother wouldn't have it.

"Think of Aunt Ruth and Uncle Norm," she said.

They liked ballroom dancing on cruise ships. Uncle Norm dyed his hair shoe-polish black, and Aunt Ruth wore false eyelashes that he glued on for her. How could we ask them to travel all the way from Boca for an affair and not give them a sit-down dinner? But a wedding at the Plaza? Who were we, the Rockefellers? My mother opted for more bang for the buck and chose the Garden City Hotel, the best that Long Island had to offer.

My father was a radiologist but, being on a hospital salary in the Bronx, he wasn't rolling in dough. Although I was his only daughter, he squabbled with my mother about the cost of my wedding, which resulted in my firsthand knowledge of the expression "Cheap is expensive in the end."

Take the flowers. My mother and I spent several Saturdays studying arrangements at floral shops on Long Island's South Shore. We decided on a big name in Cedarhurst, forking over a deposit. Two weeks before the wedding, my mother's best friend told her she had just been to a bar mitzvah with centerpieces by our florist. They were pathetic, the withered blooms dropping all over the tables. My mother panicked. What would everyone say if my wedding turned out to be a funeral of flowers? My solution? Forfeit the deposit and sign on the florist's rival. My mother agreed: Better to lose the five hundred dollars than the freesias. We hired the competition but that wasn't the last of the original con-tender. He smacked my mother with a lawsuit, and she was even-tually forced to pay the balance of the bill. Plus damages.

Then there was the photographer, a woman recommended to me by another Great Neck girl, part of the local stampede to the altar. Since her wedding was tasteful but hardly extravagant, I figured she had found an affordable, yet talented photographer. I gave my mother the go-ahead to hire the woman, but we never bothered to check out her work. Her style turned out to be candid camera: lopsided shots of guests with wind-tunnel expressions and their hands cropped out of the picture, making them seem like amputees. The pictures of me were no better. I appeared to be a stroke victim, with either one eye closed or my pink tongue glistening at the side of my mouth.

One year after I got married, my mother took me to Bachrach Studios in Manhattan where another hairdresser and makeup artist were waiting for me. (The ones who had done me up for my real wedding day were both dead of AIDS by then.) We unpacked my gown from the dry cleaner's storage box, and I clasped a fresh bouquet of white roses, posing for a new set of pictures, pretending to be a bride-to-be rather than the wife I already was, with my natural flowing brunette hair now cut into a Donna Reed bob, artificially brightened with blond streaks.

The highlight of this circus of appearances was the walk down the aisle itself. My father paused to lift my veil and tenderly kiss me on the cheek before handing me over to the groom. The whole ritual of giving the bride away was a joke. I figured my father was so happy to get rid of me, he'd kick up his heels and dance between the rows of guests, singing, *"Heaven, I'm in heaven . . ."* During the reception, he pulled a pocket calculator out of his morning coat and took Charlie aside. Punching in several figures, my father showed the tally to my new husband and said, "That's how much money you'll save me once she's off my payroll. Thanks."

Did I come with a dowry of kitchen appliances, too?

Watching their feudal exchange, I wondered how the hell I'd wound up here. One year earlier, I had entered an art history graduate program at New York University's Institute of Fine Arts. I roomed with Jessica, a fat banker suffering from severe adult acne, who'd placed an ad in the *Village Voice* looking for someone to share her railroad studio on York Avenue. I stayed because the rent was affordable—six hundred dollars a month—the maximum my father agreed to.

After my second semester, my parents announced they were cutting the cord, severing me from financial support. I would have to get a job and pay my own rent. Now plenty of students do it but, being from Great Neck where *poor* was considered a four-letter word, I panicked. Entry-level art world jobs paid minimum wage, and I had at least one more year before completing my master's—and plenty more if I were to continue for a doctorate. How would I make enough to cover the cost of housing and finish school before memory loss set in?

Let's face it. I was a turbo-JAP who foresaw the worst: becoming a squatter in Alphabet City living without electricity, spending the next twenty years completing my higher education by candlelight. My parents offered an alternative. I could marry Charlie and, while he was in law school and I grad school, our fathers would split the tab. There would be no worry about creature comforts, let alone the Con Ed bill.

"Did Mom and Dad also tell you you'd have to get a job to pay your rent?" I asked my brother Warren. "Because they told me I have to, otherwise I've got to get married."

Now in his second year of dental school at Boston University, Warren was planning on a maxillofacial surgery residency before continuing on to medical school—a decade of postgraduate studies that my parents had no complaints about funding.

"Maybe they don't see you going anywhere," he said with a shrug. "That was a nudge. Get a job. Be an adult. Stop mooching. They're pushing you out of the nest. What are you going to do with an art history degree anyway?"

He had a point. I had chosen art history because my mother and

Charlie encouraged it. My college courses had been inspiring and I could always teach—if it came to that. With the pressure on, I gave Charlie The Ultimatum.

"What am I supposed to do?" he said. "Ask you to marry me?"

Satisfied by that most unromantic of proposals, I said "Yes."

As a liberal young couple, Charlie and I arranged to have an unconventional ceremony: a lesbian rabbi would marry us. We assumed she'd be on our wavelength when we said we didn't want a traditional Jewish wedding with Hebrew prayers and yarmulkes. We wanted to keep it simple and secular, a brief pledge to love each other till death do us part.

Once we were under the canopy, our lefty rabbi turned Lubavitch on us. She started speaking in the language of the Israelites, quoting King Solomon, and explaining the Talmudic symbolism of everything from the canopy to the hair on my head. Suddenly, it seemed as if God had thrown a switch, igniting the electrical storm. Bolts of lightning crackled outside. The stormy weather so inspired the rabbi, she had a spontaneous vision: Our wedding was nothing less than a symbol of Israel's union with God when the Hebrews received the Torah at Sinai surrounded by fire and flashes of light.

Here we were at the Garden City Hotel, a splashy marble-and-glass four-star property with valet parking, breath mints at the concierge's desk, and the faint odor of chlorine from the indoor pool wafting through the sanitized air. *This* the rabbi was comparing to the sacred desert?

Finally, it was time for Charlie to smash the wedding glass. According to custom, the groom was supposed to wrap the goblet in a napkin, place it on the ground, and give it a resounding stamp. Either his timing was off or the glass was at the wrong angle but the thing didn't break. Instead of cries of "Mazel tov" filling the room, all you could hear was Charlie's lone voice, "Holy shit."

Eventually, we said "I do"—at least, I thought that's what it meant when the rabbi told us to repeat after her in Hebrew. When

Charlie and I finally kissed, you could feel the canopy heave as the wedding party breathed a collective sigh of relief. We were husband and wife.

But what I felt was a far cry from release. I had a lump in my throat and was holding back tears. My childhood was over. Great Neck might not have been Mayberry but all I wanted was to turn back time, go home, and give myself a Tinkerbell manicure.

From start to finish, the wedding reception was a complete blur, a moving image of hors d'oeuvre platters, table-hopping, and great-aunts recounting how the last time they saw me, my hair was in pigtails. During the horah, Charlie and I were hoisted into the air on banquet chairs that tipped from side to side, like ships rolling on ocean swells. We gripped the edges for dear life while the mad frenzy of guests circled us. Although Charlie appeared both wide-eyed and delighted by all the attention, I flinched every time the shutter clicked, capturing the Kodak moments.

I was buzzing from the disappearing acts I'd made to the powder room with my bridesmaids to snort toot on the porcelain toilet tank. Squeezed into a single stall, they did their best to pep me up.

"Charlie's an idealist," said Cathy. "He makes you laugh. He's high-spirited and smart."

I had known Cathy since my junior year at Barnard. We first met in a dorm where she was eating cold peas from a can for breakfast, wearing a metallic blue raincoat, black micro miniskirt, and bronze pumps. She was tiny, smaller than me, but very bosomy. With her flaming red hair, frosted eye makeup, and hurried manner, she appeared a fiery sprite who looked so glamorous, I assumed she'd grown up in "The City," as we Great Neckers referred to Manhattan. No, she said, Lubbock, where she was raised a Southern Baptist, the youngest of six kids, all of whom played the guitar in church during Sunday hymns, and went to parochial school in a green-and-navy-checked uniform.

During my senior year, I moved to Paris to write my thesis.

Cathy was already living there, attending an international business school. When she had a free weekend, we spent it together, a pair of single American girls. One night, we went to see the Béjart Ballet at l'Opéra, met a couple of French guys, got sloshed on red wine, and had a foursome. What a memory—an up-close view of my friend being fucked from behind.

Back in the Garden City Hotel bathroom, another one of my bridesmaids, Susan, offered her support for Charlie. "He's a really good person," she said. "He'll be a good father to your children. You can be proud to be married to such a man. He doesn't try to change you."

Susan and I had become friends in graduate school. Auburn-haired, green-eyed, and six feet tall, she was the most composed woman I had ever met, never overreacting, swearing, or sleeping around, though totally nonjudgmental about those who did. I liked her immediately. She dressed up for class—fuchsia lipstick, Yves Saint Laurent jumpsuits, cinch belts around her wasp waist, and four-inch spike heels with ankle straps. We were united in our contempt for a dykey-looking student who wore cat-eye glasses and had a dark, fuzzy upper lip, calling her The Troll, and another with a vertical shaft of black wiry hair whom we named Nefertiti Head.

After the first year, Susan and I were each granted summer travel fellowships and together went to southern France. I was awestruck by everything: the silvery olive trees, the open-air markets, and, no matter how provincial the town, that French women always had great haircuts.

In Cap d'Antibes, Susan and I went midnight skinny-dipping. We were staying in a hotel on the Mediterranean shore where, beneath a full moon, I gave a blow job to the manager, a married Frenchman and Rock Hudson look-alike. When he moaned, *"Tu me fais jouir,"* I quickly pulled my mouth away, not wanting to swallow frog jism. He caught the spurt in his hand before flinging it out to sea.

None of my bridesmaids was planning on marriage anytime soon, if at all. Their parents had actually discouraged it, only wanting their daughters to be happy and self-sufficient. Cathy's would refer to her boyfriends as "*that* Drake," or "*that* Nicholas," like they were some sort of germs. Susan's mother expected her daughter to remain a virgin indefinitely. My girlfriends never gave a thought to the things that worried me: time running out, the fading of my youthful glow, and every available guy on the planet being taken. With other priorities, Cathy had transferred to Columbia University to finish business school and Susan was heading to Los Angeles to complete her PhD at UCLA.

Looking at them, I had to swallow the resentment rising in my throat. Didn't I have what every girl *really* wanted—a husband? If so, then why, on my wedding day, did it feel like *they* were the ones leaving *me* behind?

When finally the reception ended and the guests had grabbed the centerpieces on their way out, my bridesmaids said their good-byes. It was time for Charlie's and my parents to go. I could sense they were lingering. Their gazes were wistful, and I imagined them hearing the words to "Sunrise, Sunset" about how quickly children grow up.

Although the song expressed the parents' loss, it reflected mine, too. When did I become such an adult? I may have been in my midtwenties with some hard living behind me but I wasn't yet ready to settle down, run a home, and keep the refrigerator stocked. I wasn't ready to be a Mrs.

I didn't want our parents to drive away. Once they were gone, there would be no postponing the inevitable: the honeymoon suite of the Garden City Hotel. There, the sight of the king-size bed covered in a mauve sateen spread, on which my bridesmaids had strewn red rose petals, awaited us. Everyone probably thought that as newlyweds, Charlie and I couldn't wait to rip off our wedding clothes and consecrate our marriage with scented massage oils and marathon lovemaking.

When we entered the room, we pulled back the drapes to check out the view over the parking lot. Then, exhausted, we collapsed into a pair of tufted armchairs. He was still wearing his wing-collared shirt and gray-and-black-striped foulard, while I had on my gown and garter. We ordered room service. The performance of the white-gloved waiter lifting the silver-plated lids off our filet mignon dinners while we remained formally dressed made us feel like we were on Robin Leach's *Lifestyles of the Rich and Famous.*

We ate our dinner watching TV, afterward raiding the mini bar for Toblerone chocolate and Diet Cokes, gossiping about who did and didn't do what at the wedding. We showered separately, using the sample-size Crabtree & Evelyn bath products. It was midnight before we finally forced ourselves to pull back the bedcovers. Neither of us said a word. We just lay there in silence with the lights out until I finally got up the nerve to whisper, "Now what?"

CHAPTER 2

I HAD NEVER QUESTIONED WHETHER I'd get married or even when. It was what was expected. Like earning a high school diploma. Sometime in my midtwenties, after college and around the time of graduate school, I'd have a husband. Until then, I'd be in a state of suspended animation.

Growing up, I imagined the man I married to be handsome, rich, and gallant. He would know a lot about literature and Europe. Together we would discover and create a life of sophistication, though he would naturally be the one to get things done and make the right decisions for both of us. He would make me feel safe; he'd understand my needs without me ever having to voice them. My faith in his character would give him the determination to succeed. Helping him to become a provider was part of the package. Our wedlock would promote self-sustaining harmony and contentment. We would kiss in front of the kids and sleep like spoons.

I didn't expect togetherness to be such a struggle. I didn't anticipate that in moving forward in marriage, there would be so much waiting—to talk, to fuck, to return to that preternatural wonderment that inspired you to become a couple in the first place. I never dreamed marriage would be not just defining, but in fact restrictive, requiring you to squelch your own desires for the sake of a presumably greater good: commitment. I had no idea that, by and large, wives bear the emotional weight of the relationship and are more likely to become depressed and sick than their husbands.

I naively believed that signing a marriage license would silence the erotic utterances in my head and perfidious urges in my body. I could not have guessed how much I would chafe under a contract enunciating, for better or for worse, that marriage equals monogamy. I had no idea that, statistically, women initiate two-thirds of all divorces, though I would eventually understand why.

One thing I thought for certain: My future would be different from my parents'. I attributed their problems to an original clash of personalities, not to the institution of marriage itself. Had I known better, I might not have gotten married at all.

• • •

When I was a girl and the magnolia tree bloomed on our front lawn in May, my mother would perform an annual ritual—walking around our property with her orange shears, clipping armfuls of yellow forsythias, tulips, and daffodils. She would arrange the radiant bouquets in glass vases around the house and open the windows. The fresh air would blow cool and forceful off the Sound, sweeping the scent of cut flowers throughout the rooms. It was the smell of a happy home. I didn't know just how happy it was until the spring of 1972, at the age of eleven, when the magnolia shed its pink-tipped white petals, carpeting the new grass with what appeared to be tatters of silk lingerie while the vases remained oddly empty. That was the year my mother attempted suicide.

We had moved to the house in 1966 when I was five and my brothers, Warren and Andrew, were three and two. Located in Kings Point, the gold coast of Great Neck, we had a 1950s brick-and-redwood ranch with wide-open rooms covered in either terra-cotta tiles or rust carpeting. It was filled with Scandinavian modern furniture, Vasarely op art, and Robert Indiana LOVE posters.

Bobby Vinton, the pop star who sang "Roses Are Red" and "Blue Velvet," lived up the street. His house was similar except it had a basement rehearsal studio where he practiced with his backup dancers. But ours had twice as many windows, skylights, and glass doors—114 in all. The house felt so light and airy, it might as well have been filled with helium. When the weather was warm, my mother liked to sit in a white lounge chair planted on the grassy pasture of our backyard, smoking a Kent, marveling at the lush wedge of land shaded by weeping willows and Norway maples. "This is *my* backyard," she would say in disbelief. "*I* have a backyard."

She had grown up in Flatbush, Brooklyn, on Albemarle Road, in a two-bedroom apartment where the furniture was frayed and the only greenery was a tree-lined sidewalk in front of the building. Her father—an Eastern European immigrant who gained passage to this country with a pocketful of gold coins and later made several million dollars—put off redecorating because he always planned on moving. Every Sunday, he got dressed up in a dark suit, gray fedora, and diamond pinkie ring to go to Manhattan to look at real estate. He had enough money to buy an entire block. But my mother's mother, my grandmother, said no. She told him he lacked the class and his accent embarrassed her. In truth, there was another reason.

"What will I do without Sam Popkin, my butcher?" she said to her sister in secret. Could he and my grandmother have been having an affair? Or was his brisket really that good?

My grandmother was twenty years younger than my grandfather and very beautiful. Blond, blue-eyed, with milky skin, she looked like a shiksa, a gentile girl, which was to her advantage growing up in Minooka, Pennsylvania. It was a coal-mining town populated by Jew-hating Poles who liked to beat up her kind at the local dairy.

One day in 1935, my grandmother accompanied her brother, a lamp salesman, to New York City on a business trip. They took his car, a light blue Packard, and when he stopped to see a vendor on the Bowery, my grandmother waited for him in the passenger seat. At that moment, a black Cadillac backed into the car. It belonged to a man who owned a neighborhood furniture factory. At the sight of my grandmother, he fell head over heels and quickly made her his wife.

Born in Bialystok, my grandfather studied the Talmud before coming to America in his twenties. Partnering with a guy named Benny, my grandfather became a successful manufacturer of upholstered furniture, owning multiple plants. When television advertising appeared in the 1940s, he dismissed it as a fad. However, after Bernadette Castro, the four-year-old daughter of Bernard Castro, made her TV debut in 1948, demonstrating how easy it was to convert one of her father's sofas into a bed, Castro Convertibles presented serious competition, causing my grandfather's business to slip. Benny took it hard and jumped out of a second-story window of his home in Kingston, New York. He lived, though never as well as my grandfather, who, all along, had been investing in the stock market. He was quite a wiz.

My grandfather had no idea that despite her beauty, my grandmother was out of her mind, a total crackpot—paranoid, schizophrenic, obsessive-compulsive, mean, and prone to hallucinations. She had only an eighth-grade education, lapsed into a phony Gaelic brogue, thinking she was from a made-up town in Ireland, "Largalacia." She called herself Timothea McTaggert, not realizing the last name was Scottish. But that was beside the point. Her real name was Alice Tamres.

When my mother was little, my grandmother used to take her to the roof of their building and look over the edge, telling her the trees were beckoning them to jump (probably the reason why my mother suffers from acrophobia to this day). Returning from the butcher, my grandmother would bring back chicken heads and give them to my mother to play with. She never allowed my mother to pick out her own clothes and constantly attacked her appearance, from the bump on her nose to her dark frizzy hair, insisting she Scotch tape her bangs to her forehead at night in order to straighten them. Shopping and grooming were my grandmother's major pastimes. She would preen on Flatbush Avenue wearing Christian Dior and later Norman Norell, her inch-long nails painted Elizabeth Arden poppy pink.

The fact that my grandmother gave birth to a son with severe Down syndrome didn't help her mental health. My mother was six at the time and knew her mother was expecting. But after she went to the hospital and returned home empty-handed, my grandmother told my mother that the baby had coughed up green vomit and died. In truth, my grandparents had shipped him off to Letchworth Village—a turn-of-the-century state nuthouse tucked away in Thiells, New York—never expecting him to survive. Upon her father's death in 1965, my mother, then twenty-eight, discovered she had a brother. When she went to visit, she found him to be a near vegetable in diapers with a propensity for eating newspaper and pebbles. He liked having his back rubbed with baby powder. That was the state in which he lived for sixty years.

As rich as my grandfather was, my mother never had her own bedroom. She had to bunk with Theresa, the maid. My grandparents did indulge my mother's talent for both music and art. In the evening, when my grandmother stood at the stove in a housedress sautéing onions for a brisket, she allowed my mother to sketch on the apartment walls as if they were a canvas. After work, when my grandfather ate his supper at the kitchen table in an undershirt, he would chew his food, listening to my mother practice Chopin and Tchaikovsky on their baby grand Steinway. When she was a teenager, he sent her to Italy, first on the *Queen Elizabeth* and then on the *Queen Mary,* chaperoned by a woman who was hired to show my mother the splendors of Europe. Lacking an education themselves, my mother's parents enrolled her in fine private schools—Brooklyn's Ethical Culture and Packer Collegiate—claiming to want the very best for their daughter. In truth, they were breeding her to marry well.

She studied painting at Columbia University where, after completing her bachelor's degree, she was one of only three women accepted to the school's graduate program in fine arts. The painter Philip Guston was her teacher. While the male students were each granted their own massive art studios, enabling them to lay their canvases on the floor to create heroic abstract expressionist works, the style of the day, the women had to share a space together, one that was half the size. Although my mother was prone to impassioned slashes of a paint-gobbed brush, she, like the other girls, was expected to control herself, to act like a lady and dab the pigment on her easel painting. But the restrictions didn't hold her back. In 1959, she was awarded a scholarship to Hans Hofmann's summer school in Provincetown and, a year later, won Columbia's purchase prize, for which the university bought one of her paintings, called *A Drop of Sunshine*, hanging it in the engineering school.

Living in a dorm, my mother and her roommate, a novelist, planned on renting an apartment together in Manhattan after their graduate degrees, a place where one would paint and the other write. My grandfather nixed that possibility. He was from the Old Country where nice Jewish girls didn't live on their own. An apartment was out of the question.

He decided his daughter should go for another postgraduate degree, this one in medical illustration from Johns Hopkins, which would provide her with opportunities to meet and marry a doctor. After visiting the school—where students were drawing human ears pickled in formaldehyde jars—my mother, who had always been timid and compliant, refused to apply. However, part two of my grandfather's plan did pan out when she went to a Halloween party and met a twenty-nine-year-old New York Hospital radiology resident.

Neither had attended the party in costume but each thought the other was wearing one. My father had come with another doctor directly from the hospital. Still in their scrubs, they bandaged up a third guy as if he were a patient, transporting him on a stretcher, the three pretending to be part of a MASH unit. My mother had intended to go as a flapper, wearing a very short skirt, but her father refused to allow her out of the house looking so risqué. He forced her to change into a modest black cocktail dress and pearls. When she arrived at the party, the hostess, a drama student, couldn't believe her friend, the artist, hadn't arrived in costume. Wrapping a feather boa around her neck and applying some heavy makeup, the hostess transformed my mother into a prostitute. None of the men at the party was remarkably dressed—an eye patch here, a feather headdress there—so when my mother spotted my father, she was impressed by what she believed was his medical getup. He, in turn, thought she was racy and fun. (Not the virgin she actually was.) Less than a year later, they said "I do."

My father was raised in Great Neck, the son of lawyers who had grown up in the tenements of the Lower East Side where they were childhood sweethearts. My paternal grandmother had wanted to start her own legal practice but, as a woman, knew she needed a husband's name attached to it. So she convinced my grandfather, who had become the assistant commissioner to the Boy Scouts of Manhattan, to get a degree from Brooklyn Law School. She scrubbed floors for a nickel a room in order to put herself through Columbia Law, becoming one of the first women to pass the New York State Bar. It was her decision to raise a family in Great Neck, a suburb renowned for its school system.

My paternal grandparents were a cold, hardworking couple— the Jewish intellectual version of Grant Wood's *American Gothic*. My father and his younger brother were frequently ignored. Dinner consisted of whatever was in a pressure cooker that their mother filled in the morning before she went to work. Left on their own, my father and uncle became quasi-delinquents, skilled at making explosives and shooting pellet guns. Had they not also been eggheads, they surely would have wound up wearing county stripes.

My father's IQ was off the charts. In 1947, when he was in high school, he took himself to the Stevens Institute of Technology in New Jersey for an aptitude test and scored higher than 99 percent of the freshman engineering students. Attending Cornell University in the early 1950s on a Merit Scholarship, he invented an automatic transmission nearly identical to one that Buick patented soon after. Among my father's fraternity brothers, he was known as "Gizmo."

His personality was actually split: a geek drawn to feats of derring-do. In college, he rode a Triumph motorcycle to class, speeding across a narrow footbridge that swayed over a gorge with a two-hundred-foot drop. At twenty, he zipped around Europe in his red Austin-Healey. With a camera concealed in the bumper, he drove to Vienna—at the time a "four-power" city—and surreptitiously photographed the Soviet soldiers.

Marriage to my father was my mother's liberation. With him, she discovered her appetite for adventure. It was his idea to take a four-week honeymoon island-hopping around the Caribbean in propeller planes. A talented photographer, he had built his own underwater camera to shoot deep-sea fish. He convinced my mother—who was more a wader than a swimmer—to scuba dive without even taking a lesson. They stayed in hotels where lizards and bat-size bugs crawled across the ceiling, conceiving me in one of those places.

In 1961, right after I entered the world, my parents moved to Europe. Fulfilling his military service, my father was stationed at an American air force base in Wiesbaden, Germany. Living overseas gave my mother a sense of accomplishment. She became fluent in German and did one of the many things her father had prohibited—got a driver's license. As a girl in Brooklyn, she had always felt like an outsider. Now that she actually was one, she felt at home.

In 1963, just before my father's tour of duty ended, my mother gave birth to Warren at the air force hospital. Our family returned to the United States, where my parents rented a two-bedroom apartment behind the Great Neck railroad station. Less than two years later, Andrew was born.

My mother put her life as an artist on hold to raise us three kids. She single-handedly night-herded us to our beds and rounded us up each morning, wrestling us into our clothes, lassoing my brothers into a double stroller as I kicked at the door to go to the park. Whether from indifference or immunity, she remained unfazed by our constant noise and mess. Housekeepers quit without notice, swearing no children were as unruly as the Hayt kids.

My father agreed, finding his offspring about as enjoyable as mosquitoes on a humid night. Although he never said so, he was actually more frustrated with himself. He had dreamed of becoming an engineer, but his mother had put an end to that. In her mind, the profession did not welcome Jews whereas medicine did. In addition, because of her Depression-era mentality, she believed health came first and there would always be a need for physicians. Following his mother's orders, my father became a doctor, though the career left him discontented and he became short-tempered at home. While reading, he shut us kids out by corking his ears with his fingers. Watching TV, he blasted the volume to cover the sound of us in the background. If we tried to talk to him, he barked, *"Busy!"*

Occasionally, though, he shared his devilish side. Taking us with him to work, he strapped us onto an X-ray machine—a fluoroscopy table—as if it were an amusement park ride. Using a remote control, he spun the unit 360 degrees, flipping it upside down and dipping it forward, causing us to shriek with gleeful terror. Afterward, he handed out souvenirs—60cc syringes and sterile gloves—that later served as great squirt guns and water balloons.

My mother was the gentler parent. She would peel open silver maple pods, affix the little green propellers to our noses, and instruct us to make believe we were helicopters. She would stick watermelon seeds to our foreheads like bindi dots. At night, if one of us had a bad dream, we trudged with pillows and blankets into our parents' bedroom, setting up camp at the foot of my mother's bed where we could count on comfort, despite the hard floor.

Once Andrew outgrew his crib, my parents bought a house. It was in Kings Point where turn-of-the-century tycoons, including Walter P. Chrysler, William K. Vanderbilt II, Alfred P. Sloan, and Moses Annenberg, had once colonized the idyllic peninsula overlooking the Sound. They constructed rambling estates with separate servants' quarters, mosaic-tiled bathing pavilions, multicar garages, greenhouses, guesthouses, horse stables, and grounds so vast, they could accommodate a team of polo players. This was a real-life version of Fitzgerald's West Egg. But after the Second World War, the robber barons departed, parceling out their property to a new breed of plutocrats who moved up in the world by moving in.

These were the Jerry Epsteins, Sol Lefkowitzes, and Alan Weinbergs of the Lower East Side who left behind pushcarts after becoming millionaire merchants on Seventh Avenue or mass producers of trifles, like paper clips. They settled in Kings Point with their wives named Phyllis, or Harriet, or Sylvia, women who wore mink coats over their tennis whites. Right before Labor Day, a collective fashion fever gripped them—not only because the fall arrivals had hit the strip of posh shops on Northern Boulevard known as the Miracle Mile, but also because the High Holy Days were coming. You would think it was a liturgical imperative to buy not one, but two outfits, the first for Rosh Hashanah, the second for Yom Kippur. After all, how could you go to temple and not flaunt a new look as you sized up what the other congregants were wearing?

In contrast to these see-and-be-seen temple types, my family were the social misfits of Great Neck. Other than sitting down to eat at an appointed hour with proper utensils, my brothers and I had no rules and trouble was routine. Cartwheeling around my mother's Steuben Glass collection and climbing on top of the roof were ordinary activities, which was probably why we were on a first-name basis with the emergency room staff at North Shore Hospital. At five AM on Saturdays, we mounted our bikes to set off firecrackers around Kings Point until the police returned us to our parents, who feigned disapproval before falling back to sleep. Our red-alert reputation made its way to the Nassau County Health Department. Officials in white lab coats appeared at our door after receiving a tip that the Hayt children had foot-and-mouth disease, a virus afflicting cloven-hoofed animals. (We actually had *hand,* foot, and mouth disease, another illness entirely.)

My father was Captain Disaster. He viewed a blizzard as an opportunity to test his snow tires on unplowed roads and a summer hurricane as an excuse to don his foul-weather gear and set sail on Long Island Sound. When a toilet in our house backed up, he dumped Clobber—a sulfuric acid concentrate used by professional plumbers—into the bowl without first diluting the solution with water, deliberately skipping that step in the instructions for efficiency's sake. His shortcut resulted in a chemical reaction, releasing a mushroom cloud of heat and gases. To neutralize it, he then added baking soda. The toilet bowl exploded.

In 1969, my father nearly lost a limb when, mowing the lawn with his own tractor, the motor got clogged with wet grass clippings and he reached inside to fix it. He forgot to declutch the moving blades, which sliced off part of his fingers. Hand surgeons at North Shore did their best, enabling my father to return to work. I often wondered what his patients thought when they saw his stubs coming at them with a barium enema.

The older I got, the more aware I became that Great Neck was no place for us. We weren't members of a country club, my parents didn't play golf or tennis, and our backyard had no pool. Every expense from hiring a housepainter to taking a vacation caused my parents to fret about finances. Nor were my grandparents to be counted on for handouts. My parents aired their worries at the dinner table, which made me anxious and ashamed:

Clearly, we weren't rich enough to live where we did, yet they vacillated between pretending we were and panicking about it.

The difference between my father and the rest of the men in town was most obvious on Sunday mornings at Tabatchnik's, a Jewish delicatessen in town, where they lined up in Fila warm-up suits and Tretorns, their hair straight and fluffy from a blow dryer. Kidding one another, the other fathers cut ahead to place their orders.

"Gimme half a pound a whitefish spread!"

"Schmaltz herring!"

"Slice me up some nova but ya betta make it nice and thin!"

Meanwhile, my father silently waited his turn in his 1960s air-force-issue, gray plastic eyeglasses and pressed polo shirt tucked into high-water trousers, his black hair smooth and gleaming like his shoes. Checking his Timex and grinding his teeth, he shifted his weight from one foot to the other. He didn't like the crowd: businessmen, a crass and shady lot.

Bernie Mandelbaum had a monopoly on the artificial flower business and drove a white Eldorado, one hand on the steering wheel, the other holding a scotch as his chunky, gold ID bracelet spelling BERNIE clinked against the glass. Morty King was a commercial meat dealer with a head of hair plugs, a ballooning gut, and twig-thin legs. Whenever he ran into my father, Morty never tired of repeating the same stupid line. "Hey, Doc, you're not the only MD around here. I'm an MD, too. A meat dealer!"

My father was the chief of radiology at a North Bronx hospital where the patients were lower-middle-class Italians who never let their bills get past due. Because his position paid better than most, he resigned himself to it grudgingly. The job had none of the prestige of academic medicine that his mother had wanted him to pursue. At that, my mother put her foot down. Teaching and research might be noble but they wouldn't cover the bills, not to mention summer camp and college tuition.

"Go into private practice," she had lobbied. "That's where doctors make the real money."

My father's life became one of daily frustration. Leaving the house at seven AM, he drove forty-five minutes to the hospital, a constant reminder his brilliant mind was lying fallow. Every night, he headed home to Great Neck, turning onto Kings Point Road, a wide berth of freshly tarred pavement, sculpted hedges, and rustic stone fences—a landscape of signs indicating we were living beyond our means, a fact he blamed on my mother.

At six sharp, he entered the front door, giving it an angry thud, bellowing, "I'm home"—words that sucked the air from the house. That was my mother's cue to put the meat loaf, mashed potatoes, and Birdseye June peas on the lazy Susan while my father made a beeline for the rosewood bar, fixing himself the first of many dry martinis with two green olives. Tightly wound, he was quick to raise a hand to my brothers and me if we descended on him too soon. We learned not to utter a peep until the alcohol kicked in and the tendons bulging around his jaw relaxed.

I didn't dare kiss or hug my father. Not an affectionate man, he had a mean streak stoked by unwanted physical contact. Of course, all physical contact was unwanted. He was capable of punishing our Siamese cat by locking him in the shower or kicking our West Highland white terrier down a flight of steps because the dog was lazy and wouldn't wait to crap outside. He never used a belt on us kids, but I was prone to spilling things. Just the thought of his reaction was enough to make me lose my grip on a glass of milk.

Despite being fearful, I didn't hate him. More than anything, he awed and fascinated me. There seemed to be no question he couldn't answer: "How much is four hundred forty-four times eighty-seven?" "How do you spell *onomatopoeia*?" "What does the moon have to do with the size of ocean waves?" "How was anti-snake venom discovered?" "Why does a high-pitched sound make glass shatter?" "Exactly how many years was the Hundred Years' War?"

Once I was able to read, I figured out how to sustain his interest in me. In the mornings during the late 1960s, he started his day with tea and *The New York Times*. I would come up behind him, inhaling the delicious scent of his freshly laundered white dress shirt, Brylcreem slicking back his hair, and Old Spice on his clean-shaven face, which my mother compared to a movie star's, Tyrone Power. Looking over his shoulder, I scanned the morning headlines, pumping him for explanations of the Tet offensive and My Lai massacre. Listening to his geopolitical analyses, I pretended to understand everything he said. At six-and-a-half-years old, I had no clue what the man was talking about.

In the evenings after dinner, my father helped me with my homework at the kitchen table. It didn't matter how late the hour grew or if the rest of the household went to bed; he stayed by my side until I completed all my assignments, including the optional extra-credit ones. His expectations were high and many of his words went over my head, but I didn't mind. The point was being close to him.

For the most part, my younger brothers bore the brunt of his rage. Out of his three kids, my father could count on me to behave and stay put when, to give my mother a break, he took us with him on Saturdays to Sears.

By the time Donny Osmond became a teen idol (mine), I was old enough to hang out with my girlfriends at La Koo Koo—a knickknack shop filled with mushroom-shaped candles, puzzle rings, and blow-up Bubble Chairs—located on Middle Neck Road, Great Neck's main drag. I no longer wanted to accompany my father to home appliance stores. He and my brothers were beginning to form a trio bonded by do-it-yourself projects and car talk. Lunching with my mother at Lord & Taylor's Birdcage restaurant was far more intriguing. She started divulging secrets, and we became a pair.

She was a funny woman, a wonderful storyteller, observing life like a silent comedy and always casting herself as a Charlie Chaplin outsider. Melodrama was the only language she spoke. If she recounted a scene of herself trying on a dress at a store and having trouble getting out of it, you could be sure the garment "lynched" her. My father never puttered but "left a trail of wreckage in his wake." She had a flawless sense of timing, suckering you in with setups and small laughs before delivering the punch line.

"Do you think one side of my face is aging faster than the other?" she asked me.

Studying her closely, I wasn't sure what to look for but observed the right side was smoother than the left.

"Maybe it's because I sleep on that side," she said. "How long will it be before I wake up with FIELDCREST stamped across my cheek?"

The more time we spent alone together, the more aware I became that my mother was not always in the mood to laugh. Some days, she could barely smile, distracted by a tendril of smoke spiraling from her cigarette, unaware a cylinder of ash had tumbled into her coffee cup. I began to equate these spells with her shaggy appearance. Although she went to the beauty parlor twice a week, her hair refused to hold a set. She bit her nails, and spokes of raspberry lipstick radiated into the smoker's wrinkles around her mouth. The métier of matching shoes and bags, which came so naturally to Great Neck ladies, eluded my mother. Wearing a new outfit, she either spilled something on it before leaving the house or didn't realize the price tags were still attached to her clothing.

With us three kids growing up, my mother questioned the way her life was unfolding. Once, she'd been a promising artist, but now she was potting geraniums in the backyard and taking needlepoint lessons. Attempting to find a more commercial venue for her creativity, she painted nursery pictures of ducklings and bunnies, framing them with pastel bows and gingham borders in the hope of selling them at Clothes & Things, a boutique in town. The owner, Suzy, tacked a thirty-five-dollar price tag on each of the pictures, displaying them in the window, alongside a rainbow of Courrèges wool turtlenecks. The merchandise sold out. Not the paintings, the sweaters.

"Do you have any idea what my fucking life is like?" my mother would later scream at my father after she thought we children were asleep. "You know, I could walk right out of this house and leave you and never come back and then what would you do? You'd be on your own, pal. I hate it here."

Great Neck was torture for her. On Monday mornings at Gristedes, she would run into Dina Lowenstein, a part-time UJA fundraiser, blinding in her eighteen-karat-gold chains dripping with diamond pavé *Chai* pendants.

"Did you hear the news?" Dina asked, her head in profile so that her new bunny-slope nose was on full view. "My Seth is playing in the East Coast Junior Tennis Championship this year! Could you die?

". . . We're having his bar mitzvah at Leonards," she continued, referring to Great Neck's banquet hall beveled and marbled in high-Liberace style. "Kids, they have to have what everyone else has. You're taking yours south for a spring vacation, aren't you?"

More and more, my mother wondered on what planet she had landed and who the real extraterrestrials were. Women like Dina weren't doing anything interesting with their lives, yet they seemed mindlessly content. My mother wasn't doing anything interesting, either, but at least she knew it. If her own unhappiness wasn't bad enough, she also had her mother's to deal with.

After my mother's father died of a heart attack, my grandmother moved to Great Neck to an apartment off Middle Neck Road. Wandering the town like a vagrant, she spent hours at the railroad station, watching the trains. Unable to drive, she often took a taxi to our house to rail at my mother for abandoning her.

Despite the anguish my grandmother caused, I thought she was wonderful. Entering our front door in a gale of Joy perfume, she'd let out a mad shriek when she saw my brothers and me. My mother would rush to make her comfortable, installing her in our living room on a low, gold velvet love seat. Parceling out supersize Hershey's chocolate bars and twenty-dollar bills to us kids, my grandmother would launch into a series of dirty jokes about popes and rabbis.

She liked to take me shopping at Bonwit's on the Miracle Mile. Entering the store, she would introduce herself to a saleswoman as Timothea McTaggert. The minute I heard that brogue—the tip-off a spending delirium was about to set in—I knew I was getting one of everything in an assortment of colors.

It burned my mother up that my grandmother could win over us children so easily. Candy, money, and clothing. How could we not realize that by delighting in my grandmother's ribaldry, we were siding with the enemy?

More unbearable was the latest development. My grandmother had started dating my father's father—my other grandfather, the lawyer, who was now a widower. (My paternal grandmother died in 1963.) He still lived in Great Neck and, like many men, fell for my crazy grandmother's looks.

"Guess what?" she said to my mother. "Your husband's father wants to marry me. That would make my son-in-law my stepson *and* your stepbrother!"

My mother's mother demanded my father's father buy her a diamond ring if he wanted to marry her. When he wouldn't, she turned down his proposal. Soon after, he had a stroke, leaving him partially paralyzed. His infirmity erased any of my grandmother's lingering doubts about her rejection of him. The last thing she wanted was an invalid for a husband. Still, she carped about him constantly to my mother.

"I can't stand another minute of this," my mother shrieked at my father from their bedroom, which was down the hall from my brothers' and mine. "I'm on the verge of a nervous breakdown! I need a vacation!"

"Goddamn it!" my father finally exploded. "I can't keep up with the bills—Macrae's fruit and Jimmy, the butcher. You're going to cut coupons. And you'd better stop spending so much on Elizabeth!"

My mother spoiled me rotten. For my brothers' birthdays, a Carvel ice cream cake, cardboard hats, and pin-the-tail-on-the-donkey were enough but, for me, the parties were all-out pageants. Created around different themes, like Cinderella or Snow White, she transformed our backyard into a wonderland of streamers, balloons, sparklers, banners, paper crowns, and goody bags. One year, she rented out Eloise's room at the Plaza, anointing me as Eloise herself.

My mother opened a charge account in my name at Wormrath's, a bookstore in town, where I was allowed to fill a shopping bag with as many Nancy Drew mysteries as I could carry. She took me to whichever Lincoln Center ballets and Broadway shows I wanted, as well as ones she thought would be good for me. She signed me up for lessons every day of the week: piano, figure skating, tennis, horseback riding, and dance.

At the age of six, I had entered Madame Bartova's School of Ballet in Great Neck, and after several years I begged my mother to let me audition at the School of American Ballet in Manhattan. Although she didn't believe a smart girl should waste her mind by becoming a ballerina, my mother relented, if only to let me figure out for myself that I was not going to be the next Suzanne Farrell. I didn't even make it through the barre exercises before the instructors gave me the boot: I had no sense of rhythm. My mother felt so bad for her rejected daughter that she took me to Bloomingdale's, where she bought me a diamond heart pendant.

While she showered me with presents, my father never voluntarily bought me a thing, let alone a gift for her. In fact, I never saw my parents share any tenderness. They slept in twin beds, didn't touch, didn't hold hands, didn't kiss, didn't go to bed early, didn't get up late, didn't take vacations without us kids, and didn't laugh behind closed doors. The only sounds we heard coming from their bedroom at night were Walter Cronkite on the evening news or them fighting.

I tried to picture my parents as newlyweds: carefree, young, exploring a foreign country, full of hope and adventure. But it was hard to believe there ever existed a time when they weren't arguing over the bills or were happy just being a family.

• • •

Perhaps it was an omen that after a particularly harsh winter, new shoots of grass were slow to sprout in the spring of 1972 when I was eleven.

My mother was spending a lot of time in bed. When the boys and I came home from school, she was usually in the kitchen, having a cup of coffee. Instead, we now found her in her room with the drapes drawn, staring up at the ceiling, chain-smoking.

"Is Mom okay?" we asked my father when he came home from work early one day.

"Don't worry," he snapped, sliding four Swanson turkey TV dinners into the oven.

We did worry. With good reason. The next afternoon, when we came home, my mother wasn't there at all. My grandmother was. We knew this was a last resort, signaling a real emergency.

Late that night, after we were in bed, the slamming of the front door awakened us. My father had returned, my mother with him.

Busting from our rooms, we wanted to find out what had happened but, upon seeing her, were afraid to ask. She was leaning against my father, who guided her down the hallway to her bedroom. They were taking baby steps because her legs were wobbly. Her pale skin seemed especially translucent and her big blue eyes—ordinarily as luminous as marbles—were dull and sleepy.

"Your mother's been at the hospital for back surgery," my father said curtly.

Afflicted with scoliosis and a couple of slipped disks, my mother had suffered back pain for as long as I could remember. Whenever she bent over to pick up our toys, she winced, pressing her hand into her lumbar region, massaging it. His explanation seemed plausible enough. She often retreated to her bedroom to rest for an hour on a heating pad.

But this time, she retreated for a whole day. Then two. By the third, she still hadn't appeared. My father announced my grand-mother would be coming back because my mother had to return to the hospital for another operation. When she emerged from her bedroom, her long dark hair appeared a tangled nest and her skin was raked with lines as if she'd aged ten years shut away in her room.

It seemed like a long time that my mother was in the hospital, though I have no idea whether it amounted to days or weeks. I was certain my brothers missed her as much as I did, but we never spoke of her absence. She was there without being there, a void felt acutely every morning when we left for school without the brown-bag lunches that she prepared for us daily but instead with a handful of coins from my father to buy the gummy cafeteria food. At night, we stuck out a bad dream alone in our rooms, knowing there was no consolation to be found at the foot of my mother's bed.

Once she returned, things changed. Her figure had always been full and curvy, but soon became svelte and angular. She stopped biting her nails and painted them Elizabeth Arden poppy pink like my grandmother's. My mother got her dark hair frosted blond. She almost looked like a Great Neck lady.

For a time, she seemed happier, giddy almost. She talked about redecorating the house. She cleaned out her closet, getting rid of dowdy madras dresses and Bermuda shorts. She bought new, slinky outfits in turquoise, burgundy, and ivory by Halston and Stephen Burrows. She wore stacked high heels instead of loafers. For once, my father didn't yell at her for all the money she spent. To help out my grandmother asked around the train station if anyone knew of a maid for hire.

My mother transformed into the mother whom I thought I wanted all along: the kind with hair sprayed into a perfect arc around her face. I didn't yet understand that to her, a manufactured image and outward control actually meant the opposite. Her own mother proved how false appearances could be.

Soon I felt awkward and uncertain around my mother. The woman who now appeared so pulled together was not the one who'd raised me. This stranger had different priorities: Family no longer came first; finding herself did. A search that cost me a deeper sense of order.

When I got older—my late teens, I think—my mother told me what had really happened in the spring of 1972. She had gotten pregnant, but my father didn't want a fourth child. We three were a handful, and he couldn't afford another. "You'll never be able to care for so many kids," my grandmother agreed.

My mother was equivocal. She was hoping to have another girl, a sister for me, but her youngest child—my brother Andrew—was already eight. An infant would mean starting all over. Although criminal abortion laws had been repealed in New York in 1970, my mother was conflicted. A male psychiatrist advised additional therapy before she made her decision. Whenever my mother raised the question of abortion, he insisted she still had issues to work through.

It wasn't until she was well into her second trimester that he pronounced her ready to terminate the pregnancy and get on with her own life. By then, it was too late for a suction procedure, so she had to have a saline. She was already feeling fetal movement and, in the operating room, still couldn't make up her mind, jumping on and off the table. Finally, labor was induced. She had to push out a dead baby.

Back home, a few days later, she took several tranquilizers, and my father could barely rouse her. He managed to get her to the hospital, where her stomach was pumped. She claimed she was only trying to get some sleep but the doctors diagnosed her as suicidal, advising my father to hospitalize her. Knowing how unhappy she was, he feared they were right and, because he was a physician himself, had faith in their medical opinions. She never forgave him for signing the papers committing her to Payne Whitney, the psychiatric ward of New York Hospital. Following her discharge, she tried to put her pain behind her. Not a day went by when it didn't occur to her that she might have destroyed a daughter.

CHAPTER 3

My PROMISCUITY AS A TEENAGER was a no-brainer. Between my parents' money troubles, my mother's mad-housewife syndrome, and my father's career frustrations, they had an embattled relationship. You didn't have to be a member of the Freudian Institute to figure out that my running around with boys was an attempt to escape the household tension and capture Daddy's attention.

It was 1974, a bitterly cold weekend in February. Frozen gusts blew off the Long Island Sound. The willows looked as if they'd been dipped in crystal. Now and then, the wind whipped the branches against the windows of the houses, shattering their frozen shells. To my adolescent ear, overly attuned to the poetry and pathos of just about everything, the crackling sounded like bells chiming. I was thirteen years old.

Saturday, I spent the afternoon at Andee's house. When my mother came to pick me up in our white Ford Country Squire station wagon, her new friend Yuri was with her. Now in her late thirties, my mother had begun taking painting classes at C. W. Post College in Old Westbury. Yuri was one of her classmates. Fifteen years younger, he was Israeli, had grown up on a kibbutz, and fought in the Yom Kippur War. He had a dark ponytail, a silver ankh on a piece of twine around his neck, and an army shirt with cutoff sleeves. He was sitting next to my mother, not on the passenger side, but in the driver's seat. It was the place where my father would have sat had he been behind the wheel.

She was behaving strangely, fidgeting and laughing too much. Yuri was talking about art and revolution. He was swearing, something my father rarely did and only when he and my mother were having it out. I wasn't accustomed to hearing an adult curse so casually. But then again, there was a hippie where my father should have been.

Afterward, I told my mother Yuri stunk up the car. She said he smelled from sweat, that was all, and she liked it, just as she did getting dirt beneath her fingernails when she gardened. Besides, I should mind my manners since he was special, someone with whom she could talk about art.

That night, I snuck down to our basement where my mother had turned a maid's room into an art studio. When I flipped on the lights, I was surrounded by giant, garishly colored suburban scenes. One depicted a barbecue party with couples laughing like jackals around a grill on which slabs of meat were sizzling. Later, when I tried to go to sleep, I couldn't get the picture out of my head.

Sunday morning, I was cooped up because of the cold, and lay in my bed, reading. I had gotten my hands on a stack of my mother's books: *The Female Eunuch, The Feminine Mystique, The Bell Jar,* and *Fear of Flying.* Who would have known that my curiosity was a sign I was standing on a precipice, the world of smiley faces and sunny skies behind me, the calamity and confusion of becoming a woman in front of me?

"The wicked womb," "comfortable concentration camp," "shock treatments," "zipless fuck"—I had no idea what these phrases meant when I spotted them on the pages that my mother had earmarked. I wanted to figure them out, sensing they might reveal more about her.

By early afternoon, I was light-headed from reading and fed up with the shrieks and thuds of my younger brothers relay-racing up and down the hallway outside my bedroom door. I pulled on a light blue Danskin leotard, faded dungarees, and Frye boots. Looking in a mirror, I studied the dusting of freckles across my nose, wishing I could scrub them away because they made me look younger than I was. I carefully applied strawberry-flavored lip gloss. Not terrible but, God, I hated being short.

Why couldn't I look like Andee? The neighborhood boys circled her house from morning until night. Her father had actually slugged one. When her parents went out, they not only locked her inside but also turned on a security system, taking the key to shut it off with them. If she tried to sneak away, a burglar alarm rang, summoning the police.

I went into the kitchen where the sun was streaking through the skylights. Seated at the table, my mother held a cigarette between two wishbone fingers. My father was reading the paper, eating a bologna sandwich on Wonder. Those were the days when I despised my parents and refused to go out with them in public. I made my mother walk behind me on Middle Neck Road. When my father picked me up at a friend's house, I insisted he wait at the end of the driveway.

I believed my parents had no clue who I was and what it felt like to be a teenager. They had no idea what it took to be popular, or that every day I walked into my public junior high school, a brick box built in the 1950s, I had to swallow hard not to choke on my own vomit. They couldn't guess how nervous it made me pretending I wasn't a good student because you couldn't be cool if you were smart and got your homework in on time. They didn't know the only way to get the boys to notice me was to talk tough and pretend their jokes about my flat chest didn't matter.

The weekend before I'd had a massive fight with my mother over a pair of red platforms with four-inch heels. "You used to be a nice girl!" my mother yelled, hurling the shoes out of my bedroom into the hallway. Was it because they were whorish or because her mother had bought them for me?

My father wasn't comfortable with my growing up, either. I was menstruating, wearing a bra, and totally boy crazy. Unlike Andee's father, mine seemed indifferent to the fact that I was becoming sexually active. He never admonished when I left the house in low-cut, Landlubber hip-huggers that barely covered my crack and a see-through Huckapoo blouse.

He acted more protective of the household plumbing than mine. When I flushed a tampon down the toilet, stopping it up, he cursed and shouted. It would have been bad enough had he done it in private but he tore me apart in front of my stinking brothers, who were all too happy to provide the backup heckling, ensuring my total humiliation.

My father held stereotypical feminine behavior in contempt, viewing the likes of fashion and primping as frivolous. His female ideal had been his mother, who considered makeup and nail polish ridiculous. She ignored the graying of her long red locks, bobby-pinning them into a neat bun at the back of her head. Owning no more than four housedresses, she replaced one only when it was worn out—not because it had gone out of style.

I was the exact opposite—everything my father had been raised to revile—a candy-colored, festooned creature who, instead of outgrowing girlish curlicues, accumulated more and more, preening in full swing during pubescence.

"I'm going to Debbie's," I lied that Sunday afternoon in February, slamming the front door behind me.

Debbie Goodstein was a nice kid who my parents thought wouldn't get me into trouble. Sheila and Harv Goodstein, Deb's parents, were really strict. What mine didn't know was that Mr. Goodstein walked around in tighty whities, flaunting a substantial bulge. They also didn't know he kept *The Joy of Sex* on his night table, which Deb and I studied when her parents weren't home.

Throughout elementary school, Debbie would come over to

my house and we would lock ourselves in my bedroom, telling my mother we were playing with my Raggedy Ann and Andy dolls. In truth, we were masturbating. I showed Debbie how to rub the tender nub of flesh inside her white cotton underpants with the tip of a pencil eraser. Neither of us dared probe the dank part where we thought the pee came from. That was still off-limits.

Not that my parents ever told me so. They neither said sex was dirty nor confiscated my brothers' *Playboy*s hidden under their mattresses. In fact, my mother was progressive as far as sex education went. When I was seven and the boys five and four, she sat us down on the floor to read *How Babies Are Made.* Showing us a picture of a man and woman under the bedcovers, my mother explained that the man's penis, which was just like my brothers' only bigger, was inside the woman's vagina, which was like mine, only stretchier, and that's how you made a baby.

"How long do the mommy and daddy stay that way?" I asked.

"That depends on how much they love each other," said my mother.

No, on that particular Sunday, I wasn't heading to Debbie Goodstein's but to see Danny Birnbaum, a kid who gave my parents—and everybody else's—the creeps. At fourteen, he was taller and huskier than other boys his age. He wore a roach clip on a chain around his neck, his dull brown eyes were bloodshot, and his shoulder-length black hair was matted to his scalp with grease. Since both his parents worked, he was able to cut classes and either sit on a fence in front of Parkwood ice rink or kick back in his bedroom playing his Fender in between bong hits with his best friend Cowboy (so nicknamed because of his hat). Needless to say, Danny was the coolest kid in school—when he was there.

He and I had started messing around about a month earlier when Andee—who was his girlfriend until I stole him away—went to Florida to visit her grandmother. It was New Year's Eve and my parents were having a party. Figuring whatever trouble I might get into was better if it happened under their own roof, they agreed that Danny could come over. With Burt Bacharach playing in the living room, the grown-ups sipped champagne punch laced with sliced strawberries and nibbled Ritz crackers topped with Boursin cheese spread. Meanwhile, Danny and I disappeared downstairs where we sacked out on a new orange patent leather, U-shaped sofa—an accent piece for the lucite-and-chrome decorating scheme that my mother had recently imported from Bloomingdale's. We rang in the New Year by smoking doobies and making out.

Right from the beginning, he hassled me to go farther. "Don't be a wimp," "It's no big deal," "What's the matter with you?" "Everybody does it," "Don't you love me?" "You'll like it," "It won't hurt," "It'll feel good," "I'll go slow," "It'll be over quick," "How about just once?" "You won't get pregnant," "I'll pull out," "I'll wear a rubber," "I don't want to wait," "I'll never tell."

Walking the two miles to Danny's house that Sunday, I wasn't thinking about the head trip that was sure to come. I was thinking only about the good things that had led up to it. Even if I had to get stoned to play the part of being Danny's girlfriend—and I secretly hated pot because it made my head fuzzy, eyes puffy, and mouth dry—it was worth it. After all, I was the one he had chosen. Not Joyce Greenberg whose father was a big cheese manufacturer or Leslie Lieber, a nationally ranked tennis player who once modeled for *Seventeen*. And not Andee, the fox, who giggled easily and knew when to keep her mouth shut. Danny had chosen me, Elizabeth Hayt—freckled, built like a boy, and, according to her parents, too smart for her own damn good.

"Hey," Danny said, his back to me as I entered his bedroom while he jacked up the eight-track tape, drowning out my hello with Yes's "Roundabout." Coming from behind, I hugged him and pressed my cheek against his worn blue-and-gray-plaid flannel shirt, reeking of smoke and sweat. God, I was so in love. Danny knew everything there was to know about bands and stereo systems and rolling joints and breaking rules and avoiding parents and telling lies and convincing girls they deserved him. I let my hands drop to his Levi's and unbuttoned his fly.

I had seen my share of boys' private parts when my brothers were little and it was more efficient for my mother to bathe the three of us together. But the boys' had been small, smooth, and limp, like some milk-fed delicacies you'd find at the butcher. By contrast, Danny's was beastly. Sprouting from a thicket of coarse, black pubic hair, the stalk was swollen and veiny, looking like it had to hurt both him and me. But I didn't let on since the last thing I wanted was for Danny to call me a prude.

Pretty soon, we were under the covers, the only way I would ever be naked with him. I cringed at the thought of a boy seeing me undressed. How could anyone ever pose nude? Touching was one thing, looking another.

No boy had ever put his finger in me. Actually, it had taken a long time for me to work up the courage to do it to myself. You couldn't see up there so how could you know what you might find? Would it be squishy like the bottom of a lake? Sandpapery like a cat's tongue? How far could my finger reach? Would I damage something if I went too deep or pushed two fingers inside? Was the milky wetness a good or bad sign? And was it supposed to smell like that?

"Ouch!" I winced as Danny pushed in his middle finger. Because he played the guitar, he kept his nails long and sharp like picks.

Maybe he thought if he kept at it, I'd change my mind. But shoving his digit in and out, over and over again, just made me sore and dry. My whole body stiffened with resistance.

"Please, Danny, enough."

He did as I asked and we lay together quietly. Kissing again, he rolled on top of me, his body nearly twice my size. Beneath his full weight, I felt small and feminine. Arching my back to seal the space between us, I wanted to merge the way it was in love songs but there was no room. We were already pressed as close together as could be. In other words, I was trapped.

Grinding his hip bones into mine, Danny kissed me harder. Too hard. His teeth cut into my lips. When I tried to pull my head away, he held it in his hands, pushing his tongue deep into my mouth, making it hard for me to breathe.

"I can make you do it if I want to," he said, half smiling, a thread of spittle catching the light.

Suddenly, he clamped his hands over my wrists, pinning them above my head. I didn't say no. I didn't say yes. My muscles went slack. Danny had made up his mind. I now understood why he was going out with me instead of a girl who had a father like Andee's. Was that why she had been so quick to forgive me for boyfriend-nabbing? Because she knew something I didn't and better it happen to me than to her?

The music was blaring and Danny's parents were God-knows-where. No one would have heard me had I tried to cry out. And why *should* I cry? He was my boyfriend. Hadn't I been expecting this to happen? By going over to his house so often, I must have known, at least on some level, it was only a matter of time.

My body was rigid, my opening constricted, but Danny was wild with impatience. With one mean push, he stuck it in. There was no blood. Somehow, my cherry had already popped. But a sharp pain seemed to slice me apart, releasing a silent howl. The tender place, once my private playground, was now cleaved into something angry and public.

It was all happening in slow motion: Danny panting in my ear, his legs forcing mine open, his animal thrusts skinning my membranes. At that instant, I remembered a scene in *The Bell Jar* when Esther Greenwood's bones nearly splintered and her brain crackled after the electrodes jolted her temples.

As Danny continued, the wind whipped the crystalline branches against the house and the icy shards now sounded like china smashing. I fixed my eyes on the window and studied the platinum frost on the glass. How long would it take Danny to finish? How long do the mommy and daddy stay that way?

That depends on how much they love each other.

"I told you I'd take care of you," Danny said, wiggling a little so I could feel the tacky slime he had just shot over my stomach. "See? I pulled out in time."

Was I supposed to congratulate him? Thank him? Entwine my fingers in his now that he had released my wrists? I had no idea. It certainly didn't feel right, yet I wasn't sure it was wrong. I was a girl. He was a boy. We were alone in his bedroom. Eventually, the deed was going to go down, so what was the goddamn big deal anyway?

Now that it was done, nothing made sense. How could something that didn't even feel good be special? And to whom? To the girl who was taught she had something to lose or the boy who was taught he had everything to gain? If it was so easy to plunder what she should give freely, then why would she ever want to be taken?

All I could be sure of was that it really made no difference who earned the title of being first. What was lost was gone for good. When Danny reached over to his night table, I thought he was going to pull a Kleenex from the box and clean up the slime. Instead, he did something else entirely, something so unexpected, it scared me shitless. He grabbed a long, shiny scissors and drew the sharp tip along the underside of my arm.

"You won't be needing this anymore," he said.

He carefully snipped off a piece of raw cowhide that I had knotted around my wrist.

Several months earlier, Andee and I had decided to wear the leather bracelets to signify our virginity. It was our way of silently declaring that boys were on our minds, but we weren't ready to make the ultimate sacrifice for them.

Danny didn't need to carve a notch in his belt; he simply cut off my strip of worn leather and tied it to his bedpost.

And come Monday morning, I was sure he would blab all over

school. That's what boys did. It would be a coup for him and a humiliation for me. But what if I beat him to it? What if I laid claim to my virginity first, telling the world that it was me who wanted to lose it all along? Fuck the myth of the girl being the victim. It was attitude, not anatomy, that was to be my destiny.

• • •

In my final days of eighth grade, Andrew ratted me out. Worried I was on a slippery slope, my brother told my parents I'd been smoking reefer after my mother stormed through the house, rampaging because her Valium was missing. Yes, I was the culprit but it wasn't the pills I was after. Dumping them down the can, I only wanted the plastic vial to store my pot.

My parents rushed me to Manhattan to be assessed by my mother's shrink—the same one who told her to have the abortion, leading to her breakdown. His office was in a penthouse of a building with a drive-through entrance on York Avenue. He was bald, had pale blue sleepy eyes, papery skin, bony features, and a hooked nose. He reminded me of Colonel Sanders. Every time he opened his mouth to ask another idiotic question—"Do kids at school pressure you to do drugs?"—I expected him to say something about crispy fried chicken wings.

Shortly after, a letter addressed to me arrived at my house. Rather than hand it over, my parents opened it, probably because the envelope's illegible scrawl suggested the sender was certifiable. Inside, they discovered a series of Magic Marker drawings of a naked guy with a boner and a girl posing spread-eagled. An inscription read "Me and You." Signed, "Danny."

No amount of hysterics could convince my parents they'd violated my privacy. I accused them of running a totalitarian regime. Why not exile me to a Siberian gulag? Instead they had their own methods of control. They hauled me into Payne Whitney. I was unaware my mother had already spent time there and this was my induction to a family tradition. I had also never heard of something called an outpatient facility so, even though I spent an afternoon undergoing a battery of psychological tests, I thought I was being committed.

Once again, I had visions of Esther Greenwood in *The Bell Jar*. My parents escorted me on a long, silent walk through the mint-green corridors of the hospital. The echo of my footsteps on the polished floor reverberated louder and louder. Any minute, I expected a posse of orderlies to wrestle me to the linoleum and a stony-faced doctor to inject me with sedatives before sticking a fat, black rubber snorkel down my throat and cautery wires to my scalp, short-circuiting my gray matter with enough voltage to jump-start a car.

When I entered a room with kindergarten-size wooden chairs, a psychiatrist was waiting. He had thick dark hair that looked as if it was dusted with talcum powder. On closer examination, it was dandruff. The room reeked of his cologne, a scent that reminded me of an Esso station bathroom doused with disinfectant.

He spent the next three hours holding up Rorschach cards, telling me to match up shapes, identify images, arrange patterns, contrast words, complete sentences, repeat things backward, and do everything short of playing Simon Says. What all this had to do with my getting busted for toking and poking was a mystery.

The doctor finally excused me and, while I sat outside the room in a gray fiberglass chair wondering whether they lock you up right away or give you a chance to go home and collect your things, my parents were called in to speak with him. His diagnosis? I was a "maladjusted teenager." Did my parents actually need a guy who smelled like Pine-Sol and looked like a "before" model for a Head & Shoulders commercial to tell them what I already knew?

They yanked me out of public school just before I entered ninth grade, installing me in a new environment they described as more wholesome and better supervised. I assumed it was a reformatory bordered with razor wire.

Instead, horse farms surrounded Friends Academy. A private,

Quaker school founded in 1876, it was housed in an ivy-covered Georgian mansion situated on sixty-five acres in Locust Valley. Populated with blue bloods in chirpy pink or green sweaters, their faces brightened by gin blossoms, the town was a Long Island hamlet where the men didn't get manicures and women didn't wear diamonds in the daytime. It was worlds away from Great Neck.

Everything about Friends was new to me: no bells at the end of periods, no passes for the bathroom, and no after-school detention. A gentle white-haired headmaster was in charge. There was a weekly school worship at the Matinecock Meetinghouse during which everyone was supposed to think deep thoughts. The students all appeared remarkably clean: boys who, despite their neckties worn askew, had military haircuts and zit-free skin; girls who never broke a sweat playing field hockey. The classrooms were placid vistas of square jaws, broad cheekbones, and natural blonds who addressed their elders as ma'am and sir. The families vacationed in Palm Beach, not Lauderdale. For the first time in my life, I felt like a real Jew and was thankful God had spared me a telltale schnoz.

Not that it would have mattered. Unlike Great Neck, where I believed I stood out for being different, at Friends, it was the opposite. I disappeared precisely because I was different. As a minority, I didn't feel maligned. Just overlooked.

It was nice at first. Although I made no great friends, I spent my days reading Shakespeare and learning Romance languages, as well as European history. I wrote for the school paper and didn't have to hide out to study. Cloistered in a world of books, I felt calm and happy, protected from the unpredictability and upheaval at home. At Friends, I finally found a place where good grades were a goal for everyone, which made it easy for me to follow along.

I might have gotten through high school without feeling like I had horns on my head had my parents not forced me to see another psychiatrist who was handpicked by Dr. Colonel Sanders. At least the shrink was a woman, but her specialty was kids with Tourette's syndrome. Although I was trying to fit into a student body of country club gentiles raised within a tradition of proud self-repression and stiff comportment, every Wednesday I had to be excused early so that my mother could drive me to the city where I was to empty my inner septic tank in an office filled with patients jerking uncontrollably, spewing racist epithets.

I revealed to the doctor that my mother was not my mother, or rather, she didn't act like a mother, the way a mother should. Because my grandparents never let her decide anything for herself and were relentlessly critical, she was raised to believe she was incompetent, becoming a functionally dysfunctional adult.

Everyday choices, such as ordering from a restaurant menu, were crippling. She relied on waiters, shopgirls, and strangers for advice that she subsequently rejected as untrustworthy before making a rash decision, which she immediately second-guessed. She drove people crazy. "There is a point of madness they come to with me," she said, laughing at herself. "I see the torment in their eyes."

The patience and reassurance that my mother required embarrassed me. I quickly learned to take charge and choose, becoming a control freak, partly out of charity, but mostly necessity. Our relationship grew symbiotic: My capableness only increased her dependence, which made me feel even more responsible for her.

Driving me to the city for my weekly shrink appointment, she turned the trips into her own therapy sessions: discussing her sexual frustration with my father, disappointment as a homemaker, self-doubt as an artist, exploitative friends, battles with depression, anxiety and loneliness, acrophobia, as well as fear of abandonment, weight gain, and aging. Worst was the burden of my grandmother.

I knew my mother wasn't trying to be destructive by telling me so much. I was the one person she truly adored: the most beautiful, brilliant, talented, and likable girl on earth. She marveled at every poem I wrote and every outfit I put together. I bathed in her adulation, wanting to believe I was everything she said and more.

My mother was trying to overcompensate for her own early cruelties by doing what her mother hadn't: lavish her child with attention and make her feel close. But it went too far. Because we were the same sex, my mother identified with me, rather than my brothers. I became her alter ego. Emotionally unfulfilled by my father, she came to rely on me as a confidante, adviser, and admirer. I served her well. So well that I felt selfish and disloyal doing anything else.

When she asked me to explain a blow job, she crossed a line. She seemed to be competing with me or living through my youth. When Laura Ashley dresses became fashionable among high school girls at Friends, I started wearing them—as did my mother. Because my friends found her open-minded and easy to talk to, they liked hanging around her. She gave her drawings as gifts to a couple of my boyfriends. When Andee and I smoked dope, my mother occasionally took a hit.

Deep down, it made me squirm. I knew it was fucked up. There were no boundaries between us, which felt dangerous. At the same time, I didn't want to jeopardize our bond. I needed her. She was all I had. In a family dominated by men, particularly my father who decried anything feminine, my mother and I were allied through gender. So long as we were together, I had a light in the darkness.

The light, however, flickered on and off. Sometimes I could count on it, others not.

My father and brothers didn't get it. Viewing my mother as self-centered and flighty, they felt rejected by her and projected their hostility onto the remaining female in the house. For *that,* I resented my mother's independence. Looking out for herself meant abandoning me to a stag scene where the male-to-female ratio was three-to-one. My brothers and father had a caveman camaraderie, from which I was either excluded or clubbed.

"She's on the crapper taking a dump," my brothers told the boys who called me if I wasn't swift enough to answer the phone.

"Elizabeth, you spend forever in the bathroom," my father shouted.

"The phone never stops ringing because of you, Elizabeth," he complained.

"The lights, Elizabeth, turn off the lights when you leave a room."

I got the message. My name was synonymous with waste.

With my mother no longer interested in running the house, my father took over the grocery shopping, saving money by going to Pathmark. He rejected all brand names, favoring generic labels. Even the cleanup felt like a privation: no-frills paper towels that smeared rather than absorbed liquid spills, and dishwashing soap refusing to lather.

I missed Palmolive. I missed dinner napkins. Such niceties were now derided as ninny-ish. If I felt disregarded at school for being a Jew, it was nothing compared to the total blackout of being dickless at home.

Was that why I sought out the dicks of others? Psych 101: Female wants what she lacks, ergo penis envy. But in my case, could it have been something more? Like positive male attention?

Scorpion was a senior at Friends whom I met as a freshman. His real name was Frank Garoni. He had acquired his nickname after sneaking up behind a school bruiser and choke-holding him until he passed out. Driving his father's smoke-gray Porsche convertible with sheepskin-covered bucket seats, Scorpion looked like an Italian movie star, his features chiseled, eyes big and brown, hair dark and wavy, along with an athletic build. It served him well playing contact sports.

My mother was not impressed. She didn't like that he honked the horn instead of getting out of his car when he came to pick me up. My father had no comment.

The one and only time Scorpion and I went all the way was

when his parents were out of town and he threw a party. I felt pretty proud an older guy was into me, a new and younger girl at school. I was willing to follow him past the pool and Ping-Pong tables of his basement "rec" room where everyone was drinking brewskies. I could tell by the way Scorpion checked himself out in a hallway mirror—arching his eyebrow, flipping a shock of hair from his forehead—he was feeling pretty proud, too. Of course, it didn't occur to me at the time that both of us were proud of the same thing: him.

In an upstairs bathroom, he dropped his jeans fireman-style. I took off mine, and we did it on the floor. Regressing to a pre-bipedal stage of human evolution, he crouched over me, weight on his forearms, panting and watching as his member disappeared between my inner thighs. The fact that he humped me hard and fast confirmed my original impression: Sex was for the sake of the boy, who couldn't give a rat's ass about the girl.

Scorpion dodged me the next week in school. I finally found him in the parking lot in his Porsche with the top down. Cradling a lacrosse stick, he was tossing a hard white rubber ball into the air, catching it in the mesh head.

"Did I do something wrong?" I said. "I feel like you're avoiding me."

"Everything's cool," he answered, pulling on a pair of aviator's before peeling out, laying rubber on the pavement.

After that, when we'd pass each other in the hallways or sit on opposing benches in the Quaker meetinghouse, Scorpion would look the other way. Was it in disgust? I pretended not to care but it was hard when word got around that I was the new school slut.

CHAPTER 4

A S A NAIL–BITING PERFECTIONIST, I was a girl with *anorexia-prone* written all over her, the type who had applied to no less than fifteen colleges, sure that even her safety school would reject her. So convinced was I of inevitable failure that when my name was called during my high school senior honors ceremony, I congratulated the girl sitting next to me.

Yet honors piled up in my desperate attempt to win my father's approval. But even my early acceptance to his alma mater did not get me what I wanted.

"Hi," I'd say, calling home from Ithaca, New York, once I became a freshman at Cornell University.

"Who's this?" he'd reply, a few seconds lapsing before recognizing my voice.

Returning home for vacations, I hoped for a reception on par with *missing child's not dead after all*. My mother didn't disappoint, throwing her arms around me before presenting a chicken smorgasbord—fried, roasted, and barbecued—from the Poultry Mart, the finest prepared food in Great Neck.

My father's welcome was less ebullient. He checked the tire pressure and antifreeze dilution of my car.

Our relationship wasn't heading in the direction I'd wanted. He was threatening not to pay my phone bill; the long-distance calls home were too high. I was living off campus in a sagging Victorian house with hemp-wearing Dead Heads who looked as if they'd stepped out of ancient Jerusalem. *The Moosewood Cookbook* was their bible and they got all worked up about beans bought in bulk at a food co-op and cruelty-free clothing. Other than making dean's list, my only concern was a working outlet for my blow dryer.

My self-validation through grades proved elusive. It was expected, but by no means required, that a freshman would select a curriculum commensurate with her degree of knowledge. Instead, I picked classes based on course roster titles, choosing those that sounded serious and rigorous. It was failure from the start.

The outline of my political theory course began with Machiavelli's *The Prince*. Day one, the professor opened with a discussion of the virtues and vices of successful monarchies. The other students were already intimately familiar with the book. What was going on? Wasn't the first meeting supposed to be an introduction with the professor announcing a reading assignment for the next class?

Not when it's a graduate course, you schmuck. It was only after the fact that I learned we were expected to read the whole book— before classes had even begun.

I started using cocaine as a study aid, to overcome feelings of inadequacy and burn the midnight oil. I had snorted my first line back in tenth grade and still remember the initial rush: a heightened sense of alertness, rapid heartbeat, and feeling of falling head-over-heels in love. The numbness and tingling that followed were heaven-sent, a magic transport carrying me up, up, and away from the earthly present.

The stimulant provided a perfect antidote to the nervousness, inferiority complex, and fear of exhaustion that defined my college coed state of mind. Ever since I was little, people told me I was good with words, and at ten years old I decided my future would be in letters. The older I got, however, the weaker became my confidence as I compared myself with peers whose literary abilities were more lyrical and persuasive. In my head, I created a Pulitzer Prize standard, to which I could never live up.

I hated Ithaca. Gray fog rolled off Cayuga Lake, clinging like mildew in a damp shower. By early December, waterfalls formed frozen appendages from the craggy gorges. Pulling all-nighters, I stayed awake, cranked up on coke, coffee, and cigarettes. The vaso-constrictors, exacerbated by the frostbiting cold, destroyed the blood vessels in my toes, which turned blue-black with chilblains. Hobbling to class, I crossed campus footbridges and peered into the ravines. The school's suicide rate was legendary. Sick as it was, I envied all the students who had the guts to plunge to death rather than flunk out.

• • •

In the fall of my sophomore year, I went home for Columbus Day weekend. Rather than drive the six hours alone, I took a Greyhound bus. On board, I immediately noticed a man sitting by a window who, with long chestnut hair, denim-blue eyes, and fair skin, looked like a Romantic poet. As I walked down the aisle in cutoffs, he checked out my legs, offering the seat beside him.

By the time we hit Route 17, I found out his name, Madison Thomas. He was a twenty-six-year-old opera singer living in Brooklyn with a woman who worked for a designer jeans company. He was also a proponent of free love.

I told him about my boyfriend, a two-hundred-pound hockey player recruited for the Cornell team. Everyone called him Canuck because he was Canadian. Proud of his nationality, he had a fleur-de-lis, an emblem from the provincial Quebec flag, tattooed on his buttock. The first time we slept together, I was shocked, but not because of the body art.

"What the hell is that?" I said, bolting upright in bed.

"My foreskin."

No American male I knew, whether Jew or Gentile, was ever left uncut. Having heard about foreign cocks and their *odeur de fro-*

mage, I worried if I got too close to Canuck's, I might get a whiff of whey. Although I never did, there was no getting past my fear: something ripening beneath that sheath of chicken skin.

"Are you in love with him?" Madison asked.

"Are you in love with her?"

"Does it matter?"

He leaned across the armrest and kissed me. We spent the rest of the trip making out, lulled by the steady motion of the bus, our tongues forming endless figure eights. At the Port Authority, where my parents were to pick me up, Madison and I exchanged contact information.

When I returned to Cornell, our correspondence began. He had decided to break up with his girlfriend and change careers, applying to an osteopathic school in Des Moines, Iowa. He was undergoing Reichian therapy, which involved an ominous contraption called an Orgone Box where he retreated to get in touch with his body's "aura." It liberated his libido.

I wrote back that, although I felt qualified to write a coed's guide to experimental sex, no man had ever brought me to an orgasm. He replied that I was a "victim of social tyranny" and showed "classic symptoms of armoring." I had to learn how to be free.

When I returned home for the Christmas holidays, Madison and I had a date. At his place in Brooklyn, he put *Madama Butterfly* on the stereo, singing, *"Ah, ti serro palpitante."* He talked about stuff I'd never heard come out of a male mouth—psychology and female sexuality—and dappled his speech with Briticisms, such as *bloody* and *mate.* After my history of stoners and jocks, Madison seemed like a huge jump up.

"I want to make love to you," he said, causing me to cover my face with my hands so he wouldn't see me blush. *Making love* sounded too intimate and sincere, whereas *fucking* was raunchier, implying your heart wasn't in it, which meant you weren't wide open to hurt.

That night, I got my first introduction to Orgone Therapy. Madison slid his finger inside me, advising me to exhale and submit to the sensations. At first it seemed absurd, his acting like a sex coach, but as the feelings grew more intense and my muscles contracted, he applied more pressure while guiding me to go against the tension and relax. Something strange began to happen. At first, I thought I was going to pee, until the urge gave way to the physical equivalent of a time-lapse image of an unfurling flower. Hackneyed as it sounds, petals were blooming inside me. My internal efflorescence.

We began to fuck, or maybe we were really making love. Contrary to my previous encounters of rapid friction and absurd pounding, with the guy's ass bopping up and down like a martini jigger, Madison rocked back and forth. The movement was excruciatingly slow and as he orchestrated his rhythm to mine, our bodies melted together. We kept our eyes open and I felt myself being absorbed into the blueness of his irises and shallowness of his breath. The hairs of my body stood on end. Pleasure streamed from my pores. Yes, this had to be love.

Then it happened: an orgasm with a man, the first of my life.

I was in disbelief. Madison had discovered my G-spot, the Holy Grail of female sexuality. The goddamn thing had been so elusive, I doubted its very existence. But now that a man had awakened the spongy lump slumbering in the recesses of my vagina, a new sensuality commingled with my inchoate womanliness. Hello, Pandora's box.

With my cheek pressed against Madison's chest, I felt it rise and fall as he sighed with satisfaction. Reaching over to a night table, he picked up a worn paperback, D. H. Lawrence's *Lady Chatterley's Lover*. The cover read: "The only unexpurgated version ever published in America."

"I'd like you to read it," Madison said. "Will you grant me that last wish?"

"Last wish? Aren't we going to see each other again?"

"I don't know how. There's hardly time. I've been accepted to osteopathy school and leave for Des Moines in a couple of weeks."

"What if I come visit you there?"

Ohmigod. What did I just say?

"Well . . . it would be all right . . . I suppose."

Okay, so his wasn't the most enthusiastic response, but it was enough to convince me that a sexual pilgrimage lay before me, a final excuse to leave Cornell, where I was miserable. Besides central heating, I missed my mother's coddling.

"You'll wind up a perfume girl at a department store!" However, when I announced I wasn't going back to school, she cried.

"Don't get any ideas about sitting around this house!" my father threatened.

I must have been high when I thought they'd spot me the money for a plane ticket to Iowa.

Breaking up with Canuck and moving back home, I went to work and school part-time. At New York University, I took a five-day-a-week French conversation course, lasting from nine AM to noon. In the afternoons, I had a job for $3.35 an hour as an archival assistant at the Institute of Electrical and Electronics Engineers near the United Nations. By three o'clock, I was already counting the minutes until my rush-hour commute.

Traveling to and from the city by Long Island Rail Road, I sat between stockbrokers in London Fog raincoats and secretaries in stirrup pants while reading *Lady Chatterley's Lover*. Savoring the erotic passages about the gamekeeper, Oliver Mellors, and his lover, Constance Chatterley, I never wanted the trip to end. More than once, I missed my stop.

By the middle of February, I'd saved enough for the plane ticket to see Madison. I imagined us stripping naked, decorating our pubic hair with posies, and dancing in the rain like Lady Chatterley and Mellors. But after I arrived in Des Moines, there would be no chance for streaking.

"You look as if you've put on weight," he said at his apartment.

"Where?" I asked, frantically patting my body as if ants were crawling all over it.

No one had ever come close to calling me fat, but since I'd returned home, quit smoking, and stopped drugs, my clothes had definitely gotten snugger.

"You just look fuller than I remembered, that's all."

That's all? Try telling a nineteen-year-old girl she has a smidgen of cellulite and you'll see her start popping Dexatrims as if they're Tic Tacs.

"It was wrong for me to have agreed for you to come here in the first place," he said, explaining that he'd recently met someone with whom he wanted to start a new and committed relationship. His free-love days were over. He never meant anything to come of us or believed I'd actually appear in Iowa.

"But doesn't it matter that I discovered my body with you?" I whimpered.

He said nothing. I gulped. It felt as if I were trying to swallow crushed glass.

What the fuck had I done? My return ticket wasn't for another five days. How could I go back any sooner? My parents were furious with me for leaving Cornell and chasing after this osteo-quack in the first place. Which was worse, to slouch through their front door, tail between my legs, or to linger where I wasn't wanted?

I procrastinated booking a flight for a couple of days in the hope that Madison would change his mind. The wait was purgatorial. At night, he slept on the couch and during the day, went to the library. I found a jug of Gallo under the kitchen sink and started drinking. Heavily.

When the morning finally came for me to leave, I placed his copy of *Lady Chatterley's Lover* on the bed. But at the beep of the airport-taxi horn, I had a change of heart. Certain things are for keeps. I grabbed the book. Maybe it could still be my story.

• • •

The spring of 1981 was my wandering in the wilderness period. Lost, I had moved back home, and while Great Neck was as civilized as a topiary garden, I managed to find some pretty treacherous territory. My brother Warren was a Great Neck North High School senior, heading for Tulane University in the fall. My other brother, Andrew, was a sophomore and star athlete who bore a striking resemblance to John Kennedy Jr. My mother was temporarily veering away from art to try acting, taking lessons at Manhattan conservatories—Stella Adler's and Herbert Berghoff's—and auditioning for off-off-Broadway plays. My father still worked at the same Bronx hospital but drug dealers and gangs now infested the neighborhood, filling the emergency room with gunshot victims. While my days were routine—French class, office job, and public transportation—my after-hours activities were anything but.

Frank Garoni, aka Scorpion, unexpectedly resurfaced. We'd had little contact since high school but, in early March, he called me out of the blue and asked me to spend a weekend at his Vermont ski house. Although I didn't ski, I was still raw from Madison's rejection and it made me feel better that there actually existed another guy who wanted to be with me. Putting the memory of Scorpion's lousy loving out of my mind, I accepted the invitation.

When we arrived after a long Friday-night drive, he fucked me like a jackrabbit: multiple, short thrusts, ending in a shallow squirt before dropping dead asleep. So much for giving my G-spot another go. Early the next morning, he headed to the mountain and I hit the kitchen. With nothing to do, I baked quiches.

In the late afternoon, he walked through the door and I proudly presented a buffet—Lorraine, broccoli, and tomato-mushroom—along with an open bottle of red wine. He dined without commentary while I overate and overdrank. When I steadied myself to do the dishes, he neither protested nor assisted, instead settling into a La-Z-Boy for a night of college basketball on TV.

I locked myself in the bathroom. Why was I even there? I

wanted to go home but, without my own car, I was stuck. Hadn't I just been through this scenario in Iowa?

For the first time, I bent over a toilet, shoved the pointer and middle finger of my right hand as far as I could reach down the back of my throat, and released a hot porridge of wine and custard. It felt good, like piercing a blister with a needle.

The relief was all too brief. The next morning when Scorpion went skiing, I went running. The snow-covered woods and mountains reminded me of Ithaca—what I imagined hell to be if it ever froze over. After five miles of pounding the country roads, the bones in my legs ached and the balls of my feet stung. Forcing myself to go on, I wanted the punishment.

Thereafter, I began a cycle of bleary sexual encounters with older men: A dentist ate my pussy on a frozen golf course; a guitarist for Lou Reed liked getting head and shooting smack; a hairdresser took me to a Kraftwerk concert and fucked me behind the bleachers. I contracted and was treated for the clap.

I started cooking elaborate dishes for my family and introduced a new practice: wine with meals. Sophisticated dining was an attempt to veil my own shameful habits—drinking, bingeing, and purging. Rationally, I knew I wasn't fat, so I claimed my compulsive exercising was done in the name of fitness. As for amenorrhea and shin splints, I ignored them in favor of achieving a desexualized, sinewy strength.

Articles about anorexia and bulimia were just beginning to appear in women's magazines. I read the stories as a blind voyeur, not recognizing they were about me. My family sensed something was wrong but had no language to express their concern.

"You're wasteful." My father shook his head over veal chops, his serrated knife screeching against the plate.

My mother sat in silence, trying to will me to put a morsel in my mouth. Warren and Andrew only wanted to eat and beat it, to get as far away from their loony, attention-grabbing sister as fast as possible.

When the meal was over, my parents exchanged nervous looks, anticipating my next move—a retreat to the bathroom where I turned on the faucet to drown out the sound of retching.

I knew I was torturing my mother. By now, I had turned against her and wanted to cause her pain as payback for years of laying her problems on me. Her trust was a burden, and I resented being her caretaker. Her needs seemed so great, her inner emptiness so vast, I could never make her happy.

Turning my rage inward, I committed acts of self-abuse that hurt her more than if I'd actually lashed out. Of course, she didn't deserve retribution. I knew she loved me and would never have done anything intentionally malicious. Still, I took grim satisfaction when I stepped on a scale and the needle quivered below the triple digits.

Why hadn't my father intervened? He was well aware there needed to be dividing lines between parents and children. *His* was an impenetrable wall. At least he never made me feel responsible for him. Then again, I never felt he was responsible for me, either.

Too old to be living at home, I knew the time had come to move out. As a girl, I often went to the beach behind our house and stood on a dock, gazing westward across the Sound toward the Throgs Neck Bridge where the mighty pilings and cables framed Manhattan in the distance. If the sun was hitting at a certain angle, the light bounced off the buildings and a faint skyline appeared like a long-lashed eyelid, seductively winking at me in the distance.

I loved my French course at NYU where Washington Square was a show a minute. The teacher was relaxed and the students weren't competitive. I had a new friend, Joanna, who dressed like a cowgirl and took me to Café Un Deux Trois—a Eurotrash canteen off Times Square—where a skinny black guy with Arabian Nights facial hair kissed me on the mouth before disappearing in a black limousine. I later found out his name: Prince.

"So I'm thinking of transferring to NYU," I told my parents.

"Finishing college there. I want to live in the city and get an apartment in the Village. Maybe someone is looking for a roommate."

"Think again," said my mother. "NYU is not a good enough school and you're not living in some apartment in the Village. You're not ready for that kind of independence. You need a more protected environment."

"I'm almost twenty. Of course, I am independent."

"No you're not. You're out of control. You're running around at night doing God-knows-what, picking up garbagemen off the street. You're wasting your time. Get back to a real school."

"I agree with your mother," my father said, nodding. "If you want to go to NYU, you can live at home and commute."

"You just want me to live here because it's cheaper."

"We'll pay for you to live in Manhattan but only in student housing at Barnard," my mother said.

"But that's all women!"

Barnard, the sister school to Columbia College, was part of Columbia University. It was located in Morningside Heights, a neighborhood where there'd be no one the likes of Prince chilling on a bodega stoop, or even a decent restaurant—not for thirty blocks south. But my visit surprised me. Centralized with traditional architecture, the campus was an urban Ivy League enclave nestled on Upper Broadway. Students wearing saris, chadors, yarmulkes, and crocheted Muslim skullcaps crowded the walkways.

At Barnard, the women walked briskly, talking about futures in architecture, law, and government, as well as ticking off famous alumnae, from Margaret Mead to Laurie Anderson. Shining with purpose and self-possession, the students were inspiring. What the hell? I transferred to the college. Maybe their gleam would rub off on me.

CHAPTER 5

*I*T WAS THE FALL OF 1982, my first semester at Barnard, when I met Charlie, a senior at Columbia. We were in the same astronomy class. With his faded army jacket, black beret, wire-rimmed glasses, and dark, scrappy beard, he was working a Trotsky look. Reeking of rat poison, his apartment on 110th Street was decorated with Marx and Lenin posters. Mao's Little Red Book sat on the night table. Charlie was a lefty, the first I ever knew.

After the Soviets invaded Afghanistan and President Carter instituted a draft registration, Charlie joined forces with other college activists to found an organization called Students Against Militarism, or SAM. He staged a so-called die-in to support the nuclear freeze movement. Local newscasters covered the event, but the real coup for Charlie came when *Pravda* showed up.

The turning point in our friendship occurred one chilly autumn night during a lab assignment. We were roaming the campus, trying to locate the North Star. Although it was a clear night and there should have been gazillions of twinkling bodies visible to the naked eye, we couldn't see any of them. Who would even think of stargazing in New York City? The ambient light from the buildings illuminated the dark sky, making it impossible to detect anything bright.

"We might as well be looking for the North Star in the daytime," Charlie grumbled. "This assignment is designed for failure. What idiot thought it up?"

The professor walked by, clipboard in hand.

"Dr. Jastrow," I called out. "We're having trouble locating the North Star. What should we do?"

"Have you tried determining the right ascension and declination? You've got to figure out the maximum and minimum latitude and add and subtract eighty degrees from the declination."

I looked at my lab partner, praying he understood what the professor was talking about. Red in the face, Charlie was hyperventilating, as if marshaling some inner atomic strength.

"Just tell me, where is the fucking North Star?" he exploded.

I was not only speechless but also scared. How could he yell at a teacher that way? I'd always been pretty cheeky but never had I talked back to or challenged a person who knew more than me, especially not one doling out my grades. More incredible was what happened next: The professor pointed overhead at the North Star.

And that was it, the moment Cupid's quiver zinged through my heart. Charlie's outrage, insolence, and courage to confront authority represented manliness at its best. He was strong, righteous, and able to effect change.

We slept together that night. But the guy who was so brazen only an hour before turned out to be Mr. Bashful in bed. His macho swagger disappeared, revealing unexpected modesty and self-deprecating humor. Although I anticipated doing the nasty with Che Guevara, I wound up fumbling with Woody Allen instead.

"You're beautiful beyond comprehension," Charlie said, showing up at my dorm the next day with six yellow roses. "You're stunning, smart, and, best of all, you're below my height." (He was five foot eight.)

To him, I represented the popular girl at a school dance who he never imagined would give an unpolished guy like him a chance. In his eyes, I had it all: a Jewish doctor's daughter, full of beauty, brains, and flair.

To me, he promised kindness, which was long overdue. My love life had included a laundry list of assholes whose sexual swaggering went hand in hand with their capacity for cruelty. Charlie was just the opposite. Tender and unsure of himself, he gave me courage to be the same. I dropped my protective Teflon coating, revealing the vulnerability within.

As my college sweetheart, he called me "Toots," his grandfather's term of affection for his grandmother. Because Charlie and I had met in astronomy, I named a star after him through the International Star Registry. At night, if I couldn't fall asleep, he read Sherlock Holmes aloud until I drifted off. Waking up, he was always in a good mood, serenading me in a campy baritone voice with "Oh, What a Beautiful Mornin'." He was so devoted, I was 100 percent certain that if ever I were lost at the Meadowlands, he would somehow find me. His love was unlike any I'd ever known.

• • •

In the spring of 1983, Charlie graduated from Columbia, planning a career in public service. He had worked for a New Jersey congressman, Andy Maguire, a post-Watergate insurgent and principled Democrat who didn't give a shit about his image or pissing off the party regulars. He was Charlie's role model.

Moving to Washington, DC, my boyfriend landed a job at the Center for Science in the Public Interest, an organization founded by Ralph Nader followers who were self-appointed nutrition police. They hired Charlie to co-author a book about the marketing tactics of the alcohol industry, which manipulated young people to drink to excess.

The irony was that I, his girlfriend, had both an eating disorder and an alcohol problem. Did he know? Not really. Afflicted with a myopic optimism, he could see only the good, blinding himself to anything that contradicted his picture-perfect view.

It never crossed his mind that I might be any less resilient and emotionally together than him. After all, he'd been able to overcome *his* childhood obstacles.

At six years old, during his first month of first grade, he had slipped off a ten-foot slide onto a cement playground and fractured his skull. A neurosurgeon in Bronxville saved Charlie from permanent brain damage. When he returned to school, his head was shaved, stitched, and covered in a protective football helmet.

For years, he experienced "auras" or "petit mal" syndromes, episodes of queasiness and déjà vu, followed by temporary amnesia. Unsure there was anything wrong and not wanting to be labeled whiny or weird, he hid the symptoms for several years until the age of sixteen, when he suffered his first full-fledged epileptic attack.

Besides his neurological problem, he'd been a sickly child, suffering endless colds and allergy attacks, which led to lots of school absenteeism and unimpressive report cards.

In eleventh grade, he realized that what he lacked in brawn, he could make up for in brains. He became intellectually voracious, reading whatever he could find on his older brother's bookshelves. Harold had gone to Columbia College and later Yale Law School. Because his older brother had always been perceived as the brighter of the two boys, Charlie was as amazed as everyone else when his own GPA soared.

He sailed through Columbia in only three and a half years, graduating with a Phi Beta Kappa key and a goal of getting to DC. He believed the Beltway was the best graduate program for an aspiring politician. No, he wasn't leaving me behind, he insisted, only doing what he had to do for his future.

I took it hard and wanted him back. With a year and a half left at Barnard, I couldn't bear the separation. I cried and cried and cried, centering my life on our visits, clinging to his words *down the road* and *staying together*.

Marriage was on my mind. Ever since ninth grade, my parents

had judged (and rejected) all my boyfriends according to high Jewish son-in-law standards. Now, at twenty-one, that future wasn't far off. There were already a couple of girls in my class at Barnard flashing pear-shaped diamond engagement rings.

Charlie was a real prospect, the first to qualify. He possessed my father's admirable qualities—dependability, diligence, and self-sufficiency—but not the nasty habits like screaming at or criticizing me. Upbeat and funny, Charlie always made me laugh. When he described green crud at the base of his electric toothbrush as a "Louis Pasteur paste" and promised to "marinate it in Fantastik," I not only snorted out loud, I became mildly incontinent.

Soulful and compassionate, Charlie, I believed, could make a difference as a public servant, and being his partner would also ennoble my own existence. But did *I* have what it took to be a politician's wife? Did I even *want* to be? It wasn't as if he'd make much money, and his career—our future—would depend on a capricious electorate.

"Charlie, you should get a law degree if you're going to go into politics," I told him. "It'll give you security. Something to fall back on. So you don't wind up just a lackey on the Hill."

"Law school's a waste of time. It's not me. I have to do this *my* way. Just like you have to do your thing *your* way."

What thing? What way? I had no idea what I wanted for myself, so it was easier to imagine what I wanted for Charlie, which, ideally, would be best for us both. By the start of my senior year, I still hadn't been hit by any lightning crack of careerism.

As a history major and art history minor, I considered my options: an archivist? I would rather have a real Valium drip. When I took a Stanley Kaplan LSAT prep course for law school, I scored higher on practice tests by filling in the circles at random than by applying reasoning and logic. In my painting and drawing classes, I showed talent, but a graduate degree in fine arts? No, thanks.

As for my girlhood fantasy of becoming a writer, that was long gone. Once I got to college, the sight of my Smith-Corona brought on heart palpitations and shortness of breath.

I looked upon single-minded women like Cathy—my closest friend at Barnard, who had graduated a year before me—with bafflement and envy. Coming from a lower-middle-class family in Lubbock, she received scholarships to school and never relied on anyone for help, knowing she would always have to look out for herself. With a far-reaching dream of being an international financier, she was now studying at the Ecoles de Hautes Etudes Commerciales, a business school in Paris.

Paris? Now that was an idea. With my college credits nearly complete, I was planning on writing my senior thesis about cubism and changing notions of time and space in prewar Europe. Why not do it there? I could rent a room someplace and research my subject at the Bibliothèque Nationale. I had a small savings from summer jobs so I could afford a plane ticket. With Charlie in DC, and without a ring on my finger, I had no one to whom I had to answer—my first real chance for freedom and self-reliance.

My parents were bent out of shape.

"The most expensive city in the world," my father growled.

"You can't go unless you apply to graduate school beforehand," my mother declared, fearing that an errant semester, without proper housing and campus confines, would throw off her master plan for me.

Years earlier, she had befriended a vanguard woman, the founder and director of the New Museum, who changed my mother's life by advancing her art and sense of autonomy. Because the woman had been educated at New York University's Institute of Fine Arts—a graduate school for art history and archaeology—and suggested to my mother that I might do the same, her mind was made up.

I had no reason to object. I liked art well enough. A couple of years of graduate study seemed a fine way to bide more time before my real future started—whatever that was going to be.

"Okay, I'll apply to the Institute if I can go to Paris," I said, words that caused my mother to clasp her hands, casting her eyes heavenward.

"You'll have to manage on the same amount as your living expenses at Barnard," my father added. "Not a cent more. Do you understand?"

"Thank you!" I leapt to hug my parents. "Not to worry. I'll be back before you know it."

And I was. Paris was lonely and cold, and after several abortive attempts to research my thesis at the Bibliothèque Nationale, I was at the end of my rope. Fortunately, I received a long-distance phone call from my mother:

"You got into the Institute! Are you ready to come home yet?"

I thought you'd never ask.

• • •

By the time I returned and was nearly done with my thesis, Charlie moved back from Washington, renting an apartment in Hackensack. New Jersey Congressman Robert Torricelli hired Charlie as a political liaison to unions, civic groups, and ethnic communities in Bergen County. Coming to his own conclusion that he didn't want his success to depend on the goodwill or fate of another elected official, Charlie was even applying to law school. He told his parents he'd changed his life, partly because of me.

It was a Great Neck girl's dream come true, and yet it suddenly didn't feel that way. What if things didn't work out? There was no chance I could turn back. Not now. My mother, ready to organize the wedding, wrote Charlie a letter:

I feel blessed that yours and Elizabeth's lives touched. I know how painful it was for you two to be apart. So often, I've wanted to call

*you and thank you for giving my daughter what she never had in
her life—for all her years of feeling lonely, confused, hurt,
unloved—it's all been changed by you and that touches my life, as
well. I've long felt you're like one of my sons.*

In fact, Charlie treated my mother better than her sons did.
When her wallet was stolen at Saks, she was too frazzled to contact the credit card companies so Charlie took over. In addition
to her artistic interest in the abnormal and grotesque, he adored
her horrific descriptions of everyday suburban life. Sharing inside jokes, they had a close relationship that, quite honestly, made
me claustrophobic.

Usually, a boyfriend is never considered good enough for a
daughter and her mother is always a nuisance to him, but in my
case it was man-bites-dog. If Charlie and I fought, my mother always took his side, reminding me how fortunate I was to have
him.

Although my father disliked Charlie at first, viewing him as a
pinko, his admission to New York University Law School earned
my boyfriend the paternal rubber stamp. As for my brothers?
Charlie became the Third Musketeer.

The more my family rah-rahed him, the more I felt boxed
in. Between their expectations and enthusiasm, as well as Charlie's career change, so much seemed to be riding on our relationship. But what no one knew, and what Charlie and I
couldn't admit to each other, was that we had a problem. A big
problem. Sex.

We had never gotten past that first night of adolescent awk-
wardness. From the very beginning, we established a routine of
no action on weekdays, during the daytime, or when I had my
period. Our intimacy felt forced, not organic and uncontrollable,
as it should have been, given the hormonal drive typical of
twenty-something-year-olds.

A malfunction that should have lasted a couple of hours became our status quo. I kept telling myself we'd get over or grow out of it. As husband and wife, we'd practice and improve. I had no idea that if two lovers don't start out by fucking all night long, afterward is always too late.

CHAPTER 6

*I*T WAS A FRIDAY NIGHT, spring 1987. Hors d'oeuvre platters were balanced atop every flat surface in my kitchen, including the step-on trash can lid. In the fridge, twenty-four bottles of icy Perrier Jouët stood in perfect line formation. One last misting of Rigaud Room Spray and I was ready for my cocktail party to begin.

I was a newlywed on domestic overdrive. I took to hostessing like a trophy wife on the charity circuit, except that I entertained not in a Fifth Avenue floor-through, but an eight-hundred-square-foot one-bedroom in the Normandie Court, a self-proclaimed luxury high-rise on Third Avenue and 95th Street, one block south of lower Spanish Harlem. Newly constructed, the building was amenity-laced: valet, housekeeping, dry cleaning, video rental, health club, and twenty-four-hour convenience mart. There were no children or pets, not because they weren't permitted, but because the tenants were too young and upwardly mobile to have accrued any responsibilities other than maintaining their Beamers.

When my intercom buzzed, the first guests were soigné aristobrats, Matthew and Fraser, nicknamed Kibble and Bits during their Princeton undergraduate days. My good friend Susan from graduate school soon followed, accompanied by her West Side apartment mate, Debbie, a gossip columnist for *Avenue*, a society magazine.

Susan and I were co-writing reviews of gallery shows for *ARTnews*. We were now friends with artists whose status was fringe, at best. Free food lured them to my uptown digs.

After my brother Andrew went off to Middlebury College, my mother celebrated her empty nest by investing her inheritance from her father in a SoHo loft, which served as her art studio. Since my father disliked Manhattan, he remained in Great Neck while she spent the week in the city, returning to Long Island to be with him on weekends. But not this Friday night. She had guilt-tripped me into inviting her to my party.

Cathy was last to show. After completing her MBA, she was now a trader at Salomen Brothers. She made up for her delayed arrival with several glasses of bubbly. She was easy to piss off and we had quite a history so I knew the warning signs: a higher pitch to her voice, quickening of her speech, and flinching at the corners of her mouth. But that night, I was too smashed to see it coming.

One minute we were clinking champagne flutes, the next attacking each other with all the venom of Hunts Point street whores.

"What the fuck is your problem!"

"How could you!"

"Crazy bitch!"

"Get the fuck out!"

The last words I remember vividly, a power surge momentarily grinding my party to a halt before scattering the guests to the street.

After that, my brain short-circuited and I crashed. It was late Saturday morning when I awoke to an immaculate apartment. Charlie, who rarely drank or did drugs, had already sponge-mopped any residue of debauchery.

"When did you wash those?" I asked, gesturing toward the flutes drying on the kitchen counter.

"After you cooked last night. We did them together. Don't you remember?"

"After I did *what*?"

"Cooked an omelet."

Not only didn't I remember, I had no recollection of getting undressed, washing my face, or going to bed. But clearly I had done those things. How else to explain my pajamas and makeup-free skin?

Slowly, a pasty image of the night before spread inside my head. Cathy, our screaming, the madness, excreted like mental sludge, making my stomach roll over. Somersaults of shame. I wanted to be sick.

I needed to talk to Jonathan, my current therapist, who offered biofeedback treatments. He had started treating me six weeks earlier, after I had experienced a bleeding ulcer and doctors prescribed Tagamet along with advising me to see a shrink, who could help me reduce stress.

"So, tell me about Friday night," Jonathan started once I'd arrived at his office for an emergency session.

"I had a party and we were really drunk and—"

"I thought you weren't supposed to drink because of your stomach."

I was never diligent about following medical instructions. Chalk it up to latent passive aggression toward Dad.

"Cathy and I got into a ferocious fight," I continued. "Afterward, I blanked out. When I woke up, I felt awful and thought biofeedback could help me relax."

"Back up. What do you mean, *blanked out*?"

"You know, passed out, blacked out, whatever. I was too drunk to remember but Charlie told me I cooked and cleaned."

"Are you saying you can't remember doing those things?"

"So? It's not as if that hasn't happened before."

"Is Charlie aware of your problem?"

"My problem?"

"You. Are. An. Alcoholic."

Me, an alcoholic?

Jonathan explained I'd experienced "clinical blackouts," severe amnesia that occurs during drinking periods when a chemical shift occurs in the brain, a symptom of a dire, long-term alcohol habit.

"Take the next plane to Hazelden, a rehab center in Minnesota," he ordered.

Rehab? But that's for real drunks.

I still wasn't getting it. Leaving his office, I stopped at Barnes & Noble and bought six books on alcoholism. Each included a standard twenty-question test created by Johns Hopkins University to determine whether or not you had a drinking problem. If you answered yes to three or more, the diagnosis was *definitely alcoholic.*

I scored a ten.

Charlie was shocked. I was never a sloppy boozer. But all the books recommended total abstinence, so I quit cold turkey. Changed my lifestyle immediately: For the next year, I avoided restaurants and social gatherings since I associated them with liquor; gave up cooking entirely—for me, an activity inseparable from swilling; and ordered in from pizzerias and delis, food that didn't go well with wine. The cocktail party for which I was so prepared resulted in an ending that I never anticipated: a future on the wagon.

• • •

Being married to a teetotaler made it easier for me to stay dry since there was no temptation on the home front. But "no temptation on the home front" represented more than just sobriety.

For years, I had relied on wine to stimulate sexual chemistry between Charlie and me. Now, without a minimum blood alcohol concentration of .10, I suffered precoital anxiety attacks. As a young husband and wife, we were *supposed* to want to have sex with each other. Instead I thought a lot about fucking our building's Puerto Rican handyman who looked as if he'd stuck a pair of tube socks down in his pants.

Although my preoccupation with men was intense, Charlie was not one of them. After a week or so had gone by without any intimacy, my stomach would tighten and my chest would constrict at the realization that we *had* to do it. If too much time passed, sex would become an elephant in the bedroom. Who was I kidding? The bedroom already was the elephant camouflaged in Ralph Lauren chintz.

"I'm glad you don't taste like stale wine anymore," Charlie said, when I asked whether he'd noticed any difference in our sex life with me off the sauce.

"Why didn't you ever tell me my breath bothered you?"

"I didn't want to make you feel bad."

That was our marriage. Forsake the truth to spare the feelings.

"Maybe we could do something different," I hinted.

"How do you mean?" Charlie said.

"Try something new in bed. More spontaneity. What do you think?"

"Talking about it isn't the answer. It's a contradiction. Sex should be natural. The kind of thing you have to just do."

Charlie's rejection dampened my instinct to offer a hands-on tutorial about the finer points of my anatomy. Instead, I left a how-to-make-love manual on his pillow, a nudge for him to be bold. Take the initiative. Go for it.

He never read the book.

My sexual experience and candor intimidated him. He'd had fewer partners than me. If I said something crude, he told me I lacked a "discretion gene" and appeared to retreat inward, averting his eyes, enfolding his body in an imaginary vacuum of compressed space.

It was understandable that Charlie preferred his wife on a pedestal than on a floor mat. To make him comfortable, I steered clear of dirty talk, Tantric positions, and blindfolds, reminders that I was familiar with more than the missionary style.

Although I didn't start out repressed, I eventually channeled my husband's inhibition. Perhaps I unconsciously hoped that by adopting his Victorian demeanor, I could restore my own lost virtue. That never happened but I did learn to feel exposed walking around the apartment undressed, grabbing a towel for coverage. The ordinary muck of the human body—from morning breath to cum stains—became so shameful, there was no way I would ever suggest anything kinky, let alone fuck with the lights on.

I now harbored a fantasy of being overpowered, of—dare I say—rape. I wanted to be smacked around a bit and beg for mercy while being mercilessly fucked. I knew it was a taboo, which was precisely the point. In reality, sexual violence was more sickening to me than murder. But the abstraction of male dominance and female submission was arousing. It freed me of responsibility for my own desire, expiating any guilt—a way to let myself off the hook for years of being an easy lay.

Never did I allow Charlie into my sin-sational imaginings. To me, he was a lily angel, uplifting the human race. The very idea of him as the aggressor not only contradicted what I believed were *his* views of women and equality, it appalled and grossed *me* out. I had my own Madonna–whore complex: My husband was my Virgin Mary.

But my conceit was not quite consistent with the man I married. He was a tongue-wagging breast lover, furtively flipping through my Victoria's Secret catalogs on high alert for a doughy rise over Stephanie Seymour's bra cups. On the street, I could hear his mental whistling when he spotted full figures, the types whose elastic-waisted underwear left pink indentations around their soft hips.

Given the chaste tone of our marriage, the push–pull of probity and prurience was confusing. The fact that Charlie liked fleshy women meant he probably found me about as succulent as a quail bone. Don't get me wrong. He always told me I was beautiful. But his titty satellite tripped a switch—my adolescent feelings of mammary deficiency. Although I told myself I was sexually superior to him, I camouflaged my curveless frame in the bedroom with soft-core clichés: merry widows, garter belts, and the like. Had I invested in a camcorder, I could have starred in my own adult film productions.

Charlie and I reserved conjugal relations for Saturday nights. To get into the mood, I had a stockpile of atmosphere enhancers: candles, Opium perfume, and Marvin Gaye cassettes. While my husband waited in our chintz-blitzed bedroom, I retreated to the bathroom where I practiced a repertoire of hubba-hubba moves, puckering my lips and batting my lashes. Next came the contortions of hooking, clipping, and strapping my costume into place. Never mind the architectural challenge of keeping my hosiery seams straight.

Come curtain time, I fought cold feet. Taking one last look in the mirror—my lips painted the color of beet juice and hair artfully waved—I held my breath before making an entrance. Why was I pretending to be a stripper for a man who seemed more like a saint than a spouse?

• • •

What Charlie failed to conquer in the bedroom, he more than compensated for in the boardroom. Putting his political career on hold, he took a first step toward his new future: shaving off his beard. After passing the New York State Bar, he was now a fresh-faced attorney-at-law.

It was the era of corporate tycoonery, when power and money were encrypted in uppercase letters—LBO, M&A, S&L, KKR, RJR—the coded vernacular of a new breed of imperialists, soaring on golden parachutes, poison pills, junk bonds, and greenmail. When one by one, these men began to crash, they hired five-hundred-dollar-an-hour lawyers to cushion the fall.

Recruited by the litigation department of a white-shoe firm,

Charlie worked in a monolithic steel building with tinted glass and recessed overhead lighting, which, like solitary confinement in a maximum security prison, was never turned off. I loved to visit. It was like infiltrating Maxwell Smart's CONTROL headquarters. A lobby security guard phoned a faceless "Chief" for permission to grant my entrance, another escorted me to an elevator, and overhead surveillance cameras panned the entire operation.

Ascending to Charlie's floor, the elevator traveled at warp speed, and the change in air pressure caused my ear canals to pop. When the double doors snapped open, I was deposited, slightly wobbly, into a reception area staffed by headset-wearing females who seemed to be enveloped in a Cone of Silence. I never knew which was responsible for a disembodied voice automatically paging my husband: *"Sir, your wife has arrived."*

Once he closed the door to his office, we had to laugh. Hard to believe that Charlie—whose idea of a Mecca pilgrimage was a trip to Saugerties, New York, to visit Big Pink, The Band's house— now recorded notes-to-self in a mini Dictaphone and had a personal secretary addressing him by the honorific *Mr.*

As a spectator, I was turned on by my husband's spotlight in a theater of power. His Woody Allen shtick had long ago lost its charm. I now understood that Charlie's self-ridicule was a coping technique, a cover-up for his insecurities. But Charlie-the-blood-thirsty-lawyer was no act, his confidence and aggression being all that and more.

I wanted to tackle him. Demand he fuck me on the fax machine. On the one occasion I tried, he arched his eyebrows in surprise and said, "Oh, yeah?" before returning to his work. Later, when he dragged himself home after a fourteen-hour day of an eighty-hour week, his voltage had expired along with my heat.

Practicing law was Charlie's extreme sport. Instead of free-climbing a three-thousand-foot rock face against a clock, he passed his own version of a three-day endurance test: traveling to London for a morning arbitration between global advertising firms; taking an afternoon flight to Japan while reading 1,250 pages of deposition testimony for a defamation case against a New York publicist; landing in Tokyo to interrogate a witness for a derivatives scandal between J. P. Morgan and Korean banks; and catching a return flight to New York during which he wrote a fifty-page brief for the defamation matter, which wasn't even his in the first place but something he'd taken on as a favor to a senior partner. My husband's final adrenaline rush came when he got word upon returning home to catch his breath that the partner had circulated an interoffice memo throughout the firm: "If you have an emergency and need a brief written, just put Charlie on an airplane."

With that, he did another about-face out our front door.

CHAPTER 7

MARRIAGE TO THE IRONMAN MEANT adjusting to days without end, last-minute business trips, and interminable cases resuscitated by a crash cart of appeals. "No worries," I'd say, Stepford-smiling, not wanting to stand in Charlie's way when he called from the office to say, "It'll be another late night."

"Your father was called to the hospital at all hours for emergencies," my mother responded when I complained. "My own father was a workaholic. We never had supper with him. It's what a man does to make it."

Like the widows of Wall Street, I knew she was right. There would be a payoff for being patient. Besides, it wasn't as if I were some whining hausfrau with nothing to do but wait on a hubby. I had a job, too.

After earning my master's, I was hired by an organization that tracked stolen and forged art. My pay was twenty-one thousand dollars a year—four grand more than any starting salary at a gallery, museum, or auction house. Since art world positions were as scarce as Vermeer paintings, mine seemed a rare find.

But my title—director of art theft—proved to be far more intriguing than my day-to-day duties: entering crime reports from insurance and law enforcement agencies into a massive database. The office wall clock held greater fascination for me than some sixteenth-century polychrome statue of St. Sebastian clipped from a church in Meerbruck, Belgium. Had the clock's hands made enough rotations that my boss—a fat old maid with rubbery lips who ate ham salad with her mouth open—wouldn't give me a dirty look when I took another break from my hypoglycemic stupor to go out for a cappuccino?

The only thing that spared me from total soul rot was the Indiana Jones allure of my office location: the Explorers Club, a Tudor mansion on East 70th Street. Permeated with taxidermy gloom, the building had musty rooms displaying expedition artifacts, such as the dingy wooden sled that Robert Peary and Matthew Henson took to the North Pole in 1909, and a stuffed, twelve-foot polar bear with yellowing fur and spiked black claws. The average club member was sixty-two, and there was always a hoary geezer climbing the creaky stairs in a pith helmet.

Oddly enough, the Explorers Club was among Manhattan's choicest party rentals. Leaving my office one summer evening, I stumbled upon a cocktail reception in full swing. With Charlie working late and no plans of my own, I made an impulsive decision to slip into the party for a Perrier and eavesdropping.

"This is really the season for figs," said an elderly man in a wheelchair to a *Sports Illustrated* swimsuit model. "In Greece, you drizzle them with Muscat wine. Always remember, they never ripen after they've been picked. Only eat soft figs."

With a caramel-colored suntan, he was impeccably dressed in a custom-made navy-blue suit, his crisp, white shirt cuffs glinting with gold links. Behind him, a sunset filtered through stained-glass windows, creating a radiant corona around his head.

"Excuse me." I stepped forward after the model floated off. "I just had to meet you. I don't know who you are but something tells me you're the coolest guy in the room."

"I am," he said in a croaky voice veneered with a Continental accent. He took my hand, flashed a tobacco-stained smile, and introduced himself: a record mogul.

I spent the rest of the evening perched on an arm of his wheelchair. He chatted about music icons with the same offhandedness as someone recounting the ingredients for a family recipe. At the end of the party, he told me to call his office to schedule a lunch together.

Lunch. Daytime. He was in his seventies and had a broken hip after a polo accident in England's Ascot Park. Both of us were married. The invitation was perfectly innocent, right?

"He's been expecting your call," said his secretary when I phoned the next day. "One o'clock tomorrow, his office?"

What made him so certain he would hear from me? How exciting. It sure beat an Interpol report about a Persian carpet heist. Did I need to mention my appointment to Charlie? Nah. Why bother? He was pulling all-nighters, working on two different cases, drafting emergency papers for both, with two separate sets of secretaries. No reason to distract him with the ho-hum details of my day.

When I arrived at the record mogul's building, a table for two was set in his office. Piping through in-wall speakers was "Emotional Rescue" by the Stones. The room, lined floor-to-ceiling with gold albums, platinum albums, Grammy awards, and photographs of everyone from Aretha Franklin to Eric Clapton, was a private rock-and-roll hall of fame.

Who knows what the record mogul and I ate: something light and elegant, perhaps Caprese salads and risotto. I was too dazed to recall anything except keeping up with his conversation. He talked about Biarritz and Bel Air, his conversion from Catholicism to Judaism, how overrated the Concorde was, and the countless famous beauties he had fucked.

Here I was lunching with a legend—me, a Jewish girl from Great Neck whose only claims to sophistication were marriage, a graduate degree, and a dubious ability to speak French. My world seemed to expand tenfold just by proximity to him. When it was time for me to go, he hoisted himself up on a walker to stand. What a gentleman.

A hug seemed appropriate. I leaned to give a filial squeeze. Suddenly, he turned his head and his lips met mine. He opened his mouth. This geriatric, hobbled by broken bones and mottled with age spots, was French-kissing me.

Whoa.

"I'll call you," he said as I fled.

I had always been fearful of going too fast—in cars, on skis, in boats. But that kiss had the kind of horsepower I liked and realized how much I missed since getting married. It propelled me to a zone where my lack of control was energizing, instantly lifting me from my dead-end job, sad sex life, and husband slipping away. The kiss seized me from going through the motions of morality, pretending to be a good little wife, when at heart I still yearned to be a Backstage Betty, a band bitch ponying for a rock star to saddle her.

One night back in 1980, when Andee and I were nineteen and home from college for Thanksgiving vacation, we took her father's LeSabre to the city to go clubbing at the Ritz. As teenagers, we had made a pact not to marry until one of us slept with Mick Jagger. The challenge, as we saw it, would be finding him. The fucking, a cinch.

Although we didn't get to Mick, we came pretty close—enough to later forfeit our agreement. At the Ritz, we strutted past a table cordoned off with a velvet rope. Behind it was Keith Richards. I took a dollar bill, tore it in two, and wrote my name and number on one half, passing it to a guy at the table. Inviting us to join them, he was named Vlad and claimed to be the prince of Poland, as well as the son of the painter Balthus. I assumed (wrongly, I later found out) he was full of shit but who cared? Wearing white leather pants and mountain-climbing goggles with reflective lenses, he appeared to be Keith's right-hand man not to mention very hot shit.

The hour got late and Andee had to return her father's car so we left before any mischief started. The next day, Vlad called, inviting us to drop by Keith's apartment on Lower Fifth Avenue that night. Dressed in our finest Fiorucci, Andee and I once again shanghaied the LeSabre.

At the apartment, Vlad led us inside, but Keith was nowhere to be seen. The place was barren of furnishings except for half a dozen harem-style pillows on the floor, as well as a scattering of Polaroids of the Stones.

Vlad offered us "merck," claiming it was pharmaceutical cocaine. He cut us each a single line, which Andee and I thought was pretty chintzy until we started to fly. An apparition then emerged from the bedroom. His hair was dark and ratty. He had on jeans, an orange chiffon sash through the belt loops, and no shirt. A skull medallion on a silver chain hung like a target on his bare chest. Walking toward us, he held an ether-soaked gauze pad over his nose and mouth. A few seconds later, he fell face-first. Keith.

Regaining consciousness, he fortified himself with "merck" and hand-rolled cigarettes. Once everyone got sufficiently wasted, the conversation rambled. Out of nowhere, the guys got a craving for shepherd's pie. They wanted Andee and me to go to a nearby restaurant to pick it up. She got offended—*What are we, the maids?* Before splitting, she lifted a souvenir: leopard-print rolling papers from a makeup bag in the bathroom, which belonged to Keith's girlfriend, Patti Hansen. I lifted a souvenir, too: Vlad.

In the wee hours of the morning, Andee dropped off him and me at my house in Great Neck. Tiptoeing down the pitch-black hallway to my room, we went to bed. I remember nothing of the experience except wondering what color eyes he had. He wore his mountain-climbing goggles the entire time. Afterward, I hijacked my father's Mercedes from our garage to drive Vlad back to Keith's. I made the return trip from Manhattan before dawn, my parents having no idea that while they'd been sleeping, their college coed had been fucking a hellion nearly twice her age in the next room.

• • •

The encounter with the record mogul brought back memories of that rock-and-roll milestone. His kiss catapulted me back to a glittering height of hedonism, the mirror ball of my youth, beneath which my current existence, dull and rule-driven, now receded. That peck of defiance—of deviance—made me realize I was a twenty-six-year-old newlywed living like a middle-aged empty-nester. I didn't have a meaningful career, children to tend to, or a husband who came home on a regular basis. Yet marriage had meant retiring my black leather miniskirt for nights no more sizzling than whatever vicarious thrill I got from reading the latest *New York* magazine.

This was not the way my life was supposed to turn out. Although I'd never had expectations of achieving fame and fortune in my own right, I had dreamed of a man who would—someone like the record mogul, only a lot less shriveled. Despite having a husband, I secretly fancied that a son of Ganymede, flush with money and creativity, would fall from the heavens and land at my feet. After all, once you got past the blond hair, height, and rockin' body, what did Alana Stewart have over me?

Rod, which Charlie knew himself not to be. "Rather than adjusting your expectations to what is possible and getting joy out of it, you're constantly disappointed," he said, feeling hurt and disgusted.

It was true. The left side of my brain knew I should thank my lucky stars to have gotten a guy like Charlie in the first place. He far surpassed all my previous burnouts and plenty of my girlfriends' boyfriends, too. But the right side of my brain regretted I hadn't *actually* reached for the stars.

A couple of weeks after our lunch date, the record mogul asked me to attend an anniversary party at the Village Vanguard. I do not remember where I told Charlie I was going, if I told him anything at all. Perhaps he was away or working late. He never kept tabs on me. His nonintervention was well intended: a disavowal of the patriarchal notion of women as property. In principle, I agreed, but privately I wished for just a little jealousy.

Heading downtown to the Village Vanguard in a chauffeur-driven Mercedes, the record mogul and I sat in the backseat, enveloped by its sweet-smelling leather. Since I wouldn't have known the difference between Dexter Gordon and Stan Getz, I couldn't say whether I met any jazz greats that night. Not that I cared. My only interest was my date. No longer wheelchair-bound, he worked the room on a pair of sterling-silver–handled canes, his shuffling punctuated by flashbulbs popping.

Afterward, he instructed his driver to take us back to the record mogul's West Village town house. No formalities like, *Dahling*—he called me that instead of my name, which I was pretty certain he didn't know—*would you like to come back to my place?* He assumed that since I'd agreed to go out with him, I was his for the night.

Once we arrived, he showed me around, mentioning that his family was away in Tenerife. In the library, he offered a drink and a joint.

"Neither, thanks."

"Ah, girls always like a little coke. Unfortunately, I'm all out."

Seated in a pair of armchairs, we talked awhile longer. Although it would have pushed the envelope of bad girl behavior to sleep with someone knocking on death's door, I wasn't into it. Not because of his age. He still had sex appeal, thanks to his cocksureness. My unwillingness stemmed from a realization that for him, infidelity was mortar for his marital bond, satisfying his need for novelty in order to reinforce his commitment to a long-term marriage, whereas for me, a meaningless betrayal of my husband might risk the opposite effect. We hadn't even celebrated our one-year anniversary yet.

As I got up to go, the record mogul rose to escort me to the door. Supporting his weight on only one of his canes, he reached to hold my hand and we stood face-to-face.

Suddenly, with the swiftness of a pro, he placed my palm on his bare penis. Somehow, he had managed to unzip his pants and whip out his willy. This coot was the David Copperfield of cocks.

My jaw dropped. The record mogul was in the eighth decade of his life, nearly crippled, but still had the moxie to initiate a hand job. However, instead of pulling away, my fingers remained, drawn to touch a relic: an organ of long and venerable history before which a pantheon of infamous pussies had spread themselves. After more than half a century of service, it was still a physiological miracle. So solid, you'd never know it was a senior's.

I gave the wundercock a few quick strokes before tucking it back in the record mogul's pants.

"Now I've really got to take off," I said, putting on my coat.

"But I want to see you take it *all* off," he announced.

At that instant, both my fantasy of female subjugation and my acquired sense of modesty evaporated. I became Lady Godiva, ready to flaunt my nakedness, and a seductress shifting the balance of power in her favor. Here was a guy: rich, famous, and enshrined in the history of pop culture. Some of the most sought-after women in the world had been his sexual conquests. He was worldlier than I could ever hope to be. The chance to turn him on meant that, for one brief moment, I would be in control.

"Sit down," I commanded.

Slowly, I pulled my top over my head and let his eyes roam over my breasts in green lace demi-cups. He took his prick out of his pants again. Still fully dressed, he started jerking off.

He had on mother-of-pearl cuff links. Trying to keep my cool, I glued my gaze to those lustrous white orbs as I slid out of my skirt. Wearing a matching green thong and black fuck-me stilettos, I turned and let him have a good look at my ass. With my back to him, I undid my bra and faced him.

"Please, let me touch your tits. I love little tits."

Yes!

"No way. You're only allowed to look."

I peeled my underwear down my thighs and watched him focus

on my pussy. He masturbated harder. Imagining myself as a con-
cubine in Ingres's *Turkish Bath,* I sat down in a chair and opened
my legs, draping them languorously over the arms.

If only I were wearing a turban.

"What a beautiful pussy you have," he panted.

Suddenly, I froze. There I was, trying to act all sultry and enticing, but I had forgotten about a skinny white string now dangling
in full view. I had my fucking period.

With as much discretion as possible, I tucked the tampon pull
inside. Blessedly, the record mogul was on the brink of coming. A
few more moments and it was over.

Like a magician drawing a handkerchief from a hat, he pulled a
white linen square from his jacket pocket to wipe himself off.
Reaching for his fancy canes, he made like Quasimodo, limping to
the bathroom. Meanwhile, I got dressed, the vixen in me vanished.
The string thing had blown the whole goddamn show.

"Ready to go home now?" the record mogul asked. "My driver
will take you."

"I don't know if you noticed, but it's, um, that time of the
month for me, if you know what I mean."

*Hit the brakes, Elizabeth. Shut your motor mouth. Haven't you
humiliated yourself enough?*

"Indeed," he said nonchalantly. "Nothing I haven't seen. I enjoyed myself immensely, dahling."

Being driven uptown to my apartment, I was no longer co-
cooned in the sweet smell of leather but suffocating from guilt.
How to cope with my violation of conscience? Rather than take
the high road by being honest with my husband and pleading for
forgiveness or, better yet, admit our marriage was tanking, I stooped
to televangelist tactics. Swaggart blamed Satan for his sins of the
flesh. Me? I pointed at Charlie.

"Do you know how lonely and boring my life is?" I taunted
when he rolled through the front door, a five o'clock shadow

looking like exhaust smeared across his face. "What am I supposed to do with myself night after night while you're at the office?"

"Do we have to do this now?" He yawned. "I've got to get to bed."

"I have needs, don't you realize that?"

"I'm sorry."

"Sorry? Why should you be sorry? I'm the one who should apologize."

"What are you talking about?"

"Can't you figure it out?"

"What?"

"I haven't exactly been the goodly wife."

I girded myself for an onslaught but was instead hit with a silence as dense as stone and so eternal, the earth could have turned in the meantime. Refusing to respond to my provocation, Charlie undressed, got into bed, and fell asleep.

Creating and functioning in opposing worlds—one public, the other private—he was prepared for confrontation in the office, but not at home. Maybe he hid from the truth because he wanted or needed to believe in my decency in order to stay married to me. But instead of spurring me to be better, his reaction only reminded me of how I had failed him, how low I had fallen, how bad to the bone I truly was.

Not only had I broken our marital covenant, I had projected my blameworthiness onto him, instead of taking responsibility for what I'd done. I wanted to engage him in battle, unconsciously hoping he'd battle for us. Wrestling with ways to redeem myself and save our marriage, I remained awake throughout the night. Even after dawn broke, I was still in the dark.

CHAPTER 8

*I*T'S TIME," MY MOTHER ANNOUNCED.

"So soon?"

"You've been married a year and a half. You'll be twenty-seven before you know it. Have a baby."

Was she crazy? I'd never held one, let alone had a babysitting job. My experience was limited to a stint when I was fifteen as a day camp counselor-in-training for eight-year-old girls. Instead of looking after my charges, I spent the entire summer in a pool shed filled with blue kickboards, practicing a dry-land version of a back float with a lifeguard named Garth.

The sole indication I had any nurturing abilities was my concern for abandoned pets. At sixteen, I volunteered at the North Shore Animal League and never once complained about hosing down and disinfecting the puppy cages puddled with diarrhea, which, for a girl from Great Neck, gives some idea of the level to which I was willing to stoop for strays.

But a *baby*? I had yet to feel any maternal longing. Never peeked inside a pram, never ogled a set of booties. Instead my heart thumped for the mothers. Gripping a spanking-clean pram, the new ones shuffled along in a maxipad waddle, ragged and shell-shocked, like Confederate soldiers returning after Appomattox. With faces clenched and bodies pitched forward, the mamas of toddlers marched on, pushing a stroller that bucked every time a pair of tiny sneakers thrust against the pavement—human brake-locks flipped into gear during a temper tantrum.

Was I ready for that? My job as a pseudo-sleuth convinced me my professional calling still remained at large. But what if my eggs were withered by the time I found it? I was in limbo, waiting for my life to take a turn for the remarkable, a reversal nowhere in sight. Once again, my mother was right.

While Charlie was more certain than me about actually wanting to be a parent, the timing was not ideal, he argued. We were living hand-to-mouth. Better to secure his professional and financial success. Although his reasoning was sound, I warned that a hold-off might end up costing us a bigger investment with a lower return rate: IVF.

He fell into line and did the deed. One, two, three months passed, each ending in a bloody failure of fertilization. Could I be barren? Following pregnancy guidebooks, I reduced stress by quitting my job and increased my BFP (body fat percentage) by forcing myself *not* to upchuck my thrice-daily meals. Charting my basal body temperature and cervical mucus, I pinpointed my ovulation day.

When the clock struck, Charlie performed his mission. I jumped out of bed and stood on my head so the force of gravity would keep his troops on the move. From that inverse perspective, it happened: conception.

I was so preoccupied with getting pregnant, I never gave a thought to actually being pregnant. What a shock: My body was preprogrammed to host, crave, feed, secrete, and swell—without any sanctioning from me.

Turning into a human cracker barrel was most terrifying. What if I developed adipose thighs jiggling for joy, the final triumph of flesh over willpower? Determined to fight back, I reverted to old habits—a cycle of minimum, maximum, and regurgitated caloric intake. By the beginning of my second trimester, my obstetrician gave me a choice: Either beef up the bump in my belly or expect a baby without a brain.

After seven years of food abuse, my priorities were clear: Ruining myself was one thing, creating a child with an IQ of a potted plant another. Finally, I had a motivation to recover. Out went the bathroom scale and in came the expandable waistbands. Squeezing between restaurant tables, I forgave my spreading ass for setting water glasses toppling. I accepted silver stretch marks glinting like minnows across my stomach—maternal badges of honor, according to *What to Expect When You're Expecting*. But what kind of honor were hemorrhoids?

In those pre–Liz Lange days, maternity wear was as stylish as walking around in a wigwam. Fortunately, fall 1988 was a season for Donna Karan's loose chemise dresses. But my high-fashion pup tents couldn't convince Charlie that his wife hadn't been body snatched. One night, standing naked in front of a mirror, I attempted to make light of the frightful sight by suggesting he hook me up to a steel cable so that I could join the Macy's Thanksgiving Day Parade floats. He advised putting on a nightgown instead.

At the start of my seventh month, we purchased a small, sunny two-bedroom co-op between Park and Madison Avenues, which stirred my Martha Stewart instinct. In the baby's room, I lacquered the walls pink, blue, green, and yellow before adding metallic polka dots and purple stencils of Matisse's cutouts. While the patterning dried, I sponge-painted every piece of furniture in a primary palette. A stimulating environment would benefit my child's cognitive development, right?

It also stimulated my uterus. By the time I realized a rhythmic tightening in my stomach was not a good sign at only twenty-seven weeks' gestation, my preterm labor had started. Halting the contractions, the hospital pumped me full of magnesium sulfate—an Epsom salt bath for my internal organs. I was put on nine weeks of bed rest and a regimen of pills to be taken every two hours, day and night. No one was surprised when I became a high-risk pregnancy. The only question: What took me so long?

On December 27, four weeks before my due date, I was wheeled into a delivery room, the baby's head starting to crown.

"Push! Harder! Push!" commanded a labor nurse.

"Breathe! Hee . . . hee . . . hoo!" Charlie coached.

"Bear down!" ordered my obstetrician. "Like you're having a bowel movement!"

Is that supposed to be encouragement?

Giving birth was as far as I could get from a Calgon-Take-Me-Away moment. There were no gauzy emotions. No trilling of a harp. Gory and harrowing, the experience was my Antietam. Panting to ease the pain? Why not just give me a Cheez Doodle to bite on?

"RAMBO!!" I screamed, summoning my inner action hero to free an alien life force thrashing to get out of me.

"You did it!" my doctor announced. "A boy! Two arms and legs, ten fingers and toes!"

"What about a harelip?" I gasped, stunned that after months of hallucinating fetal abnormalities, he had a healthy Apgar score. Charlie, expecting nothing less, burst into tears of joy.

The difference in our reactions foretold our future as parents. I needed to think the worst so that the alternative felt like a relief. Charlie was just the opposite. He refused to watch TV programs or read newspaper stories about child abuse because they hit too close to home. I couldn't get enough since they reassured me how far we were from them.

"Meet Dashiel," Charlie said, proudly showing off the baby, who was named after one of his father's favorite authors, the left-leaning Dashiell Hammett. Gathering in my hospital room, our parents and brothers all wanted to hold the newborn, the first grandchild and nephew for both families. Over my dead body. To me, the crowd meant one thing: a mounting microbe count. I ordered everyone out.

Now, when I look back, the only time I wasn't racked with anxiety was after they were all gone, including Charlie. Too excited to sleep, I spent the night in an adora-bubble, cradling my boy, marveling at a job well done: long black lashes, bee-stung lips, and a thimble-size nose. Although he was born premature, he weighed a respectable five pounds, thirteen ounces. When I slipped my pinkie in his hand, his translucent fingers folded over it. Did he know I was his mother?

"It's *you!*" I repeated again and again, disbelieving the bundle in my arms was the very being that had been using my womb as a tumbling mat.

The day we went home, a baby nurse arrived to assist me for two weeks. Wearing a white medical uniform, she had a pudgy face, around which her gray curls formed scallops, and no lips. Only a hyphen mark, her mouth.

"Hi, I'm Elizabeth and this is my husband, Charlie." I smiled, extending my hand, gesturing toward him.

"How do you do?" she said, striding past, the hyphen never flexing. "I'm Mrs. Stern. Show me to the baby."

She was of the school that fretful newborns must be ignored to break them of a fussiness they assumed to be their birthright. As a first-time mother, how was I to know any better? Trembling and weepy, I stood in the shower, cliff-hanging from a hormonal plateau of pregnancy. My hearing was newly attuned to a barely audible frequency. Like a hound cocking its ear when a silent dog whistle emits an ultrasonic blast, I craned my neck toward the sound.

"Mrs. Stern!" I shrieked, bulldozing into Dash's room, a towel clumsily twisted around my sopping torso. *"How can you let my baby cry like that?"*

"I have been doing this for over forty years. I won't pick him up every time he peeps. If you don't trust me, then I'm not the right nurse for you."

Twenty-four hours later, I agreed. Mrs. Stern was out of a job and my tour of mom duty had begun.

• • •

After eight weeks with a colicky baby, my corneas felt like pin-cushions and I was vibrating from sleep deprivation. When traffic screeched to a halt while I was pushing his carriage across Park Avenue, my reflexes refused to respond. I stood immobile, unable to distinguish between the howling of automobile horns and the howling of my son.

"I can't do this." I called my mother, sobbing. "I hate him."

"Don't *ever* say that. He's a little, tiny thing. I raised three of you while your brothers were both in diapers without any help from your father. Pull yourself together. You're *the mother*."

Two words that struck like a thunder kaboom. I threatened to run for cover.

"Stay put," my mother said. "I'll be right over."

Retrieving Dash from his Swing-O-Matic, she rocked the beet-red, raging bloodsucker, returning him to a state of gurgling grace. How did she do it? When my brothers and I were young and simultaneously came down with chicken pox, she acted a royal foot soldier and Franciscan nun rolled into one.

Now I understood why my father had no interest in his children. Standing at a distance, he observed his grandson with the same fear and bewilderment as I did. How could something so small be so irascible? With his ruched features, balled fists, and legs drawn tight against his abdomen, there was no chance of me making eye contact in order to facilitate mother–infant attachment. The kid was too busy bawling.

"How much do you think a white, Jewish, two-month-old boy would fetch on the baby black market?" I asked my mother.

Her answer was to hire me a babysitter. Irma was a live ham-mock, swaying back and forth for hours on end, buoying my squalling son in her lardy arms while humming "When the Saints Go Marching In."

Back at the work-a-thon, Charlie was coddling multimillion-dollar corporate clients with names that sounded like CIA fronts——Dycorp and Tamatzu. Resuming his global itinerary, he lived out of a suit bag. To contact him, I had to factor in multiple time zones and modern communication barriers: operators, message prompts, voice menus, faxes, pagers, secretaries, speakerphones, car phones, and plane phones. Who needed the headache? I'd pick up the fucking quart of milk myself.

Once home, he shifted gears as smoothly as a multitasking mom. Wedging a phone receiver in the groove of his neck, he could simultaneously deal with the cable company, feed the baby, and finish reading a *New Yorker* article. When Dash wouldn't fall asleep, Charlie holstered him into a car seat and drove around Manhattan until the Sandman took over. Returning the boy to his crib, his father kissed him good night lightly on the forehead, never disturbing his slumber.

I was certain my son knew I lacked the can-do spirit of his Mrs. Doubtfire dad. No matter how much peek-a-boo and patty-cake I played, I could not equal the biochemical boost that Charlie achieved just by walking through the front door. Dash's face lit up, his back arched, and his arms flapped. When it was my turn, he swatted and grimaced.

"I had no idea Charlie would be such an incredible father," cooed my mother-in-law. "The way he works. How does he do it all?"

"I've never seen a man so devoted to his child," marveled my mother. "He's exceptional. You know how lucky you are?"

Yes, and I despised my husband for it. Why did parenting come so easily to him? Were the social expectations for fathering so low that his willingness to wear a Snugli made him a superhero? Was he a better person than me, plain and simple? Between his self-confidence and the standing ovations he received, I felt more inadequate than ever. Despite being a woman, I wasn't the one hardwired to nurture.

• • •

Afternoons at the park were my version of prison yard time. Alone and bored, I staked out my turf on a slatted wooden bench, my son mewling in his carriage. Reaching into a diaper bag, I expected La Leche League lieutenants to pounce on me at any minute. While other women brazenly whipped out engorged nipples right in the middle of Central Park, I nourished my baby on what was "modern" in my mother's day but now considered contraband—a formula-filled bottle.

I wished I could have reached across the divide of snap-down nursing bras to ask if anyone else felt as overwhelmed as me. Who else broke out in hives double-checking the contents of a baby's outdoor survival kit—ointment, powder, tushie wipes, swabs, bibs, booties, bottled water, receiving blankets, and rattle keys? Was I alone in yearning for days of yore when thumbing through *People* on a checkout line was a moment taken for granted instead of one guiltily stolen?

The last person I could complain to was Andee. After a year of not speaking because of our bridal-wear fiasco, we reconciled in the final stages of her mother's breast cancer. The woman passed before becoming a grandmother.

Andee gave birth to a boy two months after me. As new mothers, we visited each other often, occasions when she wore leggings and oversize tops, not because she hadn't lost the baby weight, but because she knew better than to risk anything but Gap on child care. I, on the other hand, dressed in Christian Lacroix, deluding myself that my designer shoulders could deflect the milky appliqués that my son left behind as evidence of a productive burp.

"I really love babies," Andee said, sighing.

I'll pass on that one.

"Dash cries a lot," she said, interpreting my silence. "Mine isn't a crier. But don't feel bad. I never could hold a dog or cat right, the way you always could. I'm just, like, better with babies than puppies."

Great. So I should have had a kennel club, not a kid?

• • •

Misery loves company, and I was thankful for a new friend, Ruby. We met through her husband, Eric, an artist whose work I reviewed for *ARTnews*. Living in a renovated barn in Old Chatham, New York, the couple had a three-year-old boy and an open-door policy for weekend visitors.

"Yesterday, I was on the phone with my neighbor when my son came in the room and I didn't want to get off the line," Ruby greeted me the instant I—basically still a stranger—walked into her house for the first time, my husband and baby in tow. "Instead I shushed him and told him I was talking to a friend. I was complaining to her that people think you're a bad mother if you don't go to preschool parents' night and every meal you serve doesn't have the four food groups. Get this. The woman just left a 'Dear John' letter under my front door."

It read: "Mother of the Year you are not."

Our friendship was sealed then and there. Intense and outspoken, Ruby was a person you either loved or hated. We were a lot alike: Disappointed by the disparity between our expectations of life and its possibilities, we held special disdain for the myths of motherhood.

"Babies are supposed to be so in love with their mothers but I think Dash loves his father more than me," I oy-yoyed.

"The baby gets acclimated that when Daddy gets home, it's playtime," she said. "It's also the male personality. When the baby cries, it gets us in our stomach. Men can remove themselves. They're trained to work and get ahead. They have an attitude of endurance."

Seven years older than me, Ruby had gotten married in 1979 when she was twenty-five and Eric twenty-eight. At the time, they were an art world "It" couple, dining at Indochine and vacationing in Gstaad. Right before Ruby gave birth, they rented out their four-thousand-square-foot SoHo loft, moving to upstate New York. Shortly afterward, Eric's art fell out of favor and the family's financial struggles began.

Ruby put her career as an accessories designer on hold to care for the baby. He cried uncontrollably and vomited constantly. One day, desperate to figure out what was wrong, she decided to put herself in his place and see the world from his perspective. She climbed into the crib beside him. It immediately collapsed and the two fell to the floor screaming. "That was a metaphor for the whole experience of being a new mother," she recounted.

According to studies, one of the most likely times for a marriage to fall apart is after the birth of a first child. Seventy percent of couples report a decrease in marital happiness. By the time I met Ruby and Eric, they were proving the statistic.

"I don't love him anymore," she confided. "We haven't had sex since I gave birth. Our life has gotten hard and stressful. We never know where the money will come from. I never expected to wind up with a terrible relationship, no career, and feeling like a shitty mother."

. . .

Parenthood pushed Charlie and me into opposing corners, too. I no longer acknowledged his arrival when he opened the front door. I was mad at him for going to work and perversely mad when he came home. Without him around, I had my own way of doing things, but when he reappeared, he seemed like an intruder, disrupting the rhythm of my life with Dash. When he realized I was annoyed, he would try to engage me in conversation about anodyne topics, like movie reviews and National Public Radio. I wanted him to leave me alone, precisely because I felt so alone—with him.

We didn't fight. Never raised our voices or let each other have it. But I was spring-loaded to pounce at a slight provocation, like him leaving a film of black whiskers in the bathroom sink after his morning shave. He slithered into a shell of silence—to me, more punishing than a screaming match. Accidentally brushing up against each other in the apartment, we both recoiled as if stung by an electric shock.

Having Dash put a stop to our sex life. Not that we'd had much of one to start. Our interaction was limited to our child, who became an undeclared battleground in the marriage. "He needs a sweater." "No, he doesn't." "He won't go to sleep." "He sleeps for me." "Why is he always crying?" "You've got to see the baby through the tears."

His or mine, Charlie?

Had I been ten years older and proven myself as a professional before having a baby, I might not have been as hostile toward my husband. Every morning, he commuted in a suit and tie to an alternate universe organized around one-upmanship, returning home with a tunnel focus on fathering. I, on the other hand, had no reason to change out of my pajamas or speak in polysyllables. When I made the decision to become a mother, the timing had seemed right. Now it felt less like a choice than a duty.

Why didn't I feel blessed? I'd given birth to a beautiful, healthy child and, unlike Andee, had a mother to provide a second set of trustworthy hands. What was wrong with me? Surely, I was dooming my son to a lifetime of psychotherapy.

"I'm not happy," I told Charlie. "Something's wrong. My life is going nowhere. What if I'm fucking up Dash?"

"Nothing is wrong. You have a great kid. You should be happy. Stop worrying."

I hate when you do that: Dismiss my feelings and tell me how I "should" be. So men are from Mars.

"We started out in the same place," I continued, "but now you're the one who gets dressed up every day and has an office and a secretary and makes a living."

"Don't compare yourself with me. I went to law school. What I do is easy. What you do is so much harder."

But what exactly do I do?

Being well educated and having no use for my knowledge was the lottery prize of motherhood. Between the puzzle rings and

Barney theme song, I was living proof that autism could kick in in adulthood.

Although I still wrote art reviews, my assignments were less frequent than before my son was born. Susan, my co-critic, had moved to LA to complete her doctorate at UCLA and write about art for the LA *Times*. *ARTnews* allowed me to continue under my own byline but wouldn't grant me any plum shows, sticking me with the crap.

Hoping to work my way up to writing features, I spent Dash's nap time trying to make sense of obtuse books about critical theory, which were then au courant in the art world. Since Charlie was the smartest man I knew, I pleaded with him to be my study partner and read Jean Baudrillard's *Simulations*. Skimming the back cover, my husband called the work "bullshit," chucking it to the floor.

Once again, I envied my bridesmaids, Cathy and Susan, who were both now married. The former had started a venture capital firm with her husband in San Diego, funding bio-tech start-ups; the latter had met her husband, a film theorist, at UCLA, where he was also getting his doctorate. The couples were happy, stimulated by intellectual foreplay and a respectful volley of opinions. Charlie and I had none of that. His life was a fast track while mine was a pre-women's-movement throwback. I had become the thing women fear most: my mother.

"My marriage isn't working," I announced to her one night at my apartment while Charlie was working late. I was aiming a spoonful of pureed peas at Dash's mouth when he threw up an arm block, sending the utensil sailing and splattering my hair with slop.

"Did you remember to get me the grilled chicken paillard without any oil?" my mother asked, referring to a delivery order from our usual Italian restaurant, a meal she trusted had fewer calories than the number she would expend digesting it.

"Yes, of course, and your broccoli has to be steamed and no

dressing on your salad." I sighed. "I know. You're on a diet. Now will you listen to me? My marriage sucks. Charlie and I have problems. Sexual problems."

"Like what?" she asked, my intimate disclosure suddenly causing her ears to prick up. "He can't . . . does he . . . you mean . . . perform?"

"No, not that. There's something missing between us. It's gotten worse since we had the baby. We have nothing in common. Our life isn't panning out the way I thought it would."

"I understand. It was the same for me with your father. After I had you kids . . ."

Damn. She was doing it again. Turning the tables to talk about herself. My anger started to rise and my face heated up. Once more, I tried to feed Dash, but he whacked the spoon away and a green dollop hit my cheek.

"Fine, so you don't want to eat? Don't eat!" I brusquely handed him to my mother before leaving the room to wash up.

Whenever she got me mad, I took it out on my son, the one who couldn't fight back or reject me. I was afraid of standing up to her. What if I pushed her away? It was too lonely being home at nights with only the baby. Despite the degree of attention my mother demanded, her adult companionship was better than none at all.

"Even if you're upset about your husband, keep your cool with the baby," she admonished when I returned to the room. By then, she had retrieved a jar of applesauce from the kitchen. Spooning his vegetables, she added a dab of fruit, touching the mixture to his lips. Tasting the sweetness, he gobbled everything up.

"See?" my mother said proudly. "I'm teaching you an old trick. Put the fruit on the tip of the spoon. Are you calm enough to feed him again?"

As if the fucking feeding was what set me off.

"Mom, you don't get what I'm telling you. I want a divorce."

"A *divorce*! You have a baby. You don't make an income. Your father and I can't help you. You'd have to get a job. But there's no money in art history. You're my daughter and I'm thinking about your security. No one will ever love you like Charlie. What about taking a vacation with him?"

If my mother was trying to ensure that I remained her mini me—a discontented wife and mother with no faith in the possibility of her own success—doing it in the name of my best interest was genius. Suddenly, a Bateaux-Mouches dinner cruise down the River Seine with my husband seemed very, very appealing.

"Let's go to Paris for a long weekend," I proposed, calling Charlie at the office.

"That's ridiculous," he responded.

"Ridiculous? Why ridiculous?"

"It's kooky, zany. Impossible. Have you forgotten that we have a baby?"

"My mother will stay with him."

"We can't afford it. Anyway, I have to work."

"But I really want to do it."

"Toots," he said, exhaling. "Just because you want to do something doesn't mean we can. That's not a reason. It's irresponsible."

• • •

I gave up trying to fix my marriage and tried to fix my own life instead. One Friday evening in June 1990, I had plans to attend a gallery opening and arranged for Val to babysit late. She'd been with me for close to two years, replacing Irma, whose heft prevented her from mobilizing once Dash started crawling. When Val interviewed for the job, I immediately liked her: a slender Jamaican with mocha skin, a white-white smile, and a bounce to her step. Since she could beat my son to the wall outlets, I hired her on the spot without bothering to check her references.

I had been accepted to the art history doctoral program at the Institute but my adviser died of AIDS before I got started. Deferring my enrollment, I continued writing about art and also landed a part-time position as a New York philanthropist's assistant. Although he promised I'd be in charge of his traveling print collections—Goya's *Los Caprichos* and Canaletto's views of Venice—I never got to handle anything more valuable than his wife's dry cleaning.

While Val bathed Dash, I was all set to leave for the opening when the phone rang.

It was my editor from *ARTnews*. After a quick hello, he got right to it.

"I'm sorry to tell you but since you've been working as a solo critic, your reviews just aren't working."

"What does that mean, *aren't working*?"

"Your writing has no edge. We're letting you go."

No edge? Letting me go? Please, no!

Stunned, I dialed Charlie at work, desperate for words of comfort. All I got was a voice prompt to leave a message. With the sound of Dash splashing in the tub suddenly erupting like a sonic boom of my maternal responsibility, I tore ass out of my apartment.

At the gallery, I struck up a conversation with a smart-alecky critic in a black motorcycle jacket. Walking through the show with him, I tried to put up a sharp front, offering a stream of what I believed was brainy commentary.

"Don't you have a kid to get home to?" he interrupted.

Back at my building, I stepped out of the elevator at my floor and heard Dash crying down the hallway. It was eight thirty or so. Although he always pitched a fit at bedtime, my heart rate quickened precipitously.

With her back to the door, Val was on the kitchen phone, unaware that I'd just walked in. Dash, clutching Mitzi—a stuffed dog loved to pathetic limpness—was clinging to the bars of his crib, shrieking at the top of his lungs.

"Later, later . . . ," Val said, hanging up, spotting me.

"What's going on here?" I demanded, rushing to Dash.

"He's only started fussin' since ten minutes," Val defended. "I just put him in and you know how he hates bed."

She was smiling her white-white smile reassuringl[y] red flags—which I'd chosen to ignore so that I could child was safe under someone else's watch—were n[o] madly in my skull: change from the grocery money she never returned, endless phone messages for her on my machine.

I sent Val home. With Dash on my hip, I went to my next-door neighbor and asked if she heard much crying when I was out.

"All the time. I've even gone over and rung the bell to see if she's hurting him. She leaves him in his crib while she's on the phone."

My stomach instantly hurtled into my throat. Why hadn't I checked those goddamn references?

I did my best to get Dash to sleep. Neither a bottle nor a lullaby consoled him. Bad enough I was a mother who chafed easily. I'd also sicced a negligent nanny on him.

I had no idea how long he cried, his sobs seeming to amplify and multiply over time. I couldn't take it. Right or wrong, I swear my next move was a protective measure. The last thing I wanted was harm to come to my son.

I walked out of my apartment, leaving him in his crib, his wails following me down the hallway. At a stairwell marked EXIT, I ascended to the roof but the door was locked. Sitting on a step, I took several deep breaths, trying to clear my head. Was it possible, even hidden away in that concrete chamber, I could still hear Dash screaming?

Back at my apartment, I found the door wide open.

"What happened to you?" Charlie asked, wild-eyed, hugging Dash, his soft brown hair shellacked to his forehead with sweat.

"I went out."

"What?"

"I had to take a break. There was an . . . incident. Just before I went to an opening, I got fired from *ARTnews*. When I came home, I found Val on the phone ignoring Dash. He was hysterical. I tried to get him to sleep but he refused. I was really upset and

I thought it would be better for us both if I took a few minutes to collect myself."

"You left him alone?"

"It wasn't very long."

"I don't care if it was five seconds. Are you out of your mind? Why didn't you call me at the office?"

"I *did* call," I said, my voice rising. "I left a message. You ignored me. As usual."

"I ignore you?" Charlie exploded. "You don't even say hello when I come home. I'm not just your ATM machine."

"Then why do you act like one? You have no emotions. You're an automaton."

"What do you want from me?" Charlie cried, lifting his foot to display the sole of his wingtip. "I've got holes in my shoes because I'm killing myself to provide for my family."

"Quit playing the martyr," I hissed. "I can't go on this way with you."

"Well, I can't go on this way, either. So do what you want to do. I'll take care of *my* child."

"*Your* child?"

"I'm his father."

"And what am I? Nothing?"

With that, I grabbed my purse and ran out. Tears streamed down my face as I headed toward Park Avenue, flagging a cab.

"To SoHo," I told the driver, giving my mother's Wooster Street address, knowing she was on Long Island with my father.

Using my spare key, I entered her loft, her sanctum sanctorum of artistic freedom and self-expression where conventional life— marriage, motherhood, suburbia—was excluded. I knew I didn't belong there either, but it was as close to the bosom as I could get on short notice.

The place smelled like fresh paint. There were a couple of worktables strewn with dismembered plastic action figures and di- nosaurs, as well as rhinestones and sequins—materials for her current project, an apocalyptic tableau vivant. My mother's inspiration rested on a night table: Dante's *The Inferno*.

I had everything, yet it wasn't what I wanted. What I wanted was never what I had. I wanted out of my life but, as a wife and mother, it seemed so permanent. I believed Dash could thrive with only Charlie, a parent whose devotion was undivided. I believed Charlie would be relieved without me, a hundred pound noose around his neck. How could I help? In the despair of the moment, I saw no other option than the controlled substances in my mother's medicine cabinet.

I counted a handful of Darvon and swallowed them in one gulp.

CHAPTER 9

*I*NSTEAD OF LEAVING A LAST NOTE, I made a last call.

"I will always love you and Dash," I slurred to Charlie, the drugs deadening my words.

"WHERE ARE YOU? TOOTS, TOOTS, WHERE ARE YOU?"

Either he put two and two together, figuring out my getaway, or he had the call traced. I didn't know how long I was out before a banging at the front door of my mother's loft jogged me from my narcosis.

"ELIZABETH HAYT! OFFICERS DOMINGUEZ AND LEAHY! OPEN UP!"

When I stumbled to let them in, there was Charlie behind the two cops. He had contacted the First Precinct, as well as my brother Andrew, who, now a student at New York Law living in Gramercy Park, had rushed over to stay with Dash while the men in blue revived me.

"Have you taken any drugs, lady?" one said. "We've got to bring you to Bellevue. Police protocol."

"I'm fine," I protested, as if I were speaking through a mouthful of rice pudding. "I just needed to get some sleep. I took a couple of pills. I'm okay. Really. Charlie, tell them I'm okay."

No response.

"Talk to my father," I bargained. "He's a doctor. He'll tell you."

With the police breathing down my back, I called him on Long Island, explaining that Charlie and I had had a fight and I'd taken some medication to relax. I didn't know if my dad believed me but when I put one of the cops on the line, my father reassured him that a padded cell was unnecessary.

Normally, my mother could be counted on in a crisis. It was no coincidence that after a vet ruptured the bowel of our family's Burmese cat, he clung to life until returning home, waiting to die in my mother's arms. Peacefully.

But she would have required a medevac to the nearest ICU if she had been the first to receive the news of my Rx overload. My father's emotional consistency made him a more reliable emergency contact. I had never fully appreciated the security he provided until I put him to the test. He was the rescue blanket in my hour of exposure.

Not long after, he wound up in the hospital due to coronary artery disease, requiring an angioplasty. I visited, bringing red licorice and sliced cantaloupe—some of his favorites. Lying in bed, he wore a bloodstained cotton gown revealing his pasty calves and yellowed toenails. His sleek black hair was mussed and graying at the temples. The sight was unbearable. I noticed his water pitcher needed refilling and he could use a clean gown so I tracked down a nurse to assist him. It took the damage to his heart to bring out an unexpected love for him I felt in mine.

None of my family ever spoke of what I'd done at my mother's loft, though she did demand I return the key. Charlie said nothing, either. When I tried to tell him how trapped I felt in our marriage coupled with my longing for a more fulfilling life, his eyes welled and the corners of his mouth quivered.

"I know, I know," he cut me off, not wanting to hear any more, which drove me farther from him and deeper into myself. At home, he did what he could to make up for it, ministering to me like a hospice nurse and reminding Dash not to disturb me. But the special treatment ended abruptly in the face of the next emergency litigation.

From beginning to end, the flow of events illustrated what was wrong with our relationship. It took a dynamite of a crisis to hurl Charlie into action. Once the smoke cleared, he turned his back on the catastrophe, not wanting to relive it by discussing why it had happened in the first place.

After I half joked that Charlie should consider adding a suicide prevention hotline to his speed dial, he conceded to couples counseling. Dr. Ruttman worked out of an Upper West Side brownstone, which was chock-full of macramé plant hangers, quartz crystals, and long-haired cats. When he referred to our marriage as a "journey," I readied myself for a sing-along of "Kumbaya."

The love-in ended at the mention of my recent episode. The doctor threatened that if I "pulled one more stunt like that," it meant I wasn't committed to therapy and he wouldn't treat Charlie and me. Ruttman probably thought he was practicing tough love but it ruined my commitment to therapy. I rationalized Charlie's asthmatic reaction to the aerosolized cat dander to be a silent expression of his resistance, too.

However, hope on the home front seemed to arrive with Gwendolyn, a devout Christian who had four teeth in her head and blue-ribbon ironing skills. She was Dash's new babysitter.

"Eh, boy!" Gwendolyn called out to him in the morning. He greeted her with a full body slam, following her around like a pull-toy. At the park, she pushed him on a swing until his head bobbled, dashboard-accessory-style. When I made spot checks, she not only kept close watch over my son but kept his hat on, too.

Deciding that a major change might do me good, I applied to the Columbia University Graduate School of Journalism. On the first day of the fall semester of 1991, I rode the M4 bus to Morningside Heights with a brand-new five-subject notebook. I stood outside the university's iron gates and was unable to cross the threshold. How could I become a *real* writer? Surely the entire admissions committee was on the pipe when they accepted me.

I took the next downtown bus to Fifth Avenue and 78th Street, the location of the Institute of Fine Arts. The school occupied a limestone Louis XV–style mansion formerly owned by James Biddle Duke, a turn-of-the-twentieth-century tobacco tycoon. A ballroom, illuminated by crystal chandeliers, served as a lecture hall and, on Fridays, afternoon tea was held in an oak-paneled library. The imposing architecture was no match for my determination. Marching through the marble foyer to the academic office, I enrolled in the art history doctoral program, having deferred my admission some years back.

I was looking for a way to refuel my brain and rest my body after Dash's turbine toddlerhood. A zestful boy, he gobbled hot dogs like a Nathan's champ and turned finger painting into a paintball game. Now that he was in pre-K, and Gwendolyn was on board, I could kiss my days of touch-and-feel books good-bye. Footnotes lay ahead.

After a five-year hiatus from school, my return confirmed I'd been locked in a cryonic state. I discovered art history was no longer a study of line, color, space, movements, and biographies but a "discourse of re-presentation versus similitude." My son's Pokémon-speak made more sense.

One late afternoon nearing the end of October, I was pushing Dash in his stroller around the Great Lawn in Central Park. I spotted a young man surrounded by a bunch of schoolboys in matching red team jerseys. He appeared like a bird in flight. He had just kicked a soccer ball, and the force of the blow lifted him off the ground. With one leg swept in front of his body, his arms were outstretched as wide as wings, and his flaxen hair was fanned in the air as if he had a headdress of platinum feathers.

His silhouette was perfectly proportioned—limbs long, chest broad, and hips tapered. I recognized him from school, one of the few students in my class who didn't run at the mouth. I'd been studying his good looks from across the room and now zoomed in for a close-up. His eyes were as crisp and bright as the cloudless blue sky. He had a smattering of freckles across his nose. When a green bug settled on his arm, he delicately placed it on a blade of grass instead of swatting it away. Such a poetic gesture, it almost hurt just watching it.

"I'm Elizabeth," I said.

"I know." He smiled, his sparkling teeth straight and square. "I'm Lark."

"Who are these kids you're with?"

"I coach after-school sports at Saint Bernard's on Ninety-eighth Street. Who's this?"

He nodded toward Dash.

"My son."

Clutching Mitzi, Dash gave Lark the hairy eyeball.

"You have a kid? I don't know anyone who goes to school and has a kid."

Thank you. I now feel old enough to qualify for assisted living.

I invited Lark to join me at a Cindy Sherman opening the following week, knowing I could depend on Gwendolyn to stay with Dash. Lark and I agreed to meet beforehand at his place: a one-bedroom in the East Village, a neighborhood right out of *Rent*, where everyone was postpubescent, poor, and pierced.

Facing an air shaft, Lark's apartment got no sunlight. He slept on a mattress directly on the floor in a makeshift bedroom divided from the rest of the space by plywood papered with magazine decoupage. His roommate, a gay, bald paralegal, occupied the official bedroom. He had placed a centerpiece on the living room's glass coffee table: a rubber cast of porn star Jeff Stryker's ten-inch penis.

That night, Lark and I never made it to the opening. We wound up having sex, a transforming experience, first because I lay recumbent on the floor mattress, risking my bare flesh as roach bait. Second, he was outdoorsy and uninhibited, an eco-humanist preferring any- and everything au naturel.

He asked to see my pussy. Lights on. Up close. I hesitated. A vagina, with its anemone forms and slimy texture, looks like an internal organ wrong-side-out and is, in my opinion, best not experienced at close range—unless you're a gynecologist or an Eastern European depilatory specialist.

No man had ever taken a good look at mine, although I felt confident it was as attractive as they came. I kept it in tip-top condition: freshly bathed and neatly shorn. Neither sloppy nor skimpy, the lips were slender, yet pillowy, and flush with my clit, a rosy, pliant stem as demure as my pinkie fingertip. Although flexible, my vaginal entrance never gaped (unless it was put to good use). Penetration required gentle pushing, whereupon all the parts that made up the hole responded in a grip of warm reception. After so many years of bashfulness with Charlie, Lark's exultation in the body electric was liberating. I opened my legs wide.

Although his cock looked like a newbie's—freshly scrubbed and barely full grown at five inches max—he maneuvered it with confidence. Grasping the base, he pointed the tapered head at the cleft between my labia, wedging between the fronds of my flesh, wetting his member. When he kissed me, his mouth tasted like summer sorbet. I dripped messily.

Fucking, we fit together beautifully in a pornographic pas de deux. Lark took the lead without ever dominating, divining when to raise my hands over my head and nibble my underarms; when to swing my legs over his shoulders, burrowing his cock in my canal; when to smear the bisque running from my cunt over my asshole, wriggling a finger inside. There were no awkward rollovers, strained muscles, or uncouplings. Like solids sensitive to heat, we stretched, contracted, and lingered in a legato of molten shapes. Staccato sounds and smutty murmurs rose from our throats, punctuating our billows of ardor. But just as my climax was starting to crest, Lark slipped out, limply.

I was too close to stop. Jamming two of my fingers where his cock had been, I used my other hand to tenderize my clitoral knot. In seconds, my torso torqued in spasms and my limbs convulsed. Watching me get myself off revived Lark. Diddling his now hard prick, he rose to his knees and I got on all fours, burying my nostrils in his russet pubic hair, orbiting my tongue around his balls, first one, then the other, before engorging them both.

"Turn around," I told him.

I had never done what I was about to do. Was it Lark's sensuality or sheer physical beauty that made me want to? Covered in fine, blond hairs, his ass seemed powdered in gold. I pressed my fingers into his sturdy cheeks, parting them to peer at the tissues pinched together protecting the tiny puncture. Holding my breath, I flicked my tongue over the tender asterisk. Not much taste but, when I inhaled through my nose, the aroma was ancient and oaken like truffles.

Swaying his back, Lark pushed his bunghole into my face, forcing me to tongue him deeper. I was driving him crazy and he was beating his cock black and blue, wailing, "Oh, baby . . . baby." Holding his balls in my palm, I felt them spring upward, ready to burst. Ducking between his legs, I latched my mouth around his dick. Cum never went down so easily.

"You've ruined me," he said, collapsing in a winded swoon.

"No, *you've* ruined *me*."

That was the start of our affair. It lasted two years, thanks to Gwendolyn, Dash's capable caregiver who unwittingly abetted his mother's furloughs for fornication.

With Lark, I felt coltish and callow, as if I had never been married. When we went to a party in a basement studio off Tompkins Square, U2's "Achtung Baby" was a soundscape to my disavowal of domesticity. Singing along to Bono's moody ballad "One," Lark taught me to play pool and throw darts. In the winter, we iceskated at Wollman Rink where, instead of coffee, we took a break for hot cocoa with whipped cream; in the spring, we Rollerbladed through Central Park. Smart and sarcastic, Lark got me. Totally.

I couldn't wait to introduce him to Ruby. She was involved in a furtive fuck-a-thon with Luke, a married architect and father of three small daughters, who lived upstate near her. She often came to the city to hustle for design jobs and, on one of her trips, met Lark and me at the Second Avenue Deli.

"How would you describe your relationship with Elizabeth?" she asked him, taking a sip of her Diet Dr. Brown's Cel-Ray Soda.

"Obviously, I'm living on the edge," he said.

Choking on her drink, she dragged me into the bathroom. "He's only twenty-four." She laughed, gasping for air. "He's a sweet, wholesome guy. It's not like he's married. What edge is he talking about?"

Breaking the Ten Commandments, maybe?

I kind of felt bad about corrupting Lark and, like Wendy with Peter Pan, took it upon myself to watch over my young lover in the nasty Neverland of New York City. I bought him burritos when he was penniless or orange juice and vitamin C when he caught a cold. Noticing a missing button on his denim work shirt, I demonstrated my seventh-grade home-ec skills with a needle and thread. Once, I washed his sweaty gym clothes, not only fabric-softening but also ironing them.

Although Lark was a buck, he never rose to the status of a stud. He had trouble getting it up and, when he did, went soft too soon. I didn't know whether he suffered performance anxiety or some underlying physiological disorder but it could easily take an hour for him to ejaculate. In those pre-Viagra days, there seemed no solution, yet I couldn't have cared less. Our lovemaking was so sublime, his hard-on, or lack thereof, was beside the point.

Ever since *Lady Chatterley's Lover*, I'd been waiting for a man to strip me of my tough-girl defenses, to lay bare my inhibitions and to touch me in places that should have made me die of shame but instead would divest me of it. I had been wishing for gluttonous, unblushing, and transcendent sex—a transport to true love.

It happened with Lark. Once we started kissing, the physical schism between our bodies seemed to dissolve into a permeable membrane of shared blood and breath. His touch turned my corporeality into plasma, a metamorphosis that was preverbal and ungovernable, like a libidinal spin painting. I felt so alive and my emotional release felt so primal, I was no longer me. I was more me. Pure me. Without social, family, or gender identity. No husband. No child. No aspirations or disappointments. Having an orgasm could trigger a rain of tears down my face. It was my id, unplugged.

Ruby understood completely. "Luke and I are so enveloped in each other," she said, swapping stories with me over the phone. "I count the hours to see him. It's never enough. I'm always sore and it always feels so good. I've never had this kind of love. We're one person."

My oneness with Lark culminated on a July afternoon in 1993. Abed on a sand dune and beneath a blue sky, we made love on Fire Island. For once, Lark stayed hard. When he came, so did I, a simultaneous eruption. At the time, it seemed the height of pantheistic pleasure. In retrospect, it was an antimiracle of fate.

Three years earlier, on August 21, 1990, I had sent a letter to Ruby of which I had no recollection until she dug it up:

> *You're not going to believe this but since Dash has been talking more and is much nicer to be with, I've been yearning for another one! Charlie said it's out of the question. We have to have more money. So I figure I'll give him three more years and then I'll hope for an "accident." By then, I'll be thirty-two.*

Right after I turned thirty-two, the accident happened. But not with Charlie.

I wanted Lark's baby. My intuition told me it was a girl. She was my love child. By the time she was born, Dash would be five, a good age for a sibling. But how could I do it? I had a husband. Should I seduce him in an attempt to pass off the child as his? Even if he believed it, I could never live with the lie. It was too big. What about getting a divorce and being a single mother? Lark wanted no part of parenting, and I had no money. How could I afford to raise the baby on my own? And what about Dash? How would he feel once he found out his mother left his father to have another man's child? Who would my son hate more—his sibling or me?

I knew what I had to do.

Whether because of caution, luck, or low fertility, I was the only one of my friends who'd never had an abortion. The closest I'd come was secondhand.

In 1979, when Andee and I were seventeen, we got matching Farrah Fawcett feathered cuts at Great Neck's Peter's Place, a unisex salon. Our hairdressers wore butterfly-collared shirts, high-waisted gabardine flare-legged pants, and square-toed Dingo boots. Their names were Gary and Mitch, though I wasn't sure which was which.

After they got off work, Andee and I met them for screwdrivers at Mushrooms, a bar in town. We went back to Mitch's apartment under the 59th Street Bridge to mellow out on ludes. Andee and I let the guys demonstrate their tonsorial skills on our bikini areas, customizing our pubic triangles (a heart for her and a downward arrow for me). Circus sex and partner swapping followed, a saturnalia recorded with a tripod-mounted video camera.

Andee got pregnant and I accompanied her to the Bill Baird Center, a Long Island birth control clinic where they didn't tell your parents or require their permission for an abortion.

"First I'm going to swab the inside of your vagina with a Betadine solution," the doctor said to Andee who, lying on an examining table fitted with metal stirrups, was holding my hand. "Then I'll inject novocaine into your cervix so you won't feel it being dilated. You'll feel pressure, and then it'll be no more than a pinch."

"Just a pinch, right?" he repeated, withdrawing a foot-long needle.

From Andee's expression, it looked like she'd been skewered.

When the doctor flipped on a suction device to vacuum the lining of her uterus, the room sounded as if it were a gargantuan Waring blender. Was it only my imagination or did I detect an odor? A meaty smell? Yes, blood.

In the recovery room, a handful of girls were having apple juice and graham crackers, maxipads pressed between their legs. A nurse was making rounds, taking blood pressure and offering cool compresses for flushed faces. One of the patients was sobbing loudly, another was drenched in perspiration, and everyone was shaking. I got a diaphragm shortly thereafter.

I didn't use it that day with Lark. It was the third week of my menstrual cycle and I calculated the coast was clear. Apparently it wasn't. The doctor informed me I'd have to hang in there a few more weeks until the embryo was bigger in order to undergo the procedure. The wait was agony, a slow countdown for a day I wished would never come, a duration of despair that I endured alone.

Every night, I lay awake beside my sleeping husband, who had no idea his wife was pregnant with someone else's baby. Every day, my son was a reminder of what I was choosing to terminate. Although my mother helped me out by paying for the medical cost, I couldn't talk to her because my crisis brought back memories of her own experience, the gory details of which she couldn't resist reliving whenever she got me on the phone.

Meanwhile, Lark was AWOL. He had a summer weekend job leading bicycle tours, making him conveniently unreachable. During the week, he worked part-time as a gallery-sitter. He stopped returning my phone messages. One day, I did a gallery drive-by and spied him having a picnic lunch on the floor with a young woman I'd never seen before. Barging in, I introduced myself and she flew out the door, presumably knowing my situation. Lark explained they'd met on his last bicycle tour and he liked her smile.

"SHE WOULDN'T BE ABLE TO SMILE IF SHE HAD TO

HAVE A FUCKING ABORTION!" I screamed, pulling off my shoe, throwing it at his head.

My double life had finally caught up with me. At the start, the duplicity was merely stressful. I was always looking over my shoulder, convinced I was about to be caught. I loathed myself for betraying Charlie, a good man who deserved better. But I justified my assignations because they made my existence more tolerable, enabling me to cope with the sexual deprivation and loneliness at home. Now I realized the paradox of my infidelity: It was only due to the security I felt as a wife that I was able to test its perimeters by being unfaithful. Had I not had a husband, there would never have been a Lark.

Once I got pregnant, I could no longer have it both ways. The consequences were pretty clear and pretty bad. Forget a scarlet letter. An ultrasound confirmed I was carrying a neon signboard of sin.

On August 23, the morning of my abortion, Lark did the right thing and met me at New York Hospital. While he remained in a waiting area, I went into an operating room. It was déjà vu. Standing beside my gynecologist, the doctor who had delivered Dash, was a nurse—the very same one who had coached me during labor: "Push! Harder! Push!" The symmetry—or was it asymmetry?—was cruel.

"Relax," said an anesthesiologist, sliding a needle into my vein. "You won't feel a thing."

Just a pinch, right?

When I woke up, sharp cramps yanked my pelvis, reminding me how fortunate I was to be in safe hands, spared the horrors of back alleys. As a placard-carrying protester for women's reproductive rights, I had a new position on abortion. It is not an option that a woman wants to "choose." It was a last resort.

Soon after, Lark moved to Seattle, where he got a teaching job. In lieu of a good-bye, he left a letter with my doorman:

Dear Elizabeth,

No other woman in my life has meant as much to me as you. When we met, I was immediately struck by your beauty, sexiness, sense of humor, and intelligence. I had no idea why you wanted to be with me except that I was so far from your existence at the time that I was exotic. What I did know, though, was that I wanted you . . . totally. I wanted to see, hear, touch, smell, and taste you. I could never get enough of you. For me, you are New York—its edginess and its splendor. I needed you as a protector. I looked to you as a guide. At the beginning, I saw my relationship with you as exciting and temporary, for I knew that my stay in New York was finite and that you were tied to it by your marriage and son.

Then I fell in love. I had no intention of this. You remember how we mapped our relationship according to the phases of our sex life? I fell in love with you before the fantasy and anal phase (sounds like Erikson's Childhood Development). I fell in love when I realized I had something real to offer you. I believed in you. I believed in your inherent goodness. I believed the dramas in your life needed my balanced perspective.

Falling in love with you has also been difficult on me. I've been in an adulterous affair. Although I wanted to be in it, I've been ashamed. I can't be honest with my family. My friends are intrigued by our relationship but they are also justifiably critical.

The future for us would become rockier as I came to terms with you being a mother. I want a family of my own. Getting you pregnant remains the most tumultuous moment in my life. I am unsettled because I feel I have to be an asshole. I hate myself for it. I want to be a father when I'm in a stable situation. I can't picture us as a family, or creating one. I don't approve of the way you are a mother to Dash, but I am the reason for my disapproval.

One love,
Lark

Murder is a pretty effective way of getting rid of someone, as well as an unconscious proclamation of independence from the hold that person has over you. That was probably why I had recurring nightmares of brandishing a pearl-handled silver pistol at Lark's golden head and blowing his brains out. I was filled with rage for ever-changing reasons: He failed to be my Lancelot; he benefited from my infidelity, only to use it against me by criticizing me as a mother when it suited him. Even if he was right, he had no understanding of the complexity of my conflict. Once, upon waking from another bad dream, I wrote him this note:

"There isn't a bourgeois alive who in the ferment of his youth, if only for a day or for a minute, hasn't thought himself capable of boundless passions and noble exploits. The sorriest little woman-chaser has dreamed of Oriental queens; in a corner of every notary's heart lie the moldy remains of a poet."

—Gustave Flaubert, *Madame Bovary*

There was no need for a return address. Lark would know the sender.

• • •

I made it through one more semester at the Institute before calling it quits. The halls felt more hollow than hallowed once Lark was gone. The prospect of completing a PhD seemed as wearisome as a steady drip on a stone. I applied for a job at the Hudson River Museum to be curator of contemporary art, a new position for which I would have free rein. The hitch? The museum was in Yonkers.

Driving an hour to work each morning, I wouldn't return to Manhattan until nearly seven at night. Dash was prone to illness, nothing serious, but wellness was an exception in his history of strep, bronchitis, conjunctivitis, and stomach viruses. Although Gwendolyn was on hand if he stayed home from school with a fever, I had visions of myself bumper-to-bumper on the Henry Hudson, anxious to make it back to my apartment before his abscessed eardrum ruptured.

A safer bet was the Museum of Modern Art. I was offered a part-time position in the Education Department, to teach high school students how to look at art critically, give public gallery lectures, and provide teachers with slide sets to integrate into their curricula. The job was low level and low paying—thirteen thousand dollars a year—but its midtown location was logistical compensation. I was only ten minutes by cab from home.

By now, the tenor of my marriage was heavy and flat, a dirge of punitive indifference and grudging self-sufficiency. Charlie dropped off his own shirts at the laundry because I let the pile mount to a point where he had nothing clean to wear. He stopped giving me gifts for holidays and birthdays. When he presented a dozen flowers on Mother's Day, it was an afterthought: a nosegay of guilt grabbed from a Korean market at the behest of our six-year-old son, who wanted the bouquet to accompany a card he'd made for me at school.

Our marital decay affected Dash. A combative child, he was difficult to please, insistent about getting his way. Regimented about food, he consumed only deli-bought tuna salad, Chef Boyardee, and Swiss Miss chocolate pudding snack packs—for lunch, dinner, and even breakfast. If I tried to vary his diet, his uncompromising appetite, underscored by locked lips and Frisbee-tossed plates, was more vigorous than my will to countervail vitamin deficiencies.

He established a color code for those closest to him, designating me red, Charlie blue, my mother yellow, my mother-in-law orange, and himself green. When one of us made a picture with him, or he depicted the particular family member, there could be no deviation from the assigned Crayola lest Dash mutate into a human paper shredder. He was not truly violent, never physically aggressive toward other people, but his GI Joe collection reflected his inner rage: the soldiers stripped, bound with black electrical tape, and lynched from faucets or door handles with shoelaces, belts, or twine. Even on a good day with my son, I was always on edge that a transition to another activity, removal of an article of clothing, or the absence of Mitzi would cause a cavalcade of airborne Lincoln Logs.

"He can sense the tension between you two," said a child psychiatrist whom Charlie and I consulted. "He sees his mother as the bad guy, the disciplinarian, and his father as the softy. He is trying to unite you by asserting his own control over a situation that makes him feel insecure."

We attempted an indivisible front. Charlie was stricter about toothbrushing and soccer playing inside the house while I tried to lighten up. Inspired by *Green Eggs and Ham,* I added verdant food coloring to scrambled eggs, hoping the protein source disguised as Dash's favorite hue would serve to diversify his menu. While other kids dressed as pumpkins for Halloween, mine wanted to be a Christmas tree (green!). With a three-foot square of cardboard, a box cutter, acrylic paint, cotton balls, and rubber cement, I transformed my trick-or-treater into a consumer holiday hybrid: a cutout, stand-up, snow-covered evergreen, ornamented with an orange plastic jack-o'-lantern candy basket.

In truth, I was often more present physically than mentally. At Six Flags Great Adventure in Jackson, New Jersey, while Charlie and Dash plunged down a forty-foot chute on a rubber raft into an Olympic-size vat of water, I waited by a concession stand, conjuring a giant split screen: on one side, the real me, head between my legs, motion sick from whirling on Enchanted Tea Cups; on the other, the fantasy me, solo, string-bikinied with Steve Tyler at St. Barth's Le Ti.

The family unit was a noose around my neck. I hated processed kiddy culture and the pabulum of fireside homilies on which a mother was expected to thrive. I hated being the third wheel to Charlie and Dash, ignorant of and excluded from their tag-team gags and games. When we three went to Snug Harbor Cultural

Center on Staten Island to see an exhibition of my mother's art-work, I spent the entire ferry ride not waving at the Statue of Liberty with my little boy and his daddy, but peering over the railing, wondering: If I flung myself overboard, could I fight the instinct to swim and succeed in drowning myself?

• • •

"I want a divorce," Charlie announced over Au Bon Pain sandwiches. It was April 1995 and he had called me at MoMA, asking me to meet him for lunch in the Sculpture Garden.

"Couldn't you have waited?" I stammered. "Your timing isn't great."

I gestured toward my foot, encased in a clunky blue protective walking boot, propped on a chair. I had broken a metatarsal bone in Tae Kwon Do, which I'd taken up a few years earlier. The symbolism was trite: After a ten-year marriage, my husband, now a powerful attorney, had found the legs to move on while I, still aimless, had become a gimp.

"There's never a right moment with you." He shook his head. "It's always something. You're upset. You're sick. You can't sleep. You're never happy just being in the moment. For years, I've been intimidated to tell you how I feel. You're unloving and uncaring."

For the first time, Charlie was volunteering his feelings without any needling from me. Had I known it would mean him slogging me with years of pent-up emotional puke, I would have been more careful what I wished for.

"When we met, I thought you were so powerful, so sophisticated, so perfect," he continued. "I thought *you* would be the one to shape our lives. I never imagined it would be this much of a struggle. You're needy and you've neglected my needs. I just want a woman who digs what she's doing and digs being with me."

"All I've wanted is for you to see me as I really am," I pleaded. "You've put me on a pedestal, but I'm a real, live person with body fluids and emotions. Whenever I express myself, you shut down."

"You're so self-absorbed. Everything is always about how something affects *you*. Whether *you'll* be happy going somewhere, how *you'll* feel when you get there, what if *you* don't like it. You're unbearable."

He departed the Sculpture Garden without so much as a backward glance. Bad enough I had to collect myself and go back to work on crutches, I also had to hobble to a job interview later that day.

Wearing a navy-blue Jean Paul Gaultier skirt suit—my power look—I put on a happy face, tottering on my broken foot into Paine Webber, a massive, metropolitan office with panoramic windows and dark wood paneling. The corporation had an opening for a curator of its art collection, which came with a salary of seventy-five thousand dollars, full benefits, and a retirement plan. Directed to a conference room, I took my place at a grand mahogany table opposite Donald Marron, the company's unsmiling CEO.

"Tell me about yourself," he said.

I sounded off my qualifications, a cartoon bubble floating over my head:

Please, Mr. Marron, I really need this job. My husband is divorcing me and I don't make much money and the alimony and child support payments won't be nearly enough to cover both the mortgage and the babysitter, whom I now really need since being a working mom is no longer a choice but a necessity.

"How familiar are you with the contemporary art market?" Marron asked.

"I follow all the auction results and go to all the galleries," I lied. "By the way, that's a beautiful Alice Neel painting on the wall."

"It's not an Alice Neel," he said, in the same tone as a judge delivering a death sentence. "It's a Lucian Freud." (The difference between two artists: two and a half million dollars.)

Thank God, I hadn't jumped the gun and given MoMA notice beforehand.

That night, I called Ruby to tell her Charlie wanted a divorce.

She was surprised I took the news so hard. "Your marriage is an anomaly," she said. "You're the bad girl and he's the valedictorian. With you and him, it's a sexual problem. You go after danger and he's boring. Now you'll be free to love."

When Ruby's husband, Eric, had discovered she was having an affair, he'd kicked her to the curb, keeping their son, Joey. She was able to cozy up to the soon-to-be-divorced Luke in a lakeside cottage where deer roamed the grounds. I reminded her not all marriages ended at Walden Pond.

Charlie and I split in February 1996, six weeks after he made partner, an achievement that took nine years of our decade-long marriage. We put off telling Dash until Charlie signed a lease for a new apartment.

"Your father and I have something to talk to you about," I said, hitting MUTE on the TV remote. With Mitzi in the crook of his elbow, our son was sitting on the living room sofa, watching a sit-com, *Home Improvement*.

"I already know what you're going to say. You're getting a divorce."

Walt Disney couldn't have created more cartoonlike reactions than Charlie's and mine. Our heads practically spun 360 degrees.

"Sort of," Charlie said, recovering after a minute or so. "Your mother and I will have separate apartments but you'll live with both of us. Things will change but only for the better. During the week, you'll be here and on the weekends, you'll be with me."

"That's fine," Dash said.

"Don't you want to know why?" I asked.

He didn't answer.

"We think we'll be happier this way," Charlie offered. "Sometimes grown-ups get married and after a while, want to live apart. But they never stop loving their children. Our decision has nothing to do with you."

The *it's-not-your-fault* speech had as much impact on our kid as the daily NASDAQ average. His eyes remained glued to the aphonic tube.

"How did you know what we were going to tell you?" I asked, waving my hand in front of his gimlet stare, attempting to redirect it to us, the live audience.

"You don't act like married people on TV do," he said. "You're more like friends."

• • •

When I told my parents Charlie wanted a divorce, my father advised me to quickly find a new husband so my financial future would be more certain. My mother begged me to win back the one I already had. "I want you to have security," she said. "Why not give Charlie another chance?"

Nothing I could have said would have convinced my family the chance was not mine to give. In their eyes, I—an adulterous, demanding spendthrift—was not only to blame for the failure of my marriage but also capable of repairing it. The fact that Charlie had also been fucking around was my fault, too.

"I dallied because I needed to," he confessed when I finally confronted him. "I just never thought it was such a violation. It obviously had something to do with the fact that our sex life was dreadful. Maybe I have situational morality. I had a psychological mechanism that allowed me to detach from you, to not feel blameworthy. I had an extraordinary need for love and affection and passion. It had nothing to do with whether I suspected you were doing the same. I felt like I was the victim."

For me, his admission was a climactic moment of truth, a revelation recasting the meaning of all events leading up to it. I remembered a weekend when Dash was small and I went out, leaving him with Charlie. Returning home, I found the apartment door ajar. Poking my head inside, I overheard my husband's voice coming from our bedroom. He was on the phone. I couldn't make out most of the conversation but his near whisper, coupled with a few audible and tantalizing words—"needs," "unhappiness," and "fulfillment"—made me sense I was trespassing. It was so surreal, I backed out the front door and reopened it, calling, "I'm hoooome!"—an attempt to warn Charlie to hang up.

A couple of years later, over dinner, he casually mentioned a new case he was handling: a divorce in which he was representing the wife of a real estate scion with a history of philandering.

"If a marriage relationship is built on something firmly rooted, it won't be uprooted by a dalliance," Charlie hypothesized. "If it was, that means the marriage wasn't so firmly rooted in the first place or the dalliance was more significant. When I hear about people having an affair, I think, *Good for them.* Everyone is entitled not to hurt other people, but to be fulfilled and pleasured. I don't think you can have a deep, long-term marriage if you're fucking around but, from time to time, sex with another person? It doesn't strike me as such a horrible thing."

It never occurred to me that Charlie's words were self-incriminating. I assumed his attitude reflected a legal and social—not personal—progressiveness. In my eyes, he was too righteous and asexual to engage in extramarital activities. Amazing how little I knew him.

I always perceived big corporate law firms as dehumanizing, repressive, and sterile. It was a shock to learn what actually goes on when multiple attorneys, with a support staff of paralegals and secretaries, are all assigned to a single long-term case. Teamwork can lead to temptation—especially between tall, McTitty blondes and unhappily married men.

Charlie moved into an apartment seven blocks away, packing only his clothes, leaving me with all our belongings. With permission from my parents, my brother Andrew led Charlie to their attic, where he picked out a cast-off coffee table and a few lamps to furnish his new place. There was no dispute over the joint custody of Dash, who was now seven. Until Charlie and I hammered out a separation agreement, he would continue supporting me. On his first night at his new apartment, his family threw him a champagne party. They gave my son the cork as a memento of the cele-bration.

At my apartment, I waited alone for the Salvation Army to pick up a pair of twin mattresses pushed together to create the illusion of a single, king-size bed. That was how Charlie and I had slept: back-to-back, never touching, our bodies separated by a physical boundary. Replacing the beds with a brand-new queen size from Dial-A-Mattress, I cried myself to sleep, praying the other side wouldn't remain empty for long.

PART TWO

And the wild regrets, and the bloody sweats,
None knew so well as I:
For he who lives more lives than one
More deaths than one must die.

—*Oscar Wilde,* The Ballad of Reading Gaol

CHAPTER 10

I'D NEVER BEEN A SINGLE WOMAN. I went from my parents' home to college to marriage. Along the way, I had a couple of room- and apartment mates. Ever since fourth grade, when Seth Feinstein asked me to go steady, I'd always had a boyfriend, following the "flip principle"—flipping from one guy to another only after number two was secured in place.

I wasn't savvy about dating, the art of comparing and contrasting until you settled on someone, followed by more getting-to-know-you dinners, movies, sleepovers, a vacation or summer share before realizing your incompatibility and then surviving a breakup. At twenty, after I met Charlie, he became my anchor. Those who might otherwise have tugged at my heart never even made it as chum.

Now, at thirty-four and a half, I no longer had the mooring of a man and could let myself be carried by the currents of chance. For the first time in my life, I didn't have to behave as a daughter or wife. I was free to float as a single woman in an adult world. Maybe I would wash ashore on a tropical island. Maybe I'd be eaten alive by sharks.

There were few role models to help me navigate. Holly Golightly was out since I'd already married the nice Paul Varjak guy, though I would have liked to live the rest of my life to that Henry

Mancini score. In 1977, when I was sixteen, my mother and I went to see *Looking for Mr. Goodbar,* about a liberated young woman—Theresa Dunn, a schoolteacher for the deaf, played against type by Diane Keaton—who searches for love, self, and sexual identity in bars, drugs, and one-night stands. She brings home a murderer who kills her. The moral of the story was clear: Dating was deadly, a good reason to limit my exposure and marry ASAP.

In the 1980s, single women were career bitches—Murphy Browns—unable to deal with children. I could identify with the latter characteristic but not the former. To me, the sappy characters of *thirtysomething* were more engrossing, their yuppie angst about youthful dreams versus adult responsibilities reflecting my own.

The sympathetic bachelorettes of the late 1990s—Ally McBeal, Bridget Jones, and Carrie Bradshaw—had yet to appear on the horizon. Not that their scripts were ever to reflect mine. "They have no sense of responsibility toward another person," Ruby quipped as we watched *Sex and the City*'s infamous quartet during their first HBO season. "For women in their midthirties, they're developmentally retarded."

Which left me with Ivana. Now, *that* woman knew how to pull off being single a second time around (or third, in her case). She was no bitter, down-on-her-luck divorcée. Some might argue the twenty million she received from The Donald sweetened the split but, *puh-leeze,* to a wife rumored to have had a limousine transport her poodles daily to a hairdresser—a cost of two grand a month—the settlement was a slap in the face. She had spent fourteen years putting out to a pug-faced man and bore him three children, for God's sake.

So what did she do, this plucky Czech who, at twenty-one, had managed to ski her way out from behind the Iron Curtain? Everything: Tits, nose, lips, skin, highlights, wardrobe, personal trainers, and low-rent men. She even got a job, hawking the House of

Ivana on the Home Shopping Network. Divorce inspired her total makeover.

Being a beginner, I started small: Botox.

"Congratulations!" my father said, calling me after I had my forehead filled with pathogens in order to smooth away wrinkles. "You've been injected with one of the most powerful poisons known to man. It's used as a bacterial-warfare agent to contaminate the water of the enemy."

"Thanks, Dad. Did you have to tell me that now?"

I was propped up in my bed, wearing a neck brace to keep my head erect for seven hours so the Botox wouldn't seep from the injection site, causing my eyelids to droop, a dreaded risk of the procedure.

All my life, my appearance had preoccupied me. (What female's doesn't?) I had been both blessed and cursed with an animated face. When I laughed, my eyes brightened into a sunburst of radiant lines. When I cried, my expression molted into a blotchy pulp, creased with descending lines of anguish. Working out, I grimaced, cinching my eyebrows together, the inch of skin between them pleated like an accordion. After years of graduate study scrutinizing detailed illustrations of art history textbooks, I had squint and frown lines etching my flesh.

Following my separation from Charlie, I found myself staring in mirrors, my fingers pressed against my forehead, vainly attempting to erase the signs of fretfulness. Not wanting to look like a Sun-Maid raisin, I saw no reason to age gracefully. *Character,* it seemed to me, was simply a bullshitter's term for a hagged-out face.

I got an appointment with Alan Matarasso, a Park Avenue plastic surgeon whose breath smelled of Scope and whose tie was from Hermès. He informed me I needed no less than twelve injections—hardly the few pinpricks I'd been expecting. The two and a half milligrams of Valium, which he told me to dissolve under my tongue, calmed my jitters as I watched him fill several syringes with botulinum type A. Ingested in large doses, it causes food poisoning, paralysis, respiratory failure, and death. It had once been a Saddam Hussein favorite.

With the first injection came a disturbing popping sound—the needle piercing my skin—followed by a fiery sensation, like a bunch of flu shots in my forehead. The procedure took only three minutes (who knew how interminable three minutes could feel?) and cost eleven hundred dollars. In order to cover the check, I'd have to lie to Charlie: Either a major kitchen appliance had gone on the fritz and I needed extra cash to replace it, or somewhere between Dash's fall–winter and spring–summer clothing, there was an unaccounted-for season, requiring me to buy him a new wardrobe.

"Whatever you do, don't bend over, lie down, go to the hairdresser, try on hats, or shoe shop for the rest of the day," the nurse warned before I left the office. "Otherwise, the Botox can migrate to your eyelids."

Walking gingerly back to my apartment, a couple of blocks from the doctor's, I was terrified I'd stumble on a sidewalk crack, setting the neuromuscular blocking agent to paralyze the rest of my face. Upon arriving home, I created a throne on my bed out of shams and pillows—my perch for the next several hours. I had a new worry. The Valium was making me sleepy. What if I nodded off while sitting up and my head bobbed forward? Where would my eyelids be then?

Calling a local pharmacy, I ordered a neck support to be delivered. Looking like a personal-injury defendant, I got into bed, wearing the brace, and turned on the TV. For the occasion, I'd rented *The Picture of Dorian Gray*. The last thing I remembered before drifting off—my head safely immobilized—was Hurd Hatfield's voice: "The secret to remaining young is never to have an emotion unbecoming." Or to get Botox, I thought dreamily.

It worked beautifully, transforming me overnight from Cruella De Vil to Snow White. I was now inspired to advance to the next level of cosmetic enhancement: an eye lift.

For the last few years, I had been watching my lids dip and crease, my hazel irises disappearing beneath little swags of slackening skin. Although the peepers have been romantically dubbed "the windows to the soul," mine, framed by pleats and folds, looked like outmoded window treatments. In addition, there were now spidery lines around my mouth, webs into which my lipstick bled.

I decided on a different Park Avenue surgeon, David Hidalgo, who, in his spare time, created brilliantly colored flower paintings and hyperrealistic anatomical drawings. Carefully rendering every vein of each petal or person, he was a perfectionist with iron control over his spontaneous impulses. Not exactly the makings of a great artist but most definitely a doctor to be trusted with sharp implements on the skin. Secretly, I was hoping he'd reject me, saying I was too young to be a cosmetic surgery candidate.

"Your eyes are out of sync with the rest of your face," he observed at my consultation. "They are older than any other part of you. If you want a balanced rejuvenation, surgery alone won't turn back the clock because you have years of sun damage that makes the skin look old. Laser resurfacing of the wrinkles under your eyes will make them look the way they did when you were twenty."

I'm not a candidate. I'm an emergency case.

I immediately scheduled an upper and lower eye lift, laser resurfacing of my crow's-feet, and dermabrasion to sand off the wrinkles around my mouth. My friends thought I would be better off participating in a study of an emerging patient demographic: those suffering from body dysmorphic disorder, an abnormal preoccupation with imagined or slight defects in appearance.

"You're crazy!" said Andee when I announced my surgery date. "You're not even forty."

"I'm so worried that this is an addiction," Ruby said. "I don't want you to look like a waxwork. I think you should just go to bed—for a couple of years."

Only my mother was supportive. Instead of passing on recipes or heirloom jewelry, she provided me with plastic surgery—or at least the financing for it. As a girl, she had hated her aquiline nose, concealing the curve with her hand, pleading with her parents for an operation. Her mother refused.

My mother swore to herself to make it possible for her own daughter to look and feel her best, a commitment gaining new urgency once I became a contestant in the Manhattan singles pageant. She held my chin in one hand, using the other to pinch the skin on top of my lids, testing its elasticity.

"The eyes are always the first to go," she confirmed. "Don't be afraid to start." Not only did she remain in the waiting room during my two-hour surgery, she gave me a leg up onto the operating table.

Emerging from a thick haze of anesthesia, I felt like the English Patient after being trapped behind a plane's roaring fuselage: throat parched, lips numb, eyes swollen and smarting. I could barely see the blurry silhouette of a nurse smearing Aquaphor on my laser-fried flesh. Good thing I'd accomplished all my pre-op preparations: stocked up on frozen peas to use as ice packs once I returned home, bought Briko wraparound ski goggles to wear as a disguise if I ventured outside, and covered all my bathroom mirrors with construction paper so I wouldn't faint at the sight of my blow-torched face.

"You look so good!" complimented a private-duty nurse who sat by my side for the next twenty-four hours, her name befittingly Mercy.

Good? Compared with what? A napalm casualty?

Only my father was honest: "You look like hell."

Nine days later, after the swelling went down, the oozing and crusting had stopped, the Technicolor bruises faded, and the scabs had fallen off, I no longer appeared as if my home were a hospital burn unit. In fact, I looked better than when I was twenty. Feeling like a starlet in a swivel chair who spins around to face a mirror after a sitting with Kevin Aucoin, I gaped in disbelief at the perfection staring back at me.

Dash was undisturbed by my mutation. As a precaution, he had stayed with Charlie until I healed. Afterward, the only indication that my son noticed my altered appearance was a comment upon returning home from school: "You look better than the other kids' mothers. Are you younger than them?"

Bless you, boy.

With the renovation of my exterior completed, I turned my attention to the interior—my apartment. Enter the contractor.

He was no meathead with Spackle under his fingernails and Sheetrock dust in his hair. He was Jewish, in his late forties, and built (six foot one, 185 pounds), wearing wire-rimmed glasses and a baseball cap. His vibe? Easy and confident. When he laughed, his nose crinkled. He had spent his twenties in Europe, where he picked up masonry skills and Romance languages. I nearly melted when I heard him speak Spanish to his crew. The contractor's accent was so regal, with rolling *r*'s sounding like clicking castanets, you'd think he was reading aloud from *Don Quixote* instead of measuring my square footage.

His tile guy did a great job regrouting my bathroom. To thank the contractor, I invited him to lunch, though my motives were completely ulterior: to test-drive my sex appeal as a newly single, surgically refurbished woman. We ate a couple of blocks from my apartment, which, with Dash in school, would be empty for the next few hours. The contractor must have sensed what I was after because before I had the chance to proposition him, before the waitress even took our order, he announced that he had not only a wife but also a girlfriend.

"She's black," he added. "I love dark women—Jamaicans, Puerto Ricans, Asians. My girlfriend has dreadlocks and coffee-colored skin. One of her parents is Chinese."

"Any chance for a Jewish girl who freckles easily?"

"I see my girlfriend twice a week. I told her I wouldn't see anyone else. The only thing she wants me for is sex."

"But that's all I want you for."

"This happens to me all the time." He chuckled. "I've got one client who's married and all she wants is to blow me. She *begs* to give me a blow job. I won't fuck her because I'm not into her but she doesn't care. She tracks me down at construction sites. There are so many horny women in this city. It must be my pheromones."

I leaned in for a whiff of his neck. Oh, my God. He smelled to die for. Fresh. Like lemons mixed with pine trees.

"Irish Spring." He shrugged.

Midway through the entrée, he agreed to come home with me on the condition that it would be a one-shot deal. As we walked into my building, I wanted to pinch myself: *Am I allowed to do this? Isn't there anyone to stop me? Can I really fuck my contractor in broad daylight?*

Forty-five minutes later, his customer service proved outstanding and he became my entrée to a late-twentieth-century version of *The Ladies' Paradise*. Contrary to my prior fantasies, paradise was not an emporium of female adornment with no credit limit. Shangri-la turned out to be a free afternoon, a hot guy with good hands, and an answering machine to pick up the phone.

• • •

Knowing I was now on a hope-'n'-scope mission, Ruby took me to a party at an interior designer's on 14th Street where I saw Dick.

"He's really cute and he's got the right name," she encouraged. "You go, girl."

Bright blue eyes, small straight nose, salt-and-pepper hair, he was forty-two, divorced, and had moved to New York from Cleveland three years earlier. He worked as a photographer for Sotheby's. We had the art world in common. His only drawback:

living in Astoria, Queens. I didn't want to be a snob and hold an outer borough against him, so I handed over my number.

He called the next day and we made a date for the following Saturday to go to galleries in SoHo. He suggested meeting at Dean & DeLuca. I asked how to get in touch with him if I needed to change the time or something came up with my son. Dick said to contact him by beeper or leave a voice mail at his work phone. This made me nervous. What about his home phone? What if he didn't have one?

When I got to our destination, he was standing outside waiting for me, looking fly in black-rimmed shades with green lenses, Levi's, and a button-down shirt untucked. Upon closer inspection, I noticed he had crust in his eyes. I couldn't stop staring. No matter what he said, my focus tunneled in on those dried yellow flakes stuck to his eyelashes. Finally, I couldn't hold back.

"Dick, you've got something in your eye."

"Is it sleep?" he asked, before confessing he hadn't showered that morning.

Strike one.

We went up to the counter to order a couple of *panini*. Unsure of a payment protocol, I handed him eight dollars before heading off to the ladies' room while our lunch was being prepared. When I returned, he had our sandwiches and handed me three dollars.

"Here, I figured we should go half Dutch and you should pay for something."

Strike two.

He told me about his ex-wife and why they split. She was bossy, sending food back at restaurants, the type who played musical chairs with hotel rooms. Since he'd moved to New York, all the women he'd met were fucked up. They were only interested in sex, no commitment. Just keeping a guy on the side to screw while they looked for a "real" boyfriend—someone with money. If you fell in love with them, they didn't believe you because they were so used to getting dumped.

I pointed out that New York men were messed up, too. They thrived on rejection, needing to conquer but, at the same time, being passive and self-delusional, always letting a great girl get away because they thought a better one was around the corner. Dick assured me he wasn't like that. He wanted to settle down and have a life with someone. He couldn't just have sex for the sake of sex. He'd rejected a number of potential fuck buddies.

Walking around SoHo, he began peddling his wares at the galleries, asking if they needed someone to shoot their art. Paid minimum wage at Sotheby's, he used our date as an opportunity to hustle for extra work.

Strike three.

After a couple of hours, I told him I had to get home to my son, which was untrue, it being the weekend when Dash was with his father. Before leaving, I agreed to one more show on Dick's list. Inside a darkened gallery where a lineup of computer terminals glowed with digital art, he started kissing me. It had been awhile since I'd made out.

He asked to see me again, announcing he really liked me and thought I was hot.

Better to nip this one in the bud.

"Dick, I've got to tell you," I said. "I'm not the woman for you. If you think your wife was tough, I'd freak you out. Among other things, I don't *do* public transportation when it comes to dates. Too hard on the high heels. Right now, I'm looking for meaningless sex because I've been married for a long time. I'm newly single and horny. The last guy I screwed was my contractor. Crass as it sounds, the only thing I want you for is sex. I don't want a relationship with you. All I want is to fuck you."

"This is terrible," he said, slapping his forehead. "I know I'll kick myself in the morning if I turn you down. Well, you do have a great body. Okay, sex it is."

I told him I'd go to his place the following Thursday night and he should take me to dinner at one of those good Greek restaurants that Astoria is known for.

"Great, my house is right near the N train."

Was this guy an idiot or what?

"Dick, you don't get it. The N train? *N* as in *not,* as in *never,* as in *no way?* Talk to me about a car service."

At that very moment, a tall, handsome man walked by. I recognized him as an actor in a play, *The Penis Responds,* which I'd seen the night before. The show was a response to *The Vagina Monologues,* during which two guys lamented the fact that all women want from men is their dicks.

"You're the Penis Responds!" I yelled out. "I saw your play last night!"

"Oh yeah, you were sitting in the front row," the Penis Responds remembered.

"You're not going to believe this," I said, thumbing toward Dick. "This guy here, he's from the Midwest and this is our first date and he was complaining that all New York women want is to have sex and nothing more and he wants to settle down in a relationship but I told him I wasn't interested. All I want is to get fucked."

"Well, I'll fuck you," the Penis Responds offered. "I live nearby. Come on with me."

That got a rise out of Dick.

"Hey, you can't fuck her before I do," he protested. "How about I'll be her fluffer?"

Incredibly, they started negotiating who would get *prima notte.* Although the debate was entertaining, I stopped it, reassuring Dick that if anyone was going to fuck me, it would be him since we'd met first. I certainly wouldn't sleep with both of them together because that was more recklessness than I'd bargained for. Back in my Cornell period, I had had a two-on-one with a pair of Canadian hockey players, so there was no novelty as far as that sort of thing went. Dick and the Penis Responds exchanged business cards. Dick promised to go see his play.

We made plans for Thursday night but, by the time I got home from our afternoon in SoHo, I knew it wasn't going to happen. Caught up in the moment, the idea of screwing a stranger from Queens seemed daring and fun, but I didn't want the headache that would surely follow.

Leaving messages, Dick mailed me photographs of the Cleveland skyline with annotations about where he'd grown up. I sensed he was getting attached, or at the very least too personal, and didn't return his calls.

On Thursday, the day of our appointed rendezvous, he left another message: "Well?" Although he didn't say his name, I recognized his voice and assumed he wanted to know why he hadn't heard back from me, as well as whether we were getting together.

I left him a voice mail at work:

"Listen, forgive me for being out of touch, but I just don't think it will work out between us romantically and I've lost the sexual interest. If I'm going to have a fling with someone, it's going to be a guy who is what he is, like my contractor, not someone who is real relationship material, which you are."

Dick left this message in response:

"Contractor, my ass. Relationship material, yeah, right. You are living a dangerous lifestyle. What you need is a doctor. You are fuckin' nuts. There's lots of great straight guys in this city. Open your goddamn fucking eyes. Be straight with people and you won't burn bridges. Good-bye. Forever."

Ouch. That seemed kind of harsh. I thought of calling back and advising Dick the next time he had a first date, he should pony up for the sandwich. I thought of telling him if he wanted to make a good impression, he should wash the funky resin from his eyes. I considered suggesting he look for a day job on his own time, not when he's trying to romance someone.

Instead, I left this simple message: "Thanks for the entertainment."

And wouldn't you know it? I got a call from the Penis Responds.

* * *

Easy exploits soon lost their charm. I was ready for a challenge, a man who exceeded my grasp. That man turned out to be the art dealer.

We slept together for the first time in the late winter of 1996 at the Sherry-Netherland, where he was residing while his penthouse was under renovation. It had never occurred to me that you could actually inhabit a hotel and that transients might be rich people. Having access to room service and fresh towels twenty-four hours a day without a checkout date seemed unreal to me. But then again, so did the art dealer.

He was shameless about his hard heart. Actually took pride in it. Whenever he knocked up one of his girlfriends, he told her the choice was simple: either an abortion or lose him. A committed bachelor, he called himself a serial monogamist, the first time I'd heard the term. Apt that it had a pathological ring to it.

The man was as ruthless in business as he was in romance. He'd started with nothing, hawking velvet paintings on the palm-lined sidewalk in South Beach, barefoot and wearing little more than tanning oil. By the time he reached his early fifties, he was dressed in Savile Row suits, selling multimillion-dollar impressionist paintings out of a four-story town house on the Upper East Side of Manhattan. He could tell you off the top of his head how much a painting went for at auction. He could tell you exactly on what page of which catalog a work was reproduced—all from memory. He would fuck over his best friend if it meant closing a deal. And he'd mind-fuck a woman till she begged, cried, and resorted to violence. Not against him, but herself.

The art dealer was handsome—tall, muscular, and dark-skinned with black hair buzzed close to his scalp like a pelt. There was something more animal than human about him. His eyes were green, cold, and reptilian. He didn't walk, he slid across a room. He liked the taste of food, eating quickly and hungrily, even when he was full. His teeth were big, jagged, and discolored. When he grinned, it made you shiver a little and want to stay on his good side.

Setting his sights on something, be it a Degas ballerina or a woman who was his type—early thirties, brunette, nice legs—the art dealer turned predatory. His breathing slowed as he calculated his next move. When the hunt was over, so was his interest. He once told me if a woman wanted to leave so much as a toothbrush at his apartment, she'd have to sign a pre-nup. I took that as a warning.

I had met him one morning on 57th Street, heading toward Rizzoli. Passing glass storefronts, I caught a reflection of a man in a charcoal suit. The weather was cold, but he didn't have on a coat. I sensed he was following me. Wearing a cropped leopard-print fur jacket, I had on high heels that clicked against the pavement. With every step I took, my skirt pulled tightly across my ass. It felt like his eyes were burning holes through the fabric.

At the bookstore, I perused monographs on Georgia O'Keeffe, comparing them with a new one that had just been published, which I was supposed to review for an art magazine.

"Why O'Keeffe?" said the man, looking over my shoulder, his voice low and raspy.

"Who are you?"

He told me his name, which I immediately recognized, his reputation being scandalous. I explained my interest in the painter and he invited me to his gallery, where he had a great library. I could borrow whatever I wanted.

Lunch followed at Harry Cipriani. The art dealer silently watched me, his green eyes holding steady over the top of his red wineglass. Occasionally, he used a white linen napkin to wipe away the arrabiata sauce staining his lips. I chattered nervously. The art world may be small, but I was at a table with a man who had the biggest name in the business.

The Sherry-Netherland was next door. The art dealer didn't have to ask. He knew I was going to sleep with him. I wanted his treachery to perfume my ordinary life and, like a somnambulist, followed him to the hotel. I felt as if I were under his spell and he was willing me to enter an enchanted forest filled with tendrils of Spanish moss, menacing flowers, and poisonous plants. In his lair, a carefree whim—an urge to touch, to look, to smell—could wind up being fatal. The escapade was a far cry from my usual routine: killing time before picking up my kid outside the gates of PS 6.

The art dealer was a classic case of bad-boy attraction. A man may take pride in conquering a woman who plays hard to get, but some of us do the same. My husband wore wire-rimmed glasses and wingtips but I never could resist horns and cloven hooves. Erica Jong said dangerous men put strong independent women in touch with an adventurous part of themselves, unleashing a rebel within. I also believed those men brought out a woman's inner bitch, making her feel in control and resilient. The bitch need not be a beauty, though she acts as if she is. More likely, her confidence masks a damaged self, her jelly heart. To live recklessly without being ruined, she relies on an impersonation of indestructibility.

At the hotel, the art dealer's suite was decorated with Old World chintz and Chippendale-style furnishings. The minute I walked in, it struck me as odd that a man so smooth could make himself at home in a place so stiff. When he had unlocked the door, he didn't hold it open for me, instead gliding ahead as if he were royalty. Without a word or glance my way, he pushed a cassette into the VCR, sat down on a sofa, and clicked on the TV. His favorite sport was boxing, and he'd taped a fight from the night before. Now he wanted to watch it. I took my place beside him.

The kissing began and, in no time, he had hiked up my skirt, pulling off my underwear. He unzipped his trousers and I took out his cock. It was big, impressive, but not so large as to be grotesque. Still upright on the sofa, he maneuvered me on top of him. There was no foreplay, no interest in exploring my body, no attempt at turning me on. With me straddling him, we started to fuck. Bouncing up and down, I was like a child on a pogo stick. It was ridiculous. I felt stupid, detached, and mechanical. All the while, he kept looking over my shoulder, watching the TV, not wanting to miss a jab, an uppercut, a hook. Never once did he let go of the remote control.

Afterward, I saw myself out.

How can a man with so much allure be so rotten in bed?

I never expected to see him again but, surprisingly, he called late the next day, setting in motion a fly-by-night relationship. He often asked me out at the last minute, inviting me to accompany him to some dinner, gala, or benefit. Occasionally, he covered the cost of Dash's babysitter. I loved putting on an evening gown, being picked up by the art dealer's chauffeur, and discovering the city that first seduced me from the end of my Long Island dock.

Although my standard of living remained relatively high after Charlie moved out, I was slumming it compared with the art dealer. His lifestyle of excess and entitlement was enticing. I'd be lying if I said I never imagined what it would be like to trade up.

On his arm, I was welcomed into Fifth Avenue apartments as vast as city blocks with walls the color of ripe fruits and dining room chairs each costing as much as a European sports car.

The women were either wives ensconced in 10021 prewar classics and country homes featured in *Town & Country* or professional girlfriends recognized by—but always remaining surnameless to—a certain circle of maître d's, furriers, and real estate brokers around town. On the surface, it seemed as if being the other woman was a better deal. You got a fully furnished rental (your sugar daddy naturally holding the only other key), his Platinum Amex, and a calendar blocked off for globe-trotting.

Within a few weeks, however, it became clear to me that being the other woman wasn't what it was cracked up to be. The loot she got was hardly payback for the forty nights of pleasure he got. She couldn't have a job or kids or a social life because she always had to be available to her man. He didn't require an advance purchase of a plane ticket to pick up and go. If she couldn't make the trip, there wouldn't be a next time since another babe was always on standby, ready to claim the reservation. Given the way the system worked—that happiness for the man meant his girlfriend had to be a perpetual lady-in-waiting—I didn't think it was quid pro quo.

I knew to keep Dash under wraps as far as the art dealer went. His idea of a babysitter was to spike a juice box with Nembutal and lock the front door. He had no interest in the details of my scrambling for child care or guilt when my son acted like a Velcro strip, attaching himself to my leg, pleading for me not to go out the door.

Between mothering, writing about art, and teaching at MoMA, I soon realized I had too many responsibilities to meet the art dealer's requirements for a full-time girlfriend. And even if I didn't have my own life, slavishness and compliancy were not my nature. Unable to go with the flow, I always strained against expectations and injunctions. "You need to loosen up and get drunk," the art dealer frequently said, despite my reminders that I hadn't tipped the bottle for nearly ten years.

My feistiness was defensive, safely distancing me from a man who I knew saw my pussy as replaceable. My grandmother had always told me: "A woman better not think she's got diamonds on her schmushky because to a man, every schmushky is the same."

That was definitely the case with the art dealer. He never hid the fact that there were other women. I guess it was to his credit that he neither professed tender feelings for me nor promised any future plans. He didn't get up my hopes only to dash them. I trusted he was untrustworthy and thus demanded no assurances from him. The relationship was what it was. Take it or leave it.

Still, hands down, he was the best date in town. Once he brought me with him to a wedding at the Plaza where there was a sturgeon ice sculpture filled with twelve thousand dollars' worth of beluga caviar, the Village People performed, and I met a pet supply titan who bragged his business was so good, he could "retire on wee-wee pads alone." Another time we went to dinner at a real estate developer's town house and I spent the entire night slack-mouthed. Not because there were Modiglianis on every wall but because five out of the six male guests—power broker types— traded stories about being summoned before grand juries with the same braggadocio of war veterans showing off their battle scars.

It was hard not to feel disappointed that the art dealer didn't lavish me with gifts. The watches, the wardrobes, the trips—those he saved for the women who had no kids, no career, no strings attached. He never invited me to his fabled Greenwich estate, a neoclassical extravaganza formerly owned by a banking scion. It was only through the society pages that I learned of the art dealer's weekend parties: his pebble drive lined with limousines and guests feted on French rack of lamb and fat strawberries hand-dipped in white chocolate.

Believe it or not, I never once spent the night with him. I never even had sex in a bed with him. I never, ever saw him naked. Getting it on was merely a matter of reclining on a couch and him pulling down his pants. Generally, he left his shoes on.

For a time, the art dealer's company was exhilarating. He always noticed when I wore something new, running an appreciative hand over my rump, making me feel sexy. He loved to gossip, knowing which movie star was about to leave his wife for an up-and-coming actress before it hit the press.

He was unpredictable, too. Seated in the back of his chauffeur-driven car, he closed his eyes, lolling his head, singing aloud to "Piano Man" when it came on the radio. Riding past the Empire State Building, his mood abruptly turned melancholy. He said he was picturing a failed novelist hunched over a manual typewriter, surrounded by cigarette butts and unsharpened pencils, working in an abandoned office somewhere in the dark, empty building. The image, right out of a film noir, was romantic. Did it suggest the art dealer might also be capable of love?

Knife-witted and quick with a comeback, he expected a woman to be the same. Rising to the occasion made me feel smart and alive, as if my brain had suddenly regenerated after a marital lobotomy. The art dealer liked my sense of humor. When I made him laugh, he cocked his head to the side, flashing his jagged teeth, and pulled me close, laying a rough kiss on my lips. A bubble of delight burst around me.

But the reality check was a *fin-de-nuit* blow job. This was what the art dealer expected. Fucking was a waste of time, too much work for the both of us. Wearing a rubber, he took forever to come. I would climb on top of him, perform my pogo routine, and he would just lie there, hands limp by his sides. The quickest way to get the ordeal over was to suck him off. Once, when I complained about never having an orgasm with him, he responded: "If a woman can't come, that's her problem."

• • •

"Why do I go on seeing him?" I asked Andee one Saturday at Lazer Park where our seven-year-old sons were darting through fog-shrouded mazes, attempting to vaporize each other with phaser guns.

"He's handsome," she said. "He has dough and takes you to great places and, like, all the other things don't count."

Andee was now divorced and had fallen on hard times. "I go from one panic attack to another," she broke down to me. "I have, like, two hundred and nineteen dollars in my checking account. I had to put a carton of orange juice on a credit card at the deli."

I was fearful of living hand-to-mouth, a reality for so many ex-wives. I started keeping a log of my expenses, knowing that when divorce proceedings started, I'd have to prove my standard of living in order to negotiate a settlement. Besides the monthly electric,

phone, cable, and groceries (total: $1,550), there were unreim-
bursed medical expenses ($400), laundry ($60), household costs—
carpet and window cleaning, exterminator, detergents,
replacement appliances, miscellaneous repairs ($675), postage,
stationery, and Xeroxes ($190), as well as the babysitter/house-
keeper ($1,000). There were books, magazines, and newspapers
($65). Tae Kwon Do lessons ($150). Transportation ($400). Dash's
tutors and sports programs ($450). Did I really spend $120 on toys?
Two hundred and twenty-five on entertainment and restaurants?
The list went on and on. It didn't even include the mortgage and
maintenance payments, bills that went directly to Charlie. Forget
manicures and pedicures. The day would come when I'd have to
support myself. How on earth was I ever going to do that and
continue living in Manhattan?

Better reconsider that N train.

• • •

Were all high-octane men as beguiling as the art dealer? Was it
only the money or something special about him? Through my
new social connections, I was set up on a few blind dates, including:

- A media mogul who had sold his company for $250 million
  and took me to the Manhattan Ocean Club for dinner. Although it was a seafood restaurant, he ordered Irish oatmeal
  with clover honey and a protein shake. Not surprisingly, the
  kitchen was out. He sent his driver to find a supermarket and
  bring back McCann's, specifying the oats be steel-cut, not
  rolled, as well as a Slim-Fast French Vanilla. His unusual culi-
  nary requests were easy to chalk up to the eccentricities of the
  rich. His hygiene habits, however, were downright homeless.
  Throughout the meal, a dome of odor clung to our table. Was
  a city health inspection of the restaurant overdue? When I gave
  my date a kiss on the cheek good night, I realized the fumes
  were wafting from him. Later, I found out the problem. An ac-

quaintance of his told me the man had stopped showering regularly after a woman, whom he wanted to marry, broke his heart. She wed someone else—under seventy feet of water and in a scuba diving suit. Perhaps this explained his aversion to bathwater but I couldn't get past my aversion to his stench.

- A billionaire political aspirant who called to invite me to dinner, identifying himself by only his last name. He chose Le Bernardin, describing the jacket-and-tie-required establishment as "low-key." There, a procession of sommeliers and diners stopped by our table to pay their respects as we ate our thirty-five-dollar steamed black bass. Since the man and his money were so clearly one and the same, I asked how rich he was. He didn't know the exact figure but assured me he could buy the city. Over the meal, he railed against the corporate practice of paid maternity leave, which didn't endear me, a mother, to him. I gave him flak for supporting a system that penalized women for having children, yet disrespected those who didn't. He responded that I had a great face and great body but should lose my wiseass personality. Afterward, in the back of his limousine, he pawed me to smooch. His kissing technique—all teeth and no tongue—sucked. I, being the aforementioned wiseass, told him so.

- A Houston oil magnate asked me to meet him at The Mark hotel's lounge for a drink. My background check showed him to be a member of the Heritage Foundation. I thought that was as bad as it could get until I laid eyes on his loafers: lizard skin with low vamps. A right-winger in viper footwear. Was he trying to tempt me when he announced he always bought a woman whom he intended to bed a Cartier watch? He added that her face didn't matter because "when you turn her upside down, she looks like every other woman."

Soon after, a surgically enhanced blonde stopped by our cocktail table and purred at my date how much she missed him. "She's from California, and if you look in one ear, you can see clear through to the other side," he said after she slunk off. "New York women are just like LA women except smarter. There's a new crop every year and, after five years, a whole new turnover. The women here are insecure because they're afraid of aging and not getting married. They have crappy apartments and bosses who grab their asses. A woman needs at least a quarter of a million dollars a year to live decently. What's she gonna do? There are so few of us guys to go around."

I was willing to endure the art dealer's caddish behavior because it fulfilled my own need for penance. Life had offered me a lot of opportunities but I hadn't done squat with them. My marriage was a bust, my career nonexistent, and, with Dash many years away from being grown up, the jury was still out on what kind of a mother I would prove to be. The art dealer gave me what I felt I deserved: a magnanimous amount of mistreatment.

After a couple of months, however, it was enough. I could no longer face the final blow-job hour—too much degradation even for me. The next occasion when the art dealer called, I turned him down, telling him the truth.

"You are the worst fuck I have ever had."

You'd think his cock would have gone limp forever but he actually took the rejection as a challenge. He tried to persuade me to change my mind, pleading to give him another chance. He promised to do something different: to make me come.

How would he? Did he know the mechanics? Would I actually be able to let go? What did it mean that he was finally willing to put me first? Had the threat of rejection made him realize I meant something to him after all?

I agreed to see him again. He took me to a wonderful dinner at a French restaurant where the tables were set with clusters of fresh roses and tiny candles. The service was slow and we passed the evening at a red velvet corner banquette, he eating *loup de mer*, me filet mignon. For the first time, he let his seamless facade crack and the flotsam of his past surface.

The art dealer had grown up outside Miami, the son of Cuban immigrants. His father was a salesman; his mother worked in a flower shop. One summer, when the art dealer was a boy, his parents sent him to an overnight camp for a week. He loved it because the air smelled sweet and the grass was soft and tall, but they couldn't afford to send him back. In his early twenties, he eloped with a singer, getting drunk and playing poker before saying "I do." Within a year, their daughter was born and their divorce final. The art dealer gave up his child for adoption by his ex-wife's second husband.

Back in Miami, the art dealer did what he could to get by, peddling first T-shirts on Ocean Drive and then velvet paintings. He upgraded to photographs of palm trees, street scenes, and the local landmark architecture. Selling fine art was the next step.

It wasn't until he was in his early thirties that he boarded a plane for the very first time in his life to visit New York. With a fear of flying, he had to work up the nerve, but boy, was it worth the trip. At the Stanhope Hotel's outdoor café, he struck up a conversation with an American Old Master collector who was also a trustee at the Metropolitan Museum of Art. The collector introduced the art dealer to a shopping mall mogul. He signed on as the art dealer's backer.

In 1980, right before the art market soared, the art dealer opened a small midtown gallery. Raiding a couple of estates, he acquired more than a few gems: a Corot landscape, a Watteau drawing, and a Van Gogh pen-and-ink sketch. In addition to a gifted eye, he had a nose for the right connections and ambition so great, it could be measured only by the unremarkable past he left behind. In no time, he moved up the ladder to an East 70s town house. If there was a single character trait that explained his success, it was his Olympian self-confidence. Rather than be intimidated by rich and famous men, he looked upon them as worthy opponents, which made it all the more gratifying when he converted them into clients.

"*Powerful* is such a nineties word," he dismissed when I suggested that's what he was after. "I don't like the New York culture of who's got the power, who's on first. Winners. Losers. Thumbs-up. Thumbs-down. It's a box-score approach to life."

That night at the French restaurant, the art dealer opened up to me and I allowed the unthinkable to happen. I no longer saw myself as just another brunette with a nice figure and enough polish to hold her own in his social circles. I was someone special, the woman who had warmed his glacial heart.

We went back to his newly renovated penthouse, a high-tech bachelor pad on Sutton Place. It was a totally controlled environment where the humidity levels were constantly monitored and plasma-screen TVs, stereo systems, overhead lighting, and temperature were digitally programmed. The air-conditioning was always on high because the art dealer couldn't sleep unless it was cold as a morgue. There wasn't a single family photograph on view in his entire house.

Like always, we headed for the screening room, making ourselves comfortable on the couch just as we had so many nights before. But this time was different. We kissed more delicately. He took his time and I relaxed, inhaling his light, woodsy English cologne. He even removed his clothes and, when I pressed my naked body against his bronzed skin, it felt smooth and buttery. He entered me, gently running his hands up and down my back and over my ass, all the while whispering, "Do you like it?"

Then it happened. I had an orgasm. The aphrodisiac of unguarded dinner conversation, followed by his tender attunement to my anatomy, his Taoist knowledge of *coitus reservatus*, withholding his release while urging me to come—these techniques worked like a charm. He was a man of cunning cock, able to predicate his desire on my pleasure, putting it before his own, making my fulfillment all that mattered—when he wanted. After countless nights of me going home without so much as getting wet, he had kept his promise.

Later, with my head against his shoulder, we watched TV together, holding hands. When the time came for me to go, it had started raining. I waited in the vestibule of his building while he went outside without an umbrella, hailing me a taxi, handing the driver ten dollars to cover my fare.

"You know, I could fall in love with you." I smiled, touching the art dealer's cheek after a gentle kiss good-bye.

The next day, I was certain he would call. When the phone rang, I jumped. It was only Charlie. Would I mind if Dash spent Passover with his family? I dreaded the thought of driving to Long Island by myself and spending my first holiday as a single woman with my parents and two younger brothers. They were both now happily married, living in large white houses with a son and daughter apiece. I anticipated what they would be thinking: *How sad Elizabeth has no one to take her home.*

Imagining myself as the art dealer's squeeze was better than the reality of not being spoken for. I was already planning outfits to bring to his estate, wondering how I'd ever fall asleep in his mortician's chilled bedroom. I fantasized about the birthday presents he would bestow: a Patek Philippe watch, diamond stud earrings. Now that I had come, anything seemed possible.

But he didn't call. Not for a good two weeks.

"Hey, what's up?" he greeted, as if there'd been no secrets shared, no climax reached. "You free tonight?"

"For what?" I couldn't believe I was asking. *Hang up the phone. Just hang up the phone.*

Oh, how I regretted that orgasm.

"To a party. At the Waldorf, it'll be fun. We'll dance."

Dancing is "a perpendicular expression of a horizontal desire," George Bernard Shaw said.

"It's Monday. I have to find a babysitter and I have a class to teach tomorrow at MoMA," I hedged, the first time I'd allowed my personal life to complicate the picture, testing his determination to see me.

"You know I'll pay for the sitter."

"That's not the problem."

"Wake up early to prepare for your class."

"It's not that."

An image of the night ahead beckoned. There would be a table bedecked with sumptuous flowers and flickering votive candles where I would hobnob with faces illuminated by their celebrity status, a paparazzi affair no doubt appearing in the pages of *Vanity Fair*. The alternative was my usual ringside seat on the sofa beside my son, watching the bloody pummeling of World Championship Wrestling on TV.

"What time should I be at the Waldorf?"

I arrived in a black chiffon gown with a plunging neckline, the front of the dress trimmed in ruffles, the back trailing behind me in a train. It had a cha-cha look and made me feel frisky. Earlier in the day, right after the art dealer called, I had gone to Bergdorf's and spent way too much on a black silk stole trimmed in fringe by Dolce & Gabbana.

When I entered the Waldorf's Grand Ballroom, my heart sank. It was filled with midlevel executive types in double-breasted tuxedos with shoulder pads and pointy shoes and women in shiny rayon gowns that pulled across bulging bellies. There wasn't a real gemstone or designer dress in sight. Gidget girls in frosted makeup and midriffs exposing rub-on tattoos giggled in pockets around the room while short, pimply boys clung to the corners, like algae in a fish tank. Overtired, sweaty children were racing about, excited to be at a grown-up party. The table centerpieces were bouquets of red and black balloons trimmed in curlicues of ribbon.

If this is the beau monde, I want out.

The art dealer, already seated, motioned me over to his table. "What the hell is going on?" I demanded, like Ivana to Marla on the Aspen slopes.

"It's a charity event for some boys' club or children's hospital, I think," he said, pretending not to understand my disappointment. "A client of mine, a collector, is being honored."

So this was a fucking PR move for him. The art dealer had asked me to the cheesy affair only because it was in his business interest. He would have been bored to death alone. I wanted to kill him but I had no one to blame but myself. The party was my punishment for being a shallow shit and sucking up to a scoundrel when I—rather than Pauline, a tenth grader at Spence living below me in 10F—should have been home with Dash, pretending to be a referee counting to three as my little bruiser pinned a throw pillow.

Seated beside the art dealer, I tried to hold my tongue and eat my dinner, a lukewarm slab of gristly roast beef. When he took up a lengthy conversation with a guy—who, with his slicked-back, receding hair, could have passed for Robert Duvall—and asked him to drop by a party at the art dealer's penthouse the following Thursday night, I went batshit. The bastard hadn't even invited me.

"I'm leaving," I announced. "You bring me to this loser affair that's only for your benefit. You're having a goddamn party next week and you have the balls to invite a stranger sitting next to you but not me. What the hell am I here for? What's in it for me?"

"Don't make a scene," he said nervously.

"It took you two fucking weeks to call me after our last date. Don't you realize I have feelings for you?"

"Half hour max, we'll be outta here."

Ordinarily, the art dealer made all the decisions, but this time, when we left, he must have been feeling guilty because he asked where I wanted to go.

"Your house," I said, not wanting to let him off the hook.

Back in the screening room, I stormed up and down, reeling because of all the trouble I'd gone to for his stupid party. As I got more upset, I started to perspire and tears stung my eyes. This was exactly the kind of performance the art dealer thought he could avoid by going out with a girl like me—or at least the girl I pretended to be.

I had convinced the art dealer that I was tough and unavailable, posing no threat of being damaged or engaging in midnight showdowns. Now, with my defenses down, I couldn't fake being impervious to hurt. Wearing my shawl, I held up the fringed ends and, in a wounded voice, told him that I had even bought something new for the occasion.

"How much was it?" he said.

"Three hundred."

Pulling a wad of cash from his pants, he peeled off three C-notes and handed them to me.

"Thanks," I mumbled, feeling funny about taking the money.

I had sex with him that night, hoping to re-create the bond we had shared a couple of weeks earlier. This time, the kisses felt flaccid, and when I undressed, the art dealer kept on his shirt, merely dropping his trousers. I climbed on top and told him to stay real still so that I could find my groove and make myself come. I wasn't about to let him get away without that. At least he obeyed. Closing my eyes, I fantasized his hands were all over me and his raspy voice was whispering in my ear, *Do you like it?* I managed to eke out an orgasm.

The art dealer didn't bother to get me a taxi. The street seemed especially dark and empty while I stood there, hailing my own cab. When the driver pulled up in front of my apartment, I reached in my purse for some money. Among the lipstick, keys, and loose change were the three hundred-dollar bills the art dealer had given me.

"Here," I said, emptying all the money onto the cabdriver's seat before running into my building, bursting into sobs.

"Hey, lady," he called out. "You made a mistake!"

Didn't I know it? For a last-time fuck, I had paid way too much.

CHAPTER 11

*Y*OU'RE BETTER OFF WITHOUT HIM," my mother counseled during our usual morning phone call. "That art dealer's not real. Women are his playthings."

"Maybe I need to run around for a while. Sow my oats more. Be a she-rover. What's so wrong with that? Men do it all the time."

"It sounds like you don't want to get close to somebody and build something. Don't you get lonely? I worry what happens when you get sick. What happens when you get older. You gotta go out and meet the right people."

"What do you mean by 'the right people'?"

"Money is important but I don't mean *that* kind of money, the ultrarich. I mean lawyer- or doctor-rich. A few dollars in the bank. You should have a man of substance who has lived and appreciates you and treats you well from the very first time you go out. He's got to be A Man. Also, he should have a little paunch so that he doesn't outshine you."

"Where am I supposed to find A Man?"

"What about those personal ads? I see them in the back of *New York* magazine. Just meet him somewhere public in case he's a crazy."

I decided on *The New York Observer*, figuring anyone who placed an ad there would appeal to me because of the paper's urban sensibility. I responded to half a dozen SWMs but only two called back. The first lived in New Jersey. When I gave him my address, he referred to my neighborhood as "fancy." That was all I needed to hear. Not only would he have to cross a bridge to see me, he'd have to cross class lines. Fuhgedaboudhim.

The other guy worked on Wall Street and lived in Manhattan. I didn't catch his name but the conversation was easy and we agreed to meet at a coffeehouse with comfy sofas on Second Avenue not far from my apartment, where I would identify him by his pin-striped shirt and chinos.

When I arrived, my heart sank. The man was barely taller than I am. He had rabbit front teeth, crossed eyes, and a Newt Gingrich part in his hair. He was chewing a huge wad of cobalt-colored gum. Every time he chomped, I caught a glimpse of the bright, rubbery glob and imagined him turning blue like Violet Beauregarde in *Willy Wonka and the Chocolate Factory.*

We settled into one of the sofas and had to yell to hear each other over Los Del Rio's "Macarena" in the background. He jiggled his knee nervously. After ten minutes, the music made his head hurt and he wanted to leave. Out of politeness, I suggested we head over to a Starbucks near my apartment to finish our conversation.

It was a freezing March night and I was counting on grabbing a cab even though our destination was only a few blocks away. When we stepped outside, the guy beelined to a battered bicycle, chain-locked to a parking meter, and told me it belonged to him. That was how he got around the city. We had to walk the fucking thing to Starbucks.

By the time we got there, my fingertips were numb and I wanted to go home. When we parted, I had no interest in seeing him again. Mercifully, the feeling was mutual. I never did find out his name and, since he never called me by mine, he probably didn't know it, either.

After about six weeks passed, my sour experience had faded and my mother encouraged me to herd-surf the personals again, this time focusing exclusively on the forty-to-forty-nine-year-old age bracket. I was seeking a man who had an equal amount of baggage, or at least wouldn't be overwhelmed by my load.

I picked seven descriptions, avoiding ones that didn't include the term *successful* or *financially secure,* as well as steering clear of *spiritual, gentle,* and *sensitive.* Those kinds of guys are too sincere and rarely stylish. My requirements included a mordant sense of humor and a wardrobe updated more than once a decade.

The next day, someone named Jeff called back. We chatted briefly. He was forty, lived on the Upper East Side, had never been married but was cool with my history. I asked where he worked. Morgan Stanley. Sounded solid. When I told him I was an art historian, he thought I might know his brother, an architect. A familiar name but I couldn't place it. Nevertheless, a connection. So far, so good.

Then the conversation took an unexpected turn. Jeff boldly asked if I was cute.

"Of course," I answered. "A Julia Roberts double."

What kind of a schmuck asks if you're cute? What am I going to say, No, you'll wince when you see me?

"And you?" I asked.

"Women tell me I'm handsome."

Then he had the nerve to ask me what my breasts were like.

"Absolutely perfect."

"Are they a B or a C?"

"Full B."

"Do you need to wear a bra?"

"Nope."

"You mean, at your age, you don't need a bra? What, did you have them done?"

"Of course not," I lied.

After my eye lift, I had progressed to advanced-placement plastic surgery: breast augmentation. Although there was nothing wrong with my endowment other than a lack of it (my boobs remained nicely shaped and perky after childbirth), I had long fantasized about the life changes borne by modest-size implants: sensual curves to offset my barbed tongue, which might also stimulate the salivary glands of suitors.

In the heat of passion, lovers never seemed to mind when the distinction between fatty tissue and saline sacs melted away. Afterward, I was self-conscious lying on my back, my gravity-defying breasts like a pair of missiles on a launch pad. In the end, the surgery both failed and exceeded my expectations: Men would never drop to their knees because of my tits, but my tits would never drop to my knees, either.

Once Jeff dared to inquire about my cup size, I figured everything from his body hair to his bank account was now fair game.

"Are you bald?"

"Ah, n . . . n . . . n . . . o," he stuttered. "I have a full head of hair."

I wondered whether he was lying, too.

"What about body hair? How hairy is your back?"

"It's a little hairy," he said sheepishly. "I'm a Jewish guy."

"Are you tall?"

"Well, that's the only problem. I'm not tall. I'm five foot six."

"So, you're short. Are you at least successful?"

"Are you asking how much money I make?" he said, his voice cracking. "Wow. I like you, you've got spunk."

He suggested we get together. Now, *that* took spunk. I was impressed I hadn't scared him away. Either he was incredibly confident or incredibly stupid. Out of morbid curiosity, I had to say yes.

We agreed to meet at the Starbucks near my house. That night, I had a birthday party to attend and allotted half an hour for him beforehand. He told me he'd be sitting at a corner table in a blue shirt and khakis.

Swanning through the java-aromatized interior, I arrived in flamingo-pink halter dress, yellow calf-hair mules, carrying a matching clutch, and with a huge citrine cocktail ring glittering on my finger. I felt fabulous.

Then I saw Jeff. Incredible. They say lightning doesn't strike a second time. Yet in a city of nearly seven million people, I had managed to meet the same loser, not once but twice. He was the very guy with the battered bike and blue gum.

"It's you!" I gulped. "We met the last time I answered the personals."

"I don't remember you at all," he said, unaware he'd just insulted me. "How can you be sure it was me?"

"It wasn't that long ago. How could I forget?"

"You must have a great memory. I go out with a lot of girls so it's easy to forget who I've dated. Maybe if you had worn what you're wearing now, I would have remembered you."

Is that supposed to be a compliment?

"Care for a piece of gum?" he offered before I bolted for the door, my breasts leading the charge.

• • •

The next morning, my mother had a new strategy: the synagogue.

"The *what*?"

"I'm not talking about Friday-night services with you sitting on a bench, waiting for the social hour afterward when people mingle. Oh, is that ever lame. I mean a matchmaker."

"And a matchmaker's *not* lame? I don't want a 'Shlomo' with a beard and black hat."

"The matchmaker would get to know you and she would know him. You need a man who was raised on the same matzo balls as you. She could be a good fixer-upper."

I attended Torah classes at Congregation Kehilath Jeshurun on East 85th Street where the teacher, Rebbetzin Esther Jungreis, had a reputation for successful introductions. According to Judaism, God predetermined the union of a man and woman but it was up to us mortals to figure out His Plan. Make way for the match-maker.

Her shepherding was sorely needed, judging by the two thou-sand singles crowding the pews for her Tuesday-night Torah classes. You could hear the unwrapping of breath mints and click-ing of compact mirrors as the congregants prepared for the meet-'n'-greet that followed. After class, everyone gathered in a reception hall for diet soda and rugelach where the rebbetzin's daughters sat at card tables taking Polaroids of anyone who wanted to be set up, scribbling the names and ages as well as romantic dos and don'ts on the backs of the pictures. Like everyone else, I stood behind a piece of masking tape on the floor and smiled for the camera. Perhaps my request for a tall, good-looking, successful, creative, well-dressed hipster over thirty-five was too specific. Maybe that kind of guy just didn't hang out at Torah classes. Ei-ther way, I never got a date.

But other setups began.

There was a dermatologist allergic to New York City water who had his meals delivered from Queens. He couldn't eat out in restaurants and was always starving. Next, a real estate developer who had been a psychology major in college and began our date by retrieving from his sports jacket a "PhD-Certified Personality Profile Test," checking off little boxes of character traits to deter-mine whether our temperaments were compatible. After him came a Greek importer-exporter whom I initially rejected because his business card had a typo, but my mother said I was being too picky and to give him a chance. At Elios for dinner, he spent thirty minutes recounting the incredible sexual connection he'd had with his ex-girlfriend, a prominent New York State government official who, he was convinced, had dumped him after he lost twenty million dollars. The second half of dinner was devoted to discussing his most recent capital investment: a spermicide, which African women were testing, that could kill the AIDS virus.

"They use an applicator to insert it up to four times a day and it won't cause vaginal abrasions," he explained. "That's the problem with spermicides. Multiple insertions cause vaginal abrasions."

Just what I want to hear as I open my mouth for a forkful of striped bass.

Mom's next brainstorm: a puppy.

"You put on your makeup and look good and go to the park. A dog is good. Dog owners are social. I see in my neighborhood the dog people talking. Men like dogs."

"But all the men who live around here are married."

"Don't be naive. Who says they're all happy?"

I bought a miniature long-haired dachshund whom Dash named Marilyn, after Marilyn Monroe. My son and I had so much fun with her, I acquired two more puppies: Joe, as in DiMaggio, and Jackie, as in Kennedy. I had this Warholian idea of accumulating a pack of American icons, an Elvis, a Liz, and so on, but my building co-op board instituted an ex post facto one-pet-per-family limit. Dash's babysitter, Gwendolyn, who had immigrated from Jamaica, where animals didn't live inside the house, reached her limit, too. She quit.

My son and I didn't care. Once the puppies arrived, I no longer behaved as a Mother with a capital *M*. Rassling with them on the carpeting, Dash and I fart-kissed their bellies as they slobber-licked our faces. Crooning "How Much Is That Doggy in the Window," he and I split our sides laughing at the way they cocked their little heads in confusion. Like parents mesmerized by their baby's every blink of an eye, my son and I found our dogs' personalities—Marilyn, the boss; Joe, the lazy oaf; and Jackie, the mama's girl—endlessly dissectible.

One evening, I was walking my threesome and met a Secret Service agent on duty outside a fortress of a building on Park Avenue where Vice President Gore was at a fund-raiser. The agent's name was Jack Kensington. His eyes kept shifting back and forth, scanning the street. He had a tiny black phone wedged in his ear like a hearing aid, a mike clipped to the lapel of his blue blazer, and a handgun in a holster.

When he stopped me, it wasn't to compliment my dogs, which usually got all the attention, but to admire my red shoes. I joked that J. Edgar Hoover liked heels, too.

"What are you saying, I'm queer or something?" sneered the Secret Service agent.

I was surprised that he asked for my number and even more so when he phoned the next day. I had call waiting and was on the other line at the time. Clicking over, I asked for his number to get back to him. It was a 631 area code, somewhere in Suffolk County, Long Island.

"Secret Service," answered a woman with a nasal voice.

Strange. Shouldn't a Secret Service agent be more discreet about his identity?

When he picked up the line and said, "Agent Kensington," I cast aside my doubts. In a flash, I had visions of bulletproof vests, foiled assassinations, and late-night assignations at Spy Bar.

"It's the woman with the red high heels," I said.

We small-talked and he asked what I did for a living. *Art historian* sounded too prissy so I lied and said, "Thriller writer."

"You're not planning to write about me?" he bristled. "You can never write about me. I mean *never.* Do you understand?"

"There are no guarantees," I said, trying not to let a G-man with a walkie-talkie intimidate me. "Everyone I meet is part of the plot. Whatever happens might wind up in print."

I paused, waiting for a response. There was none. The line went dead.

My mother's take?

"To get the right guy's attention, you should have gotten an important- or unusual-looking dog, like a Great Dane. Not a small dog or, in your case, three."

She didn't realize that, because of my three small dogs, I had gotten the right guy's attention: Dash's.

• • •

Searching for style and sophistication, I decided to go shopping at the Bergdorf Goodman men's store. It wasn't the merchandise I was after but an actual man.

Heading for the European designers' floor, I staked out the Paul Smith department, calculating that the quirky English clothes might lure someone playful and droll. There, rifling through the racks, was a six-footer in a brown leather hunting jacket, perfectly distressed jeans, and chunky-soled boots. Because his back was turned, I couldn't tell what he looked like, but his bedhead hair said *Very stalkable*.

"Would you wear something like this?" I asked, holding up a hideous berry-print shirt.

"You've got to be kidding," he said with a grin. In addition to twinkling baby-blue eyes, he had a goatee and a chipped front tooth. The sight caused me a mild cardiac arrhythmia.

"But what if I was the one who gave it to you?"

"Then I'd definitely wear it."

This was too good to be true. Very Stalkable was flirting. I introduced myself and asked what he did.

"I'm a video artist."

"Really? I write about art. What's your name?"

"Rex Nelson."

Doesn't ring a bell.

"What gallery do you show with?"

"None."

Now, this just isn't adding up. An unknown video artist who can afford Bergdorf's?

As I followed him around the store, he admitted his day job was actually at an international advertising agency, but he made art off hours. Then he let it drop he was newly single.

Is this my day or what?

"I'm going to an opening next week downtown," I said.

"Would you like to come? I'm sure there will be lots of pretty girls."

"I'm only interested in one pretty girl," he said, looking me in the eye. "Should I wear Versace or Givenchy?"

Oh, my God. We both love designers whose names end in vowels (and sometimes y*). What are the chances of that?*

On the night of our big date, Rex and I agreed to meet at the opening. It was so crowded, we bailed before seeing the art and made our way over to the Odeon for dinner. The hostess gave us the once-over—Rex in a sleek charcoal suit and me in a Romeo Gigli dress—nodded her approval, and conducted us past the patrons standing three-deep at the bar, waiting for a table.

Seated in a booth, I couldn't take my eyes off Rex's constantly moving hands—lifting a cosmopolitan to his lips, rubbing his eyes as if he'd just woken up, folding and refolding his napkin. His nervousness made him seem guileless but I sensed this was entirely rehearsed, which was okay by me since I wanted to be baited.

Rex worked the magic of his blue eyes by smiling just enough so that his laugh lines flexed, making him appear constantly amused. He name- and city-dropped, his friends notable indie-film types and his travels exotic. Rex was a straight man who had figured out that the secret to looking as good as a gay came from a kind of turned-out dishabille: a dark Helmut Lang shirt with unbuttoned cuffs, a white T-shirt peeking out from the open collar, and fingernails rimmed with blue pigment from a painting on which he'd been working.

Nice. Just enough grit to sully his designer edges.

He had grown up in San Diego, a town of "surfers and cowboys," he said, where he got into bar fights (hence, the chipped tooth). He recounted his past with ironic detachment, as if he were Young Pip, arriving luckless to the world, benefiting from accidental good fortune: At birth, his mother had given him up for adoption to a middle-class, churchgoing couple from California, the Promised Land.

"A state college recruits me to play football but I get accepted to art school to paint," he said. "I move to Manhattan and have a couple of shows at galleries that close. So here I am with no paycheck, getting shitfaced every night. I get evicted from my apartment on the Lower East Side for not paying my rent, and I need a job. I get hired by a giant advertising firm and make hundreds of thousands of dollars for the company."

"What's your most recent project?" I asked.

"A video installation for a Tokyo bank. It's a floor of flat-screen TV monitors showing dozens of Japanese women diving for pearls."

"Genius."

You are so fuckable, it wouldn't matter if you were describing a rescue squad dredging a river of acid rain for bloated human carcasses.

A couple of months earlier, he had broken up with his live-in girlfriend, a fashion model. The relationship had been long term and he'd outgrown it. Later, he confessed she'd cheated on him after he gave her an engagement ring, leaving him for the other guy.

This is getting better and better. Poor Rex needs my comforting.

I slid out from my side of the booth to join him on his, pressing my hip against his body. He invited me to his country house upstate, which he was renovating and decorating with furniture he had bought on a trip to Bali. There was a duck pond in the backyard where his mutt, Stieglitz, liked to swim. When I told him about my dogs, he said they'd love it, too.

The big question now was whether to tell him about Dash. You never knew which guys would head for the hills once they heard you came with a kid.

"I have a seven-year-old son," I blurted.

"What is he into, Nintendo 64 or PlayStation? I'm great at both."

Score!

For dessert, Rex and I shared crème brûlée. Watching his spoon sink into the ivory custard, I noticed he had a tiny crucifix tattooed in the fleshy spot between his thumb and forefinger. *God is in the details.* Just before he paid the check, I leaned my face close to his, pressing my thumb against the raw edge of his broken tooth.

"When are you going to kiss me?" I asked.

"You are such a turn-on. I love confident women."

His mouth tasted of wine and cigarettes. His neck smelled of Bulgari, a scent I recognized from a bar of soap I once swiped from a Four Seasons hotel. When he put my hand on the crotch of his pants so that I could feel how hard he was, there was no doubt in my mind. His apartment was our next stop.

He lived in a Tribeca loft that was sparse and unfinished. The floor was concrete and the walls were exposed brick. There was nothing but a weathered picnic table, sofa, kitchenette, and bed covered in a cloud of crumpled white linens. When we walked in, the TV and radio were both at full volume. The only evidence of responsibility was a barking dog. I admired his faux crocodile carrier in a corner, and Rex said he'd get me one. He proudly showed me a really bad graffiti painting propped against a wall, his creative ventilation after a drunken night. I was so dick-notized, I couldn't see the slapdash brushwork as the mess that it really was. Instead, it affirmed his life of abandon, inspiring me to imagine giving up all my worldly possessions and living out the rest of my days on a Balinese beach, fucking without a care for the sand in my hair.

Taking off his pants, Rex—I saw—wasn't wearing any underwear. Naked, he was beautifully proportioned, his body long but not skinny, the muscles sculpted, not bulky, his quads and glutes superbly cast. Even his prick was good-looking.

The sight of the male member has never turned me on. Overall, I find the organ pretty hideous. The skin is stretched out in some places, shriveled in others. The form is bulbous, rubbery, and wobbly. Like a gourd, it is too long here and too stubby there. To appreciate it, I have to overcome its ungainly appearance by discovering its potential for pleasure.

But Rex's required no such effort. It was an optimal size—seven inches—and a healthy shade of pink with no blue undertones, which give so many cocks an uninviting grayish pallor. Veinless, too, without ropy lines or blood vessels marring the smooth surface. The ring of circumcision scars was invisible. His balls were hearty and hair-free. Overall, a perfect hitching post.

He took off my clothes, requesting that I wear thigh-highs the next time we were together. Turning me around, he examined my ass, grabbing fistfuls of flesh in his hands. Leading me to the bed, he pinned my wrists above my head, making my hands go numb, before lowering his weight on top of me. Despite his lubricious maneuvers, his kiss was incredibly gentle, which made me warm all over, my bones half melting in supplication. He ran his lips along the insides of my thighs, settling on the opening between them.

"I want to know your taste," he said, spreading the narrow aperture. Relaxing and flattening his tongue, he rolled it over and around my clit. As it started to swell, he fastened his mouth tightly, as if it were a suction cup leeching the blood flow to the surface.

"There . . . that's the spot . . . ," I breathed, a soft moan slipping from my throat as my knees tightened around his head and my body shuddered.

"So you've done this before," I said once recovered.

My climax had inflamed his cock, so I sat astride him, but I didn't want to fuck because I wanted to save something for later. Instead, I guaranteed him the blow job of the century, an experience so memorable, he'd get a hot, churning feeling in the pit of his stomach every time he thought of me.

Gripping the base of his cock in one hand and kneading his balls with the other, I slid my mouth down the shaft, squeezing my lips closed, pulling in my cheeks, and alternating between revolving my tongue around the mushroom head and tracing a vertical vein now defining the length of the organ. Lubricating my forefinger with saliva, I palpated his tight asshole, easing it open, working a knuckle inside. Hearing him groan, I wondered: Why do so many men prefer fellatio to pussy? Is a Hoover lined with a mucous membrane, equipped with a built-in attachment of a rotating tongue, literally more stimulating for a prick than the friction of fucking? Do men perceive a blow job—a woman lapping at the master phallus—as *that* much of a power trip? In reality, the act, if skillfully executed, does just the opposite, turning the beefiest guys into mincemeat.

Clamping his hand on the top of my head, Rex pumped into my gullet, driving the air from it. Breathing through my nose, I guzzled his cum and then sat up to kiss him deeply, lolling my tongue, now coated in viscous brine, over his.

"There's *your* taste," I said.

Afterward, it felt completely natural for us to head to the bathroom together to pee. I asked if he considered every woman he went out with to be a potential partner in a relationship.

"Never. But sometimes, it evolves that way."

So there's hope.

"Will you let me shave your goatee?"

It was an intimate thing to do but even though the sex was over, I still wanted to be close to him. He handed me a razor and I steadied his chin, coating it with shaving cream. He closed his eyes as I ran the blade over the arcs and curves of his face, thinking, *You're the one for me.*

When I wiped off his skin, he looked in the mirror, touching the new pale triangle where his goatee had been. I had left him something (or nothing) to remember me by.

Lying back down in bed, Rex smoked a cigarette with one arm under my neck. My stomach was aflutter and my head swoony. I was feeling loose and hip, far away from my suburban background and daddimony dependence on a lawyer husband. Rex didn't wear a suit and tie to work yet appeared to have the stability and confidence of a guy who did. His world of visual animation and social exposure excited me. For the first time, it seemed possible to have a lifestyle of security with a man who wasn't a nice Jewish boy.

"You know, I really like you," I said. "Since my marriage ended, you're the first guy I've met who I've connected to. I didn't even know it was possible to feel this way. It's so incredibly liberating. We really have chemistry, don't you think?"

Is it my imagination or did your eyes just stop twinkling?

At one o'clock in the morning, Rex walked me to the street to get a cab, promising to call the next day. I didn't sleep a wink. I was worried. Although we hadn't actually done the nasty, we'd come pretty close. Was it a bad move for me to have had Clinton sex on the first date? Was I wrong to have told Rex how I felt? Was there something to the hype surrounding *The Rules*? Was I too easy? Too aggressive? Too what?

Twenty-five years post–feminist revolution and after my ten years of marriage, it was hard to believe I would have to flash a fair tail and scamper away to sustain a man's interest in my scent. Wasn't it possible to get close without fearing I'd come on too strong? Couldn't two people first fuck and love would follow?

The more a guy pushed me away, the more I threw myself at him. Charlie had been the exception, which was why Andee and Ruby always said I wasn't hot for him. I wasn't so sure *that* was the reason, but my actions did prove that the more a man withheld his affection, the more pathetic I became.

In the end, the joke was always on me. By not letting a guy get to know me before having sex with him, I managed to chase him away once he did, when I revealed to him my neediness and intensity. Why couldn't I start out softer? Why couldn't I allow myself to be approachable without feeling so fragile? Where was my true strength? I had spent hundreds, maybe thousands of hours in therapy trying to reprogram my brain in order to circumvent my primary male relationship—the unattainable love of my father. But there seemed to be no getting past that original hard drive.

"You didn't swallow, did you?" Ruby asked the next morning

when I phoned to debrief her about my date. "What kind of idiot are you? Sure, he'll call. You sucked his dick. That's all he wants. You go into a fantasy and think, *This is The Guy.* You met him in the men's department of Bergdorf's. It's so sad. You're a smart person. You should change your phone number. You don't want him to call."

Squirreled away with her lover boy Luke, Ruby had no idea how unfair and confusing being single at my age was. She hadn't put herself out there—yet.

"No man wants a woman drooling all over him," said Ruby. "Just like we don't want them drooling on us. You have to behave like Kate Moss. Don't say anything. Just look drugged and bored. It's more becoming."

"Since when have *you* ever behaved like Kate Moss?"

I refused to believe that a self-respecting man would want a waif with a Dumpster for a brain when he could have a woman with hyperkinetic neurons. In other words, *me.*

"Hi," Rex said flatly, calling at the end of the day.

"Last night was great," I offered.

"Yeah, I've got a lot of work. I'm going away for a while but I said I'd call."

"When will you be back?"

"I'm not sure. Take it easy."

That was it. Not even a *Call you when I return.* I cursed myself, a fucking idiot. I was such a rookie. What had I been thinking going back to his place? Why hadn't I restrained myself from giving in to the hocus-pocus of my hormones?

Had I spent my twenties messing around instead of being married, I might not have been such a JV dater. I might have gained the wisdom to wait until a guy was as emotionally invested in me as I was in him before sleeping with him. I had never matured beyond my teenage self—putting out because I believed boys expected it and wouldn't like me if I were a tease.

I had grown up in the 1970s—the high noon of the Age of

Aquarius—when promiscuity represented more than personal liberation. Indiscriminate sex was progressive in spirit and anarchic in deed, a mind-and-body free-for-all usually accelerated by recreational drugs. Tumbling into bed was a pathway to finding a Higher Truth. Hedonism expressed an elevated lifestyle, a status symbol really, one toward which enlightened, energetic, and curious people strived. Who could deny the excitement that came with discovering a new body?

Yes, the freedom led to heartbreak. Having expectations and hopes was the great faux pas of casual encounters. Still, back then, the questions that governed my behavior were straightforward: Did I or didn't I want to do it? Not: What did sex mean in terms of a relationship and how would it be affected if I consented now or later? And how much later?

These days, the exchange of unfamiliar body fluids (latex barriers notwithstanding) was equated with moral turpitude and social decline. I no longer understood how to assign a value to fucking. To me, it was "good" if satisfying, "bad" if not. Doing it early on shouldn't jinx a future between two people. Starting out with sex was a good way to bypass unnecessary banter. My views, as I was to discover, were retro-sexual.

I was so mixed up. Why did Rex tell me confident women turned him on? Why did he claim to be a video artist rather than an adman when we first met? Was he ashamed of being a professional manufacturer of desires? Was I merely a target audience? Or was he an empty vessel for *my* unarticulated longing to be loved? Was I so infatuated it prevented me from seeing him for what he truly was: a wolf in a sheepskin coat from Bergdorf's?

• • •

One Friday night about a month later, I was home alone, cleaning out my closets, when the phone rang.

"How about I come over and cover your body in hot fudge?"

The Wolf.

"What took you so long to call?" I said.

"You've been on my mind lately."

Nice dodge.

"Why?"

"When we met, it was so hot between us, I'm getting a boner just thinking about it."

Boner? I hadn't heard that word since my brothers were little. It made The Wolf sound playful, even harmless.

"Yeah, it was hot, but you were a bastard. We fooled around and I told you how I felt and then you disappeared."

This is great. How often does a girl get to call a guy who pulls a Houdini a bastard?

"Don't you want answers to all the questions?" he said. "We never got to fuck. How about I come over?"

"What if it isn't any good?" I challenged. "Can you give me a guarantee? Otherwise, it's not worth my while."

There, I was doing it again, pretending to be bulletproof. Why, oh, why did I do that?

"It'll be great," he assured. "How can it not be? Remember how it started. Don't you want to find out how it will end?"

"I've thought about it."

More like obsessed about it. After my last few blind dates—a saliva-spraying close talker and a blubberball who tallied dinner calories (mine!)—The Wolf had become my male ideal: a juicer with a cool crib, a deck job, and 2 percent body fat.

"So what's the problem? You have a boyfriend?"

"No."

"Is it your son?"

"He's at his father's."

I was hesitating because I didn't know if I could keep my emotions in check. Would I be able to shuttlefuck The Wolf without wanting more? How much or how little was I capable of?

In the past, my promiscuity represented defiance and retaliation, a way to cash in on grudges against my parents, husband, and social restrictions. "I don't belong to one man, I belong to all men,"

Rita Hayworth once said, flipping her red mane over her shoulder. I told myself the opposite: *I don't belong to one man, all men belong to me.*

The Wolf was making it so easy. Shouldn't I take what I could when I could get it? With Dash at Charlie's, why not live it up? I'd already checked off the boxes of wife and mother. Now was my time for spontaneity and irresponsibility—and to check off my own box.

"You live all the way in Tribeca," I said. "It'll be after eleven before you get here."

"What's your address?"

Forty-five minutes later, I opened my door in a black silk La Perla slip, lace-trimmed Fogal thigh-highs, and nothing underneath. The Wolf was even more blazing than I remembered: unshaven and tan, though summer was still a couple of months off. We immediately started kissing, making our way to my bed. His mouth tasted of cigarettes and booze, at once sweet and dirty.

"Spread your legs," he said gruffly, driving his finger into my pussy.

"Take it easy!" I yelped.

Maybe The Wolf was so excited he couldn't help but act like a Roto-Rooter man plunging a drainpipe. Maybe he was caught up in the heat of the moment. Or maybe the lack of true intimacy between us made him aggressive. For all I knew, he might be punishing me, a woman, for agreeing to sex without a romantic sugar-coating.

"We'd better switch gears," I suggested. "How about going down on me?"

The Wolf took great pride in his cunnilingus capabilities. By the time guys hit their thirties, the lucky ones have figured out that the real coup comes not from being able to get off with a girl multiple times a night, but from getting the girl off multiple times a night.

As I settled back into my smooth cotton sheets, I thought, *This is gonna be good*. Handiwork might not have been The Wolf's skill, but I recalled his oral know-how. What I hadn't banked on was his stubbly face. He left whisker burns between my legs.

"It's my turn now to take care of you," I offered, figuring he wouldn't turn down a blow job.

Anything to give my pussy a break.

"Nothing doing. I'm here to make you feel good. I'm going to fuck your brains out."

Most men use that line to pump themselves up, to get their testosterone going, like a rallying cry before combat. Unless the guy really is out to hurt you, to actually commit an act of violence, he should know better than to really bang you. He should know better than to thrust so forcefully your eyeballs spring from their sockets. He should know better than to withdraw all the way before trying to push back in with one mean dagger stroke because your pussy will naturally close up and he'll wind up slamming into a wall of flesh instead of sliding into a hospitable hole. Even if he's never read the Kama Sutra, he should know the smaller and slower the movements, the stronger the sensations.

Not The Wolf. When he said he was going to fuck my brains out, he meant it.

It didn't take long before my privates felt as if they'd been put through a meat grinder. The only way to prevent further damage was my ace in the hole, the fake orgasm. I started in with labored breathing, followed by a riff of expletives before I clamped my legs around his ass, bucking and contracting as if my life depended on it. In the case of The Wolf, it really did.

Believing I'd climaxed, he exploded. Then it hit me. Like I'd been belted across the face. Using a rubber hadn't even crossed my mind. The Wolf and I were so hot for each other, neither one of us was willing to forgo the steamy interchange for the chilling effect of responsible behavior. Plus, guys always hate rubbers. Men know it's harder for them to catch something from us than the other way around so they rarely insist on them. It's up to the chicks to make them bag it. I hadn't done that despite the fact that I'd had a negative HIV test and kept a LifeStyles sampler—from Ultra Sensitive to XL—in the bathroom. How could I be so smart and still be so stupid?

"Why are you here?" I asked, when The Wolf and I finally lay face-to-face. *And how soon are you leaving?*

"Unfinished business."

"What do you mean?"

"I told you before this was about unanswered questions. You freaked me out that time at my apartment by being brutally honest and we never got to fuck."

"If my honesty freaked you out then, why is it different now?"

"Because every other girl has a tick box."

"A tick box?"

Was this guy a mind reader? How could he know I'd just been thinking about life in these terms?

"A checklist. I can see it in her eyes. The imperceptible nod of her head. The guy's good-looking? Check. Good job? Check. Sense of humor? Check. Loft? Check. Country house? Check. Car? Check. Good dresser? Check. Wants kids? Check. There's always a hidden agenda."

"You mean a hidden agenda before she'll agree to sex."

"Yeah, exactly."

"If a woman doesn't have an agenda or a type of guy in mind, then what's she supposed to be looking for?"

"A woman shouldn't be looking for anything. She should be interested in the ideal of the relationship. What two people can be together."

Now, *that* caught me off guard. It sounded so utopian: A convergence of two separate beings gives rise to love, and their relationship represents a resolution? A romantic dialectic.

Since The Wolf made no mention of his preconditions—like whether his dreamgirl had to enjoy outdoor sports—or his postscripts, such as his desire for four kids and a farm, his theory seemed to leave room for a lot of possibilities. Could one of them be me?

"What about us?" I ventured.

"Don't push it. Tonight is what it is. I thought you wanted that. You're like a guy when it comes to sex."

Under different circumstances I might have been flattered. Instead I recoiled, rolling away from him in my bed. I didn't want The Wolf to see me crying.

After he left my apartment, I looked at the empty place where the flattened pillow bore an imprint of his head. I couldn't get comfortable. My face was burning from his beard. My nipples were sore from being pinched and pulled. My pussy hurt from all the fingering and fucking. Yes, I wanted animal sex but I wanted a man to be sweet to me, too, to pull the comforter up under my chin and kiss me good night. I wished I had a guy who wanted to be with me. To wake up and start his day by my side. Was I wishing for a husband?

It hurt too much to have sex without love or, worse, sex with a hope for love that didn't pan out. The soreness between my legs was the same as my heart. Who was I kidding? I could never fuck like a man. It tore me apart. Guys seemed to be able to tell you one thing and do another, or do one thing and tell you another, without a twinge of pain or regret. Even when a new man came along, someone who seemed so promising, it always turned out to be the same. When I fucked, I was looking for love. And when I was looking for love, I got fucked.

CHAPTER 12

Once Charlie moved out and Dash was spending weekends at his father's, I was faced with a new challenge: being home alone. There was no one to talk to or listen to. No one to wait for or get away from. No one to feed, pick up after, or say good night to. The ticking of an antique electric clock in my bedroom pierced the silence with window-rattling force.

I missed my son. Despite my self-image of being a "hands-off" mother—one who didn't cart her kid to and from playdates or sell raffle tickets for the school fair—I now found myself with time on my hands. Too much time.

At night, when the dogs were asleep, I remained awake, wandering into Dash's room. I had taught my child to put away his belongings, to help me keep our small apartment neat. Parents of his classmates were always complimentary of his good manners. Studying the organized hodgepodge on his bookshelves, I re-created the child I knew so well out of the rows of Ping-Pong, baseball, Wiffle, football, basketball, and tennis balls. There were cleats and mitts and shin guards and soccer shoes. A bat and a hockey stick stood in a corner where a life-size cloth Power Ranger doll—Dash's ever-faithful wrestling opponent beaten into permanent floppiness—slumped in a corner. Books were few, my son being more a jock than a reader, though he had a small library of horror stories and refused to let me give away *Harold and the Purple Crayon,* claiming sentimental reasons: "It reminds me of when I was a child" (this coming from the mouth of a seven-year-old).

Looking over at his night table, I smiled. There was the Sunkist orange essay. He was in third grade and learning about adjectives. His teacher had given a homework assignment to write one hundred words describing something.

"One hundred words?" Dash cried, after school. "I can't write so much about one thing."

Retrieving an orange from the kitchen, I pointed out the pitted texture of the rind, asking him what he noticed about the fruit. He said the name and color were the same but the surface was not entirely orange. It had green splotches.

"On a desert island, you could use an orange to quench your thirst or put it in a sock and swing it at someone, if you needed a weapon," he said.

In the end, he found his hundred words and more.

It was only after Dash was away at his father's Thursday through Monday that I became aware of how much I missed seeing the world through him. One night before bedtime, he recited a poem that popped into his head: "The moon sails up the sky / And we fall asleep and dream / Of tomorrow's sun." I immediately transcribed the words onto a bookmark, laminating it to preserve his haiku, lasting proof of my child's latent lyricism.

Without my boy around, my daily structure started to crumble. Ordinarily, his school hours were mine to work and run errands, the evenings devoted to his dinner and bath. Bed was scheduled for nine but that never happened. He always begged to watch one more TV show and then another. It became routine: his surrender to the sack being pushed back another hour.

Before the end of my marriage, when Dash and I were apart, we still seemed to be together. I always knew where he was, whom he was with, and what he was likely to be doing. He was a part of me, an extension of my being. Our linkage felt nearly physical, a sensation as lively as pain, as if he were hundreds of fishhooks in my skin.

With him at his father's, that tension was gone. Feeling bereft and disconnected, I wanted to track him down, but calling Charlie's more than once a day was tantamount to crossing a no-fly zone.

"Hi," I said once, phoning for the hell of it.

Charlie didn't respond.

"Just wondered what you guys are up to."

Silence.

"Where's Dash?"

"In his room."

"Doing what?"

"Playing, watching TV, the usual."

"Why don't you want to talk to me? Wouldn't it be nice to have more than a three-word conversation?"

"I give you a lot more than I have to, given our situation. I'm entitled to my privacy."

What could I say? By comparison with my girlfriends who all fought with their exes and didn't get nearly as much money as I did, my relationship with Charlie was pretty warm and fuzzy. But in the pit of my stomach, I was scared: He no longer saw himself as my caretaker. I had lost my safety net.

A few months after Charlie moved out, I met Nate on Memorial Day at a clambake in the Hamptons. He lived in San Francisco but was in New York for business. At the party, I was standing by myself, drinking a club soda, when he passed me, a fat Cuban cigar between his teeth. He flashed a whopping grin and stopped. He had great hair, the color of sand and densely bristled. His eyes were hazel like mine. Most unforgettable was his voice: full-throated and velvety, a white man's Barry White.

Nate was staying in the city for the following week at a friend's apartment. The next Saturday, he took me to dinner at La Goulue.

We'd barely said two words before he told me to keep my eyes open, giving me a long, deep kiss.

"That was intense," I said, my cheeks burning.

"I've always smoked unfiltered Camels, and I drink straight scotch and black coffee. I've never diluted anything."

He'd been married twice, briefly in his early twenties and again at thirty-five. It lasted nine years and was now ending in divorce. His boy, Matt, was seven, the same age as Dash. Nate had another son, Sam, nineteen, who was adopted.

"What do you do for a living?" I asked.

"I'm retired."

Forty-four years old and retired?

"I owned a chain of retail stores, like Wal-Mart. It started as a family business but when I sold it, I had two thousand employees."

"So, you were a big *macher*."

"Are you Jewish?" he said, his eyes lighting up. "I'm Jewish, too."

Wait till my mother gets wind of this. Finally A Man! Jewish, to boot!

"You work?" he repeated after I explained what I did at MoMA. "My wife didn't work. It's so nice to meet a woman who actually has a career."

"I don't know if you'd call it a 'career.' It's more like a job. Or a bunch of part-time jobs."

"Hey, don't put yourself down. I bet you're good at what you do. People must love you."

Unaccustomed to male cheerleading, I assumed he was giving me a snow job. New York men were self-absorbed and guarded, sizing you up as they gathered intelligence, dismissing you based on trivia that didn't fit their preconceptions of a perfect woman. ("You live on the Upper East Side?" Next! "You've got a kid?" Next! "You grew up in Great Neck?" Next! "You're how old?" Next! "You don't drink?" Next!) After months of demoralizing dates, I was skeptical of Nate's candor and flattery. Then again, he was from the other side of the country.

"Do you like motorcycles?" he asked. "I've got a Harley. It's not the best-looking model but the best riding. I had it outfitted for long-distance trips. I ride by myself to Iowa or Wisconsin or Montana. You want to come on a trip with me?"

"You're crazy! You don't even know me. You might not like me. I can be needy and demanding."

"Are you trying to push me away? Because it's not going to work."

"Well, I'm a woman with a past," I said, trying a different tack. "I've been with tons of guys."

"Good. That means you know what you're doing. I couldn't care less so long as they're all before me. You're young looking but you have experience. That's why I'm attracted to you."

Back up. Did you say, Young looking?

Although Dash was at his father's, which meant my apartment was empty, I knew it was risky to bring Nate home. After The Wolf, I'd promised myself to go slower. But there was always room for an exception. Nate was leaving town the next day and I didn't want to pass up what lay beyond the city limits.

When he walked through my front door, the dogs went berserk. Like all Upper East Side pets, mine got the royal treatment, which meant my den—bed included—was theirs. They acted territorial if anyone else was in it.

"I hope you don't mind but they're not accustomed to guests. If we don't let them join us, they'll yap and whine the whole time."

"Join us?"

"We have to bring them into bed. Don't worry. They'll just sleep. We'll work around them."

"If you say so."

Hugging and kissing, Nate squeezed me tightly. Running his hands through my hair and stroking my face, he hadn't even laid a finger on my pussy but it was already warm and stirring. When I reached between his legs, however, there was nada lotta response. I figured a blow job was in order.

Dachshunds are hounds, originally bred to hunt foxes, badgers, and rabbits. Mine, being urban dwellers, hadn't much occasion to demonstrate their venery skills. Somehow Nate's scent piqued their genetic instincts and three wet snouts made a nosedive for his balls.

"No! No!" he cried, crossing his legs together. "Get away from there. Stop it. Stop it!"

"I'm so sorry," I said, laughing. The response of his johnson, shrinking like cornered prey, indicated Nate didn't share my sense of humor about the situation.

When the dogs finally settled down and I restored his mojo with my mouth, he worked his prick inside me. After one corkscrew push, he collapsed, his deadweight compressing my breast implants. Fearing he'd flattened my tires, I automatically pushed him away. His premature ejaculation was so disappointing, I had another knee-jerk reaction.

"Where's my orgasm?" I blasted, not giving any thought to his feelings.

"Why are you yelling at me? I'm a little rusty. It's been a year."

"I can't believe you didn't wait for me. You're a Jewish man."

"What does being Jewish have to do with this?"

"The Talmud says a woman's satisfaction takes precedence over a man's."

"Do you even want a man?" he asked, sitting up halfway, leaning on his elbow. "That's not the message you're conveying. The dogs, the orgasm on demand, the Talmud—what about an emotional connection?"

An emotional connection? Since when does a man want an emotional connection?

All my life, women were the ones who were supposed to want to "make luuuuuuuv" while men were supposed to want to fuck. But the older I got, the more apparent was the fact that men failed to live up to their billing: durability, potency, and eagerness. A woman was also taught to accept that sex was over when the man came, and there was no female equivalent to blue balls.

All bunk. My libido was stronger and more reliable than a good many men's. My sexuality was the part of me I loved best because it was neurosis-free (the only thing that was). Responsive and un-inhibited, I felt entitled to fulfillment and expected a man to want the same for me, even more than for himself. And yes, the Talmud stated that I come first (admittedly, my exegesis was entirely self-serving since the edict referred only to marital relations, but hey, this was no time for hermeneutics).

Nate and I were both stewing, lying in my bed without a word. He was probably making a mental map of where he'd left his clothes in order to get dressed and shazzam his way out my front door. Meanwhile, I was trying to remember where I'd put the contractor's phone number to invite him over for a repair job.

Then I began to wonder: What if Nate's right? What if I really don't want a man? Am I jaded? Cold-blooded and castrating?

"It's been kind of shitty since my marriage ended," I said softly, making an effort to open up to him. "Actually, it was shitty before my marriage ended, but being single isn't what I expected, either. I guess I need reprogramming, some kind of detox for the romantically disheartened."

"I know what you mean. I take out women and there's nothing there. They're not interesting. I don't sport-fuck. For so long, I've felt dead inside."

Nate started fingering one of my nipples. Picking up my hand, he laid a string of kisses along the inside of my arm. "Before, when you were yelling at me, I kept thinking, *Get out of here,*" he said. "This woman has gone over to the dark side. You've heard of the flight-or-fight theory? I'm not one for the flight option. I'm stubborn. I'm going to find out if there's actually a heart in that beautiful body of yours."

While our blowup might have maimed ordinary men, this guy's penis suddenly seemed anabolically enhanced. Pumped and ready to go, he took my palm, closing it around his now hard cock. When I let go, the stalk jumped slightly, springing backward. I wanted that feeling inside me, his dick flexing against the walls of my pussy. Pushing Nate on his back, I was poised to mount him.

"You don't deserve me," he said playfully, restraining my hips. "You've been a bad girl. I'm going to have to punish you. You know what happens to bad girls who get punished? A spanking."

I had long enjoyed a spontaneous slap on my bare ass but never confessed how much I desired it. I was embarrassed to reveal the truth: Beneath my brazen-hussy persona was a little missy in need of a licking. When I masturbated, the narrative that most aroused me was one of corporal comeuppance: a faceless paternal figure bidding me to lift my skirt and lie across his lap, whereupon he pulled down my underpants, striking my lower loins with a brusque hand, hairbrush, birch branch, paddle, small whip, or bedroom slipper.

Several months earlier, in February 1996, I read in *The New Yorker* Daphne Merkin's story "Unlikely Obsession: Confronting a Taboo." Here was a highbrow publication presenting the soft-porn desires of an intellectual reveling in spanking as a sexually gratifying act. This was fucking major.

A copy of the issue circulated throughout MoMA's Education Department, where the all-female staff reacted with the exhilaration of Soviet gulag prisoners getting their hands on prohibited *Samizdat* documents written by exiles and dissidents. In whispered tones, we expressed our happy disbelief and guilty pleasure that Merkin, a woman to whom we could relate, a woman who represented *us*, had the chutzpah to come clean and expose our collective yearning for a dose of the strap oil.

"I love when he spanks my ass hard," said Mathilde, the department's punkette secretary, my best pal at work, who was speaking of her boyfriend, a former USMC sergeant and civilian physical therapist. "Lots of women love it. Women want to be dominated. In your case, I know you probably feel you deserve it and so do I."

"Why do we like it so much?"

"It's stimulating because it evokes something powerful. Getting what we deserve from our daddies. We've been taught since childhood we're bad little girls."

It was with the utmost thrill that I finally felt Nate's hand systematically circling the surface of my cheeks, warming up my posterior for punishment. He targeted the sweet spot between haunches and crease where thighs and buttocks meet. His upswept smacks caused me to clench and unclench the globes in what the French call *la danse de la croupe,* the dance of the bottom. The slapping sound was as arousing as the knowledge that my insolence was betrayed by his buffets reddening my behind.

"You've been a bad, bad girl," he said, emphasizing every word with a stroke. He alternated between cheeks, varying the interval, each time resting his hand on the struck area, offering brief words of comfort and consolation to reinforce the lesson.

By the time he fucked me, I was a luna-chick: frothing at both ends, writhing, imploring, panting, apologizing, and blithering God-only-knows-what. Each crack across my rear made my pussy drip with expectation for the next blow. When he finally conceded to my entreaties for a cock of punishing force, it released a tidal wave of orgasms. I thrashed from side to side, as he flipped me from top to bottom, then bottom to top. Oblivious to my baying dogs, Nate and I were capsizing in bodily emissions.

When he left New York late the next morning, my apartment felt emptier than ever, filled with signs of his presence now gone— a damp towel on a hook in the bathroom, my bedsheets stained with our impurities. I was emotionally and physically spent. Would I ever see him again? A man who had lived, loved, worked, sired, and spanked?

At the end of the day, my doorbell rang. It was a flower delivery—a potted pink orchid—with a note: "To be continued . . . Nate."

He phoned me that night and again the next morning. And so

it went, day after day, with voice mails, late-night conversations, and early-morning wake-up calls, revving up our relationship.

With his divorce under way, Nate had to split his assets with his wife, Nina, and pay child support. He needed to go back to work. Since his background was in brick-and-mortar discount stores, he decided on a new career: online retailing of brand labels at outlet prices.

"You're going to make a bundle," I told him. "I just know it."

"You make me feel big," he said. "Like I can succeed."

He, in turn, made me feel loving. Not having grown up in a touchy-feely household, I looked upon kisses and caresses as a lead-up to sex, not for the sake of ordinary affection. Although it seemed sappy to me at first, I forced myself to interlock my fingers with his. Soon I became so accustomed to us holding hands when we were together, mine felt empty when we were apart.

The first night Nate and I slept together, I turned my back to him, balling myself up, burrowing beneath the covers while he needed his legs exposed in order to "breathe." After a couple more nights, I was curling my body inside the arc of his, making sure to first pull back the comforter from his feet. To anyone watching, the gesture would have appeared insignificant. But it made me feel good to think of his needs, proving myself capable of caring.

Nate was the marrying kind, a take-charge guy who could fig-ure out the health insurance, get the plane tickets, and anticipate a wife's "honey-dos" (as in "Honey, will you do this? Honey, would you do that?"). In addition to being right for me, I knew he would be right for Dash.

Not that my son needed a father. Charlie was 100 percent there and no one would replace him. But Nate offered something dif-ferent, a healthy role model, someone with whom I could be demonstrative. I wanted Dash to watch me fuss over a breakfast of French toast before serving it to an adoring guy. I wanted my boy to witness how a man who cherishes a woman stops reading the newspaper when she enters the room, slides his arm around her waist, and kisses her cheek when she passes. I wanted my child to know that, unlike his parents, a married couple should be more than friends and sleep in the same bed, not a pair of twin mattresses pushed together Lucy-and-Ricky-style.

"Matt needs to see me in a healthy relationship so that he can emulate it in his own life," Nate agreed, regarding his son. "In the past, he saw Nina and me fight. We slept in a king-size bed. It was very lonely. I never want my wife that far away again. A queen is as big as I'll go."

When Matt was with his mother and Dash his father, Nate and I had cross-country rendezvous. I was joyful yet agitated, unable to relax, knowing we would have to say good-bye all too soon. He was so giving and easy to be with, I wanted to lock in for life. But the distance wasn't making our hearts grow fonder.

Nate wouldn't leave his son to move to New York and I wasn't willing to resettle in San Francisco. Whatever romantic fulfillment I could derive from him would never be as great as the hurt and rejection I would cause Dash if I left him to be with a man. No child can overcome a mother's abandonment. Bringing him with me was out of the question; Charlie and I had a joint custody arrangement. Even if I somehow managed to relocate with my son, separating him from his father would have ruined our boy's life.

It was hard to accept that what Nate and I shared—a loving relationship we believed would benefit our children in their own romantic futures—might also be a source of destruction. In the end, we had to choose: us or them.

• • •

"I miss Dad," Dash said over dinner on Labor Day weekend.

"Why?" I asked.

"He's so much fun. He's soft around the middle when I hug him. You're skinny. I can feel your bones. I like his house so much better than yours. There, the sheets don't match and I can be a slob. I can swing a baseball bat around. Here, I can't do what I want. I have to clean up and act civilized. I have to be mature. I feel like I have to impress you."

He was right to complain. I didn't like living with me, either. A couple of weeks earlier, Nate had ended our relationship because the stress of the long distance, coupled with his divorce, was too much. Heartbroken, I was constantly irritable.

"The TV's too loud!" I hollered at Dash. "And no playing ball inside!"

Once he was asleep, I alternated between sobbing into my pillow and staring out my bedroom window, counting the number of apartments aglow across the street. How many were filled with loving couples? Was there another Miss Lonely Heart out there besides me?

I reminisced about a summer weekend when Nate came to New York and we went to Amagansett, stopping at an outdoor James Taylor concert at Southampton College. Every ballad made me cry—tears of happiness because I loved being with Nate. During our visit to Topanga Canyon, we fucked in an oak tree, the air fragrant with bay laurel, him straddling a branch and me straddling him.

The responsibilities of motherhood did not allow for lamentation or erotic reenactments. Mommy was supposed to be cheerful and de-sexed, otherwise her child would be mentally scarred. But I couldn't shake my sorrow. On the weekends, when Dash was at Charlie's, I languished in bed, unable to summon the energy to go outside, not even to walk my dogs, what with them being paper-trained and all. The pall grew darker and heavier.

I turned to a love affair that had begun nearly two decades earlier, but had remained a clandestine part of my entire adult life. I anticipated it with my entire body, even in the depths of my bowels. Euphoric, agonizing, delectable, loathsome, prohibited, invigorating, tragic, and volatile: My secret was cocaine. We'd started spending a lot of time together when I was in college, our relationship persisting through graduate school, my years of being an art critic, and even a teacher at MoMA. Long after I'd given up my childhood dream of becoming a writer, the actual enterprise of structuring thoughts into words to form sentences to create paragraphs to build essays still paralyzed me with fear. Cocaine was a way to anesthetize myself and get the job done.

My habit was private, hidden from my family, friends, colleagues, and husband. I stashed my works—little glass vials, mini envelopes created out of folded magazine pages, thimble-size plastic packets, short straws, rolled-up dollar bills, shrunken spoons, and razor blades—inside Tampax boxes and between credit cards in my wallet. Because I got stoned in order to be productive, it was easy to deny the problem. After all, Sigmund Freud was a user and look what he accomplished.

• • •

"Hola, flaca, como estas?" said Lunita, opening the red door of her Upper East Side garden apartment. She was wearing a turquoise tunic embroidered with gold threads, her wild black curls clipped to the top of her head like a gaggle of snakes charmed from a basket.

"Bien, bien," I answered, ducking inside.

The air smelled heady and lush, a mixture of sandalwood incense and rose oil. Candles burned in pink lotus-shaped holders, Tibetan prayer flags fluttered from the ceiling, and bamboo mats covered the floor. I perched on a meditation bench, trying to balance my chakras.

"Your mules are beautiful," I admired. "Are they . . ."

"Prrrrrrra-*Da*," she confirmed.

I loved her accent, the way she purred her *r*'s and emphasized her *d*'s. Lunita was Argentine, in her midthirties, and had been trained as an architect in Buenos Aires. She came from family money—the cattle industry. Her boyfriend, Tony, was ten years younger. He emerged from the bedroom shirtless, his muscular chest honey-colored and gleaming as if coated in hash oil, his shredded jeans hanging below his pelvis, revealing the waistband of his white Jockeys.

Our three-way exchange was like a coin trick, a game of now-you-see-it-now-you-don't. The illusion began with me slipping a hundred-dollar bill into Lunita's palm. She then embraced Tony's waist, sliding her hands down the back of his pants as he unclipped her hair, raking his fingers through it, hiding my bindle in the tangle. As she escorted me to the door, bidding me ciao, she wound a finger around her curls, retrieving the cache, and we reversed our pantomime, my hand now greased with a gram.

I have no idea how or why I came to know the choreography. Who was watching? There was a private patio with wood fencing behind her apartment. Our performance must have stemmed from the paranoia that comes with committing a felony. However, the charade of me "dropping by" on a designer-dressed South American socialite made it easy to dissimulate that we were uptown cronies when, in reality, Lunita was my down-and-out connection.

My "visits" grew more frequent after Charlie moved out, when I went from chipping—sporadic use for writing assignments—to monthly buys. Streptococcus was the inciting cause of my escalation.

It was a Saturday night in the spring and Dash was at his father's. For days, my throat had been sore. With my lymph nodes the size of kumquats, temples pounding, and shivering with a fever, I ingested yet another ineffective round of Tylenol. Like a cat hawking up a hairball, I suddenly started choking because the pills were lodged in my windpipe. The near asphyxiation induced a frightening flashback.

When Dash was little, I often caught his colds, and one in particular knocked me out. At the time, I was at the Institute, preparing a seminar presentation on Foucault. I was doing blow to write. Over the course of a week, my throat became sorer and sorer until I was unable to swallow. With my tongue out and head bent forward to prevent myself from aspirating my own saliva, I drooled my way to New York Hospital, where I was admitted with epiglottitis, an acute, life-threatening infection causing my air pipe to close up.

I spent five days as a lab rat: regulated, categorized, and observed by a host of otolaryngologists who inserted fiber-optic scopes into my nose and down my pharynx. Although epiglottitis is rare, it is more common in children than adults. A circle of medical students widened at the foot of my bed, marveling at me. I didn't want to admit to myself, let alone the experts, that my anomalous condition was probably explained by the fact that I had compromised my immune system with coke. Since there was no way to detect it in my system unless they did a urine toxicology screening, the cause of my disease remained a hospital mystery.

Now, staring at a box of tissues moisturized with aloe lotion and vitamin E, I felt big, hot tears running down my cheeks. The only comfort I could count on would come from those Kleenex.

Vivid with illness and self-pity, my imagination conjured a colony of acid-green microbes feasting on my trachea, contaminating my bloodstream, and poisoning my heart. HELEN KELLER = SCARLET FEVER and MOZART = RHEUMATIC FEVER lit up like LED signboards in my head. My fate was joined to America's founding father, George Washington, who, supposedly, died of epiglottitis.

"Get me to the hospital," I croaked, calling Charlie.

"What's the matter now?"

"I'm sick. Really sick. My throat. It's bad. Remember when I had epiglottitis? I can't wait till Monday to see a doctor."

"What do you want me to do? I'm with Dash. I can't leave him."

"Can you two meet me?"

"At this hour? I'm not going to take him to a hospital. Can't you call someone else?"

"Andee's afraid of germs. My parents are on safari in Africa."

"What about Ruby?"

Ruby? Worse off than me. Her beloved mother had just lost her battle with esophageal cancer; her son, Joey, was acting out; and

her love affair with Luke had ended after he admitted to conflicts about his sexuality, confessing to her during intercourse, "I
wish you had a penis." A strap-on wouldn't do. Quitting while
she still had a clit, she had run away to Colorado, where, house-
sitting for a friend, Ruby was currently dissipating on Ketel One
and Dunhills.

"I wouldn't ask you if I had another choice," I told Charlie.

"Just go to the hospital by yourself. You'll be fine. Someone will
take care of you."

At nine PM, I joined the other city rejects who, like me, had
nothing better to do than pass a Saturday night in an emergency
room. Two hours later, a resident appeared, swabbing white pus
from the back of my throat. I was hoping he'd admit me; I was
looking forward to the companionship—nurses, orderlies, techni-
cians, transporters, food servers, housekeepers—anyone with a
pulse. On a deeper level, I wanted someone to intervene because
my inability to care for myself was worsening. But instead of a hospital bed, the doctor provided a Z-pack and a cliché: "Plenty of
fluids and rest."

Although my throat cleared up by the following Friday, I sank
to a new low. When Dash went to Charlie's, I "popped by" Lunita's to pick up some candy to keep me buzzing throughout the
weekend, which I spent rearranging the linen, utility, and coat
closets, as well as alphabetizing my cassette and CD racks. By Sunday night, armed with a label gun and a glue stick, I was manically
dating, identifying, and mounting ten years of family snapshots in
leather-bound photo albums.

On Monday morning, I felt as if my brain were clogged with
caulking compound and my eyes pasted shut. How was I going to
get out of bed? Pull myself to work? At least it wasn't my day to
take Dash to school.

One quick snort did the trick: Up and Adam! Or was it "up and
at 'em"? What was the difference? The white powder worked like
Wheaties. I was raring to go.

Facing the next morning's torpor was no easier. Once again, I dipped into my portable supply for bumps of energy. It was amazing how much I could accomplish by increasing my metabolism to that of a hummingbird. With my voice racing at forty-five rpms, I had no time to waste, not even to pause for commas.

I had to walk kid to school run dogs through park shower dress hail cab get to MoMA give lecture skip lunch go to ATM give another lecture give another lecture teach after-school program mail slide sets to teachers return slide sets from teachers leave MoMA hail cab no cab take bus see Lunita greet son relieve babysitter feed son pick at son's leftovers help son with homework call back Mom battle son to bathe battle son to bed talk to Charlie need more money prepare next day's class for Flatbush High plan subway route to Brooklyn put away laundry inventory refrigerator make grocery list for maid take five milligrams Valium wait twenty minutes take five more milligrams Valium toss turn no sleep.

Add a Clapton soundtrack, along with some stolen handguns and wiseguys in pinkie rings, and I'm living a Scorsese movie.

There's only so long you can sustain a drug habit before your body goes haywire. I was constantly shifting my jaw from side to side. My ears felt stuffy, my teeth were sore from grinding, and my muscles ached from tensing up. I had TMJ of the entire body. I went from feeling cold to hot and breaking into a sweat faster than you could say *vasodilation*.

My perception of space became distorted: Objects no longer conformed to perspective, with those in the distance appearing smaller, but rather as a surrealist vista of compressed, overlapping, flattened forms, looming forward, tilting backward, and veering off at sharp angles. My Manhattan looked like a de Chirico painting.

The fact that my coke-encrusted nostrils resembled salt-rimmed margaritas and I was reversing the clock of my surgically rejuvenated eyes—now red, droopy, and sunken—did little to enhance my professional demeanor. At MoMA, my boss suspected something was wrong, given not only my late arrivals, early de-

partures, and growing number of sick days but also my public diss-
ing of a pillar of modernism.

Leading a class from the Bronx's John F. Kennedy High School
through the museum, I stopped to discuss Matisse's *Dance,* asking
the class how the artist evoked an Edenic setting. I expected them
to figure out it had something to do with the nudity and atavistic
movements of the figures in the painting. A girl in a North Face
jacket, Timberlands, and gold door-knocker earrings raised her
hand.

"Yo, miss," she said, flicking back her acrylic fingernails. "Why
don't the ladies got no nipples?"

Although I had never noticed the omission, her observation was
a perfect segue into a juicy discussion about nudity versus nakedness and art versus pornography. Normally, I loved moments like
this, when teaching turned improvisational.

But on this particular day my brain was too oohblah to trans-
act. Several seconds of silence passed before I heard myself de-
nouncing the painting as fleshless and G-rated to the class. Matisse
was no more than a poster designer and art history was sanitized
smut. I had given up, not on my students, but on myself.

Charlie had given up on me, too. He had filed for divorce. My
doo-dah days as his dependent were to end. With no marital assets
to speak of, there was nothing to divide, other than our apartment.
The deck was stacked against me: A matrimonial attorney at Charlie's firm was counseling him for free whereas my legal fees were
$350 an hour. I saw the writing on my walls: TAG SALE: EVERY-
THING MUST GO.

• • •

A druggie in denial minimizes her own condition by measuring it against those who are worse off. Cocaine hadn't reduced me
to a twitching wraith with rotting teeth, living out of a cardboard
box beneath a highway overpass. I never cracked up a car, pawned
my property, or neglected my child. Okay, I admit my nose bled,

but only twice, both times in private, which didn't really count, right?

Although I had been secretly doing blow during the time I was involved with Nate, it was after our breakup that I really plummeted. I experienced anticipation highs en route to Lunita's, anxiety before my supply ran out, and fear that if she disappeared, I'd bled my own veins rather than make do without her.

Who knew if I was on the brink of hitting my bottom? Maybe I was already there. But to this day I attribute an unexpected phone call from Nate to saving my life.

"She did it," said Nate, the first time I'd heard from him in six weeks.

"Who? Did what?"

"My wife, Nina. She killed herself."

The previous afternoon, she had argued with her son, Sam, who, home from college, was staying with his mother in Palo Alto where she'd been living since her split-up with Nate. Sam had bronchitis and was taking Phenergan with codeine. Snitching the bottle, she chugged it down to anesthetize herself.

"What's the matter with you?" her son shouted, trying to steady his mother as she crashed around the house, toppling furniture.

Lurching away, she ran to her bedroom, locking the door behind her. From her closet, she grabbed a loaded Winchester, which her father had provided for her self-protection. It was Mother's Day, five days before her forty-third birthday, and with her son merely yards away on the other side of the door, she pointed the thirty-inch barrel to her chest and pulled the trigger with her big toe. The blast to her body was so powerful, her face turned black-and-blue. She had left a note: "Sam, take care of your little brother."

Nina died before reaching the hospital. By the time Nate drove from San Francisco to her house, the police were already there, arranging for a cleaning service to shampoo the blood from her white bedroom carpeting. Earlier that afternoon, when she hadn't shown up at school to pick up her younger son, Matt, a neighbor had brought him to her home.

"I parked the car in the neighbor's driveway and Matt got in the car," Nate recounted to me over the phone. "He was surprised to see me because he knew I was in San Francisco. I said, 'Your mom died.' He asked how. I told him she took her own life. We just sat there and both cried."

"You sound so calm," I said, chilled by Nate's robotic tone. "Are you okay?"

"I'm numb. I'm just going through the motions. There's the autopsy, the funeral. I've got to keep it together for the kids. I'm all they've got. I can feel their fear that I may abandon them, too. I just thank God Nina didn't take the kids with her."

The insides of my stomach were roiling, imagining the reaction of Nate's children to never seeing their mother again. I wondered what, exactly, had driven Nina to do it. She was a housewife without a career on which to fall back once her younger son was grown. She was now living in a crappy two-bedroom house with Nate nickel-and-diming her over the settlement. With her marriage over, she had lost her social prominence. It was only a matter of time before her looks went, too. Was she afraid of growing old alone? Did she believe her sons would be better off without her?

In October 1996, just after Nina's death, I was sitting cross-legged on my bedroom carpeting, wearing my oversize sleep T and Calvin Klein cotton underwear. Despite the warm autumn day, I avoided going outdoors. The sun was too bright, making my eyes squint and head hurt. Working at home while Dash was in school, I was assembling a teacher slide set about art and war, trying to write an accompanying text and study questions.

In front of me was a Brother electric typewriter with an automatic memory. Since I hadn't written anything, there were no words to store. Cocaine, my once reliable mental Metamucil, now left my brain constipated. Maybe the amount of blow was the problem?

Strung out and desperate to get my job done, I eased the end of my now ever-present straw into my sore nostril. The snort went straight to my tear ducts. Salty droplets sprang forth and I blinked several times to block the spillage. It didn't work. I was crying. Weeping out of nowhere.

That happened a lot these days. Caught in a cokehead's catch-22, I did another hit, attempting to jump from the sinking ship, but instead got tangled up in the rigging. The white lines were tightening around me, pulling me down under.

As I hunched over the mirror, a female face came into focus. Resembling a Tim Burton illustration, her features were skeletal and the skin was lined, as if she'd taken a fine blade to the tissue, carving every instance of pain felt over the course of a lifetime.

It was Nina, yet not Nina. Like a double exposure, the reflection was also me. Right then, I understood an unintended purpose of Nate's call: to warn me. Whether accidentally or intentionally, I, too, was going to die.

But did it matter? What had I to live for? Charlie and I were getting a divorce; my attempts at replacing him with a new husband had failed. I had been looking for meaning through men, love, and sex. By defining myself in and through romantic relationships, I had no identity as an individual.

My existence was a vacuum. Without my own achievement, I lacked a fundamental condition to thrive—self-esteem. My writing—overly intellectualized, florid interpretations of visually challenged art—appeared in publications with a circulation of zero. My responsibilities as a wife, mother, and teacher never felt like the decisive undertakings they were but passive concessions to someone else's expectations, though whose, I wasn't sure. All my life, I had struggled against convention, but nothing positive came from my defiance. I was who I was by default.

And yet, I was consumed by a cult of the self. Never did my

conga line of psychotherapists get a break during my sessions. One look at a black Eames lounge chair was all it took to get me started, pondering aloud the who, the what, and the why of my life. Was anyone else as sick of listening to me as I was?

I had never been a woman who martyred herself for others, forfeiting food from her own plate to feed a hungrier mouth, setting aside a career to care for her child, and subordinating her sex drive to spare a man's ego. I hadn't toiled, trudged, scoured, served, and nursed. I hadn't wished I'd studied more, stayed home less, spoken louder, behaved better, or exercised my right to vote. I was no one's doll or helpmate. Consumed with my own actualization, I had never forged a self to sacrifice. A solipsistic shut-in, I needed a reason to find a way out.

Any minute, he would walk through my front door: *Dash*.

When I was sixteen, my mother took me with her one night to the Lone Star Café in Manhattan. She introduced me to a handsome young actor who was her scene partner at the time. At some point, I realized my mother was nowhere in sight. The place was packed. Searching, I couldn't find her. Was she looking for me, too, or had she taken off with some guy? It wouldn't have been the first time.

By one in the morning, I was pretty panicked and hailed a taxi to Penn Station, riding the Long Island Rail Road home to Great Neck where I called my father from a pay phone, woke him up, and asked him to come get me. I have no recollection of explaining my mother's whereabouts. What I do remember is feeling betrayed and guilty: She'd abandoned me, yet maybe I should have kept a more watchful eye over her.

Was that how it felt to be a motherless child? Missing in a crowd with no one looking for you? Wondering if it was your fault for getting lost?

At every parent–teacher conference Charlie and I attended, as well as on every report card we received, our son's behavioral evaluation was the same: self-assured, energetic, eager to participate, but needed to demonstrate self-control, avoid side chatter, and stop fidgeting. Naturally, Charlie glowed, hearing only the compliments. I scowled, wanting disciplinary measures taken.

Loud and disruptive, Dash needed to be reined in, broken of his bad habits. I suggested he sit on his hands to keep from moving while his teacher was at the blackboard and pick a seat away from his friends so as not to get distracted. When the urge to socialize took hold, he should pull from his pants pocket a reminder that I had written: "NO TALKING IN CLASS."

Nothing worked. He remained rambunctious, playful, and pleased with himself. "Stop trying to change me," he dismissed. "I'm fine the way I am."

If he lost me, how fine would he feel about himself then?

I didn't want to be one of those mothers who died and took the kid with her, either literally or figuratively. I didn't want to kill my son's spirit. There was a self at risk greater than mine and I knew what I had to do to protect it. First put down my straw.

PART THREE

"Nothing's turned out as I expected it, Ashley," said Scarlett. "Nothing."

—*Friends Academy Yearbook (1979)*
  (Elizabeth Hayt quoting *Gone with the Wind*)

CHAPTER 13

THE DAY I HIT MY BOTTOM, I called the one person who I was certain would be there for me. Ever since Charlie moved out, my mother started acting like a mother, probably because I could no longer be anything more to her than a daughter. Now, with too many problems of my own, as well as my struggles with independence, I became more reliant on her, which righted our original reversal of roles. The irony didn't end there. She now turned to my father for support and partnership, the dissolution of my marriage helping to restore theirs.

"Can you come over right now?" I asked her. "There's something I have to tell you."

"Can't it wait?" She was in her SoHo studio. "I'm gluing a mink penis bone to a dogfish shark jaw. Oh, shit, I can't find the epoxy. Oops, it's stuck to my pants."

"I know your art is important but please, it's an emergency."

Obviously, I was not in my right mind. Didn't even think to question the penis bone.

Dash would be home from school any minute. I didn't want him to know his mother was such a mess that she needed to be steam-cleaned out of the carpet. Hearing the charge of his footsteps in the hallway, I threw an emotional deadbolt across my bedroom door: "I'm working, sweetie, I'll be done soon."

"*Venga,* Dash," said Franci, his new babysitter, pulling him into his room, sensing it best not to disturb me. She was Colombian and the primary language in my household was now Spanglish.

When my mother arrived, her entrance was met with gleeful whooping and hollering. Even though she loved each of her five grandchildren, Dash held a special place in her heart because he was not only the firstborn but also mine. After disentangling herself from his chimpanzee clutches, she tapped my bedroom door.

"I have a problem," I started, my lower lip trembling, the waterworks already flowing. "A really bad problem. Will you help me no matter what?"

"Of course. But what could be so bad?"

With my back to her, I began my soliloquy, the first time I uttered aloud the words, "I'm a cocaine addict." If I faced her, the sight of her brow latticed with worry lines would make me falter. She really could use some Botox.

At first, she was unable to comprehend how her functioning daughter, who never missed a monthly facial and worked for the world's preeminent museum of modern art, could sustain a drug habit without anyone knowing. I did not fit her idea of a doper. She challenged whether I was really hooked, wondering why, if I recognized what I was doing was wrong, couldn't I just quit?

"Remember how you were as a smoker before you gave it up? I want to stop and know I should but I can't. The urge is too strong to fight."

"Have you told Diane?"

Diane was my shrink, a no-nonsense, supersmart doctor who did more than time-travel with a patient to relive childhood traumas. She offered feedback and strategies. But after so many years of telling my story to one psychiatrist or another, I was desensitized to the process. I couldn't seem to progress to a point of being truly happy with myself, whatever being happy with myself even meant. Maybe just getting through each day without wishing Dr. Kevorkian would pay me a visit was as good as my life could ever get. Of course, part of my problem was never admitting The Problem.

To confess I was a drug addict would be to confront how profoundly I had failed and how far I had to go to set myself straight. Humiliating and daunting, it was a truth I avoided until my destiny presented itself as Peruvian poisoning and a pine box.

Remaining calm but serious, my mother insisted I make an emergency appointment with Diane. If I couldn't afford the cost of whatever therapy she prescribed, my mother would cover it. In the meantime, I flushed my coke down the can and called my MoMA boss, explaining that since my husband moved out, I'd become clinically depressed and needed a medical leave from work. She readily agreed. Her husband was a psychoanalyst and she had great respect for suicidal tendencies.

"It's a positive sign that you initiated taking time off from your job," Diane said when I arrived at her office the next day. "You didn't get fired. It shows that you appreciate the seriousness of your problem."

Does that make me a good drug addict? Because I'm always looking for approval.

"Maybe my problem isn't as bad as I think," I said. "It was only recently that my use began to escalate. Before that I only did it to write, secretly, without telling anyone."

"You used cocaine like a drug or medicine," she analyzed. "Because it's a stimulant, a lot of people find it can help them focus. But eventually they get into trouble. For someone like you, who also has a tendency toward depression, it's a really bad thing because there's a tremendous crash after the high."

Eighteen years of denial instantly dissolved like the Wicked Witch of the West into a puddle of scum.

"That's why I left Cornell," I confessed. "It wasn't to chase after a sex guru in Des Moines. It was because the pressure at school was so intense and I was doing coke all the time. It was the same with the Institute and my PhD. I was afraid of writing a dissertation. How could I? Spend a year high on coke? It would be lethal. I guess I need to go away to detox, right?"

"I don't advise that. You're a single mother with a young child and his father has joint custody. The price would be high. He might say you're unfit. Child Welfare Services could take your son away."

Unfit? Child Welfare Services? Take my son away? But I'm a Jewish girl from Great Neck!

The last thing I ever expected was to wind up a case file. So, during the hours Dash was in school, I started attending daily Cocaine Anonymous meetings and therapy sessions every other day with Diane. I counted on my mother for support, along with a handful of friends in whom I confided. Feeling fragile, as if my bones had thinned, I moved cautiously, hesitating to cross streets and use revolving doors. At a supermarket or faced with a restaurant menu, I was tentative making choices, unable to trust my judgment.

My dopamine levels did a nosedive. To make it through a day was as laborious as swimming across an aquamarine lake with rocks tied to my ankles. There seemed to be a constant grating behind my sternum, as if a litter of baby mice were trying to scratch their way out. I felt fidgety and paralyzed at the same time. To get out of a chair demanded Herculean strength. Even the act of speaking was so taxing, I limited myself to the most minimal exchanges.

Diane prescribed twenty milligrams of Prozac. It took a few weeks before my bleakness and agitation began to ebb. My smile muscles, which seemed to have atrophied during my whiteout, came back. Although my cravings for a powdered pick-me-up continued, my lows became less so. I had new appreciation for the term *drug intervention*. For me, it came in the form of an SSRI.

· · ·

Dix was part of my recovery program. He was a fitness guru at Reebok Sports Club/NY on Columbus Avenue and 67th Street, a Bellagio of fitness with a red-carpet membership, including Matt Dillon, Demi Moore, and George Clooney. Because I'd been too strung out to practice Tae Kwon Do while I was doing drugs, my mother agreed to pay for a trainer so I could ease back in to physical shape. Knowing her, I'm sure she was also hoping I'd meet Mr. Right wheezing on side-by-side StairMasters.

I always imagined a trainer to be a gorgeous chunk of granite but Dix was closer to a cyborg. Neither masculine nor feminine, he seemed more android than androgynous. His skin was luminescent, his hair peroxide blond showing dark roots, and his eyes two different colors, one hazel, the other brown, which, though rare in humans, is fairly common in inbred strains of dogs, like malamutes.

Everything about him was pointy: the shape of his head, nose, lips, cheekbones, chin, and joint bones. He moved like a keyboard cursor, gliding left, right, and spinning around a room. He wore a white zip-front jumpsuit, which looked as if it was biohazard-contamination-proof.

"Why is it so hard to get an appointment with you?" I was his last client of the day; I had booked a session on Friday evening, when Dash would be at Charlie's, so that I wouldn't have to cut short my leg lifts in order to rush home to my son.

"I'm awesome." Dix grinned diabolically, revealing tetracycline-stained teeth, overlapping like roof shingles. His smile screamed out for cosmetic dentistry. "Now take off your watch. With me, you commit to your body, not the clock."

Inspired by ancient Greek athletes, he had created a so-called Hellenic workout, forbidding the use of advanced technological systems. The only modern device permitted was hydraulic—a water fountain.

His routine came in two parts. The first half included jumping jacks, jumping rope, and long jumping, both standing in place and from a running start. I had to jump on one foot, then the other. I jumped in hula hoops arranged in a circle. I jumped with my hands on my head, waist, and thighs. Luckily, I had protected my jugs with both a Jogbra and an Ace bandage that I'd wrapped around my chest like Yentl—Barbra Streisand masquerading as a yeshiva boy.

The second part of the workout involved a medicine ball. Holding the five-pound orb, I squatted, lunged, swung it overhead, as well as between my legs and back again. The session ended with a game of "catch." When Dix tossed me the ball, I collapsed.

My sweat-drenched T-shirt and shorts were glued to the floor mat. My Frédéric Fekkai layered haircut was now flat and frizzy from perspiration. The only thing worse than the way I looked was how I felt.

"Honey, what's wrong?" Dix asked when he saw tears running from my eyes. "Don't feel bad just because you're out of shape. You need more cardio, that's all."

Maybe it was the intimacy of being alone in a room with a man, or maybe I was too debilitated to activate my usual deflector shields, but out poured everything: my marriage ending, my money worries, my sexploits, my lackluster jobs, my maternal self-doubt, my squandered opportunities, my identification with a woman I didn't know who'd killed herself, and, finally, my free fall into drugs.

A client confiding in her trainer was nothing new, but having an all-out breakdown? Surely that was more than Dix bargained for, even at $150 a pop.

"Do you want me to take you to a meeting?" he asked, clasping my hands in his as I looked at him with very stunned eyes.

• • •

Born Virgil Philpott in 1959, Dix grew up in Ridgeway, Virginia—population roughly seven hundred. He was familiar with the slippery ropes of recovery but more so, with the stranglehold of addiction. His father had fallen into an elevator shaft at the Pannill Knitting Company, where he was a maintenance engineer. The accident left him disabled and depressed. He started drinking and got violent; his wife ran off to Florida, where she changed her name and become a migrant orange picker. She left behind her then thirteen-year-old son, Dix, without so much as a backward glance.

Two years later, his father died of liver disease and Dix was left in the care of his grandfather, who had been residing with the family. Congenitally cross-eyed, the grandfather was too poor to afford an operation to correct his vision. He also had Charcot-Marie-Tooth syndrome, an inherited neurological disorder atrophying his lower legs, which appeared like a stork's. Wheelchair-bound, he passed his days with a tray table on his lap, dipping into a pouch of Red Man chewing tobacco, a jar of Planters peanuts, and a fifth of Jack Daniel's. At night, he peed into a slop pot.

Throughout high school, Dix rose at four AM to work the early-morning shift at Biscuitville before school. Sometimes he skipped classes to ride his dirt bike to the Martinsville Speedway, where NASCAR races were held. In the afternoon, he retreated to his basement, where he'd built a gym outfitted with mail-order equipment from a muscle magazine.

In the evening, he hung around the King's Grocery Store parking lot, drinking free Pabst Blue Ribbon courtesy of the cashier, his plump and permed girlfriend, Sharon. The day after graduation, they got married and she moved into Dix's house; the newlyweds claimed the master bedroom, kicking Grandpa out. One night, asleep in his wheelchair in the hallway, he somehow rolled into a wall. In the morning, he was found dead.

Dix never cried after his mother's abandonment and, on the day of his father's death, he stood on an overpass above Route 220, throwing rotten tomatoes at the cars below. But at his grandfather's funeral, years of dammed-up sorrow broke free. He ripped the preacher's robe, blaspheming God and the horseshit of heavenly reunion.

"At least I have you," Dix said, weeping into Sharon's neck.

Not for long. She started screwing a skinhead art student at a nearby community college. When Dix found out, he stole her El Camino and drove cross-country to California. By the time his divorce came through, he was teaching aerobics in Beverly Hills at Jane Fonda's Workout Studio where women in Lycra leotards, cinch belts, and leg warmers flocked to his class, loving his Southern twang. His regulars started calling him "Dixie." The name stuck, though in time it was shortened to Dix.

"I'm never going to get married again," he said to me, recounting his life while we ate at Lenge, an Upper West Side Japanese restaurant. Because I had been so upset at the end of my training session, he suggested I join him for dinner.

"There's no reason for marriage unless it's to have kids," he continued. "Too many cripples run in my family so why bring more into the world? Besides, I don't want the responsibility of being someone's old man. If I ever knocked up a chick, I'd take out the coat hanger. Better yet, I'm going to get myself fixed."

I didn't know whether to be offended or laugh uproariously. I'd never met anyone who could make a right-wing shock jock sound enlightened and humane.

"Nice shade of lipstick," Dix complimented, watching me apply Chanel Matador Red after the meal. "Pass it over."

"Huh?"

"Let me have your lipstick."

Requesting a knife from the waiter, Dix used the shiny blade as a mirror, painting his mouth. "One of my clients did my colors and she said I'm an autumn. But this lipstick is really for winters. Can I get away with it?"

He pursed his lips, batting his lashes.

"The waiter can't stop staring," I whispered.

"He's probably a fruit. What do you think he'd say if he knew I was wearing a thong?"

When we left the restaurant, Dix offered to walk me home.

"Do you think that man over there is embarrassed?" Dix asked, pointing to a well-dressed Maltese owner wrapping his hand in a

Baggie before bending over to clean up after his dog. "I bet that turd feels hot in his hand."

"I can't believe you just said that," I said, suppressing the urge to crack up. In truth, I was thinking the very same thing, imagining myself performing similar sanitation duty.

Detouring to a side street, Dix stopped in front of a neo-Federal-style town house with a brick facade. There was money written all over it.

"That's what I want," he announced.

"Me, too. Along with a summer estate in Southampton, a pied-à-terre in Paris, and a winter villa in Anguilla."

"No, I really mean it. I'm going to have my own club someday in a place just like this."

"Oh, yeah? How? It's a fortune. You're just one guy working out of a gym."

"Oh, that's only temporary." He spoke quickly. "After fifteen years, I make good money and I've saved every penny. Between LA and New York, I've got clients with deep pockets. They could be potential investors or silent partners. I'm working on a business plan right now."

Dix narrowed his eyes at me. "Why, are you saying I shouldn't think big?"

"Not at all," I answered. "Unless you want your tombstone to read DIED AN EMPLOYEE, go for it."

At that instant, a pouty-lipped blond glamazon nearly caused a taxi collision as she sprinted across the middle of the street toward us.

"Ich kann nicht glauben!" she exclaimed, throwing herself into Dix's arms. *"Du hiere in Madison Avenue? Also, nicht mehr Los Angeles? Es ist ja so lange zeit wir haben uns gesehen! Was machst du?"*

She was Claudia Schiffer. Her presence was so stunning, I wanted to fold up my vertebrae and scurry into a narrow drainpipe. No chance. Dix immediately introduced us, which led to yet another surprise.

Even though he and I supposedly communicated in the same tongue, my Yankee ears could not decipher his redneck diction. His English was as sonorous as a gardening rake against concrete. But when he broke into German to converse with Schiffer, his speaking skills were magically transformed into *Die Fledermaus.*

"How did you become fluent?" I asked, resuming our walk.

"I read a lot."

"In German? That's impressive. Which authors?"

"Not the authors. The dictionary."

"How can you 'read' a dictionary? And why?"

"My mother's side was German and I wanted to learn the language of my ancestors. I'm good at methodical tasks. They have a calming effect, like meditation."

Next, a vagrant wearing only a Hefty bag and gray socks blocked our path.

"Hey man!" he greeted, knuckle-tapping Dix. "Long time. Gotta come see you. Near got me a 'fro."

"You know my schedule, blood. First Wednesday night of every month."

Grabbing his woolly tufts in each of his hands, the man nodded, ambling back to his perch on the Madison Avenue Presbyterian Church steps.

"He's a client?" I asked Dix, my mouth in an O-shape of shock.

"Back when I was in LA, I went to work for The Sports Club. They have a beauty salon and one of the stylists taught me how to cut hair. I'm not great but I do it for the homeless at the Graffiti Church at Tompkins Square. Jesus said, 'Sell that which ye hath and give to the poor.' "

Does Jesus offer advice about Barbicide?

Between our surreal dialogue and Dix's supermodel-to-soup-kitchen street encounters, the thirty-block journey to my apartment left my brain like an upside-down snow globe. When we finally arrived at my building, he followed me upstairs. I had no idea what was in store.

The dogs took to him right away. Or rather he took to them. While many pet owners (present company included) have no problem French-kissing their own pooches, it tends to trigger a gag reflex in strangers. Splaying himself on the living room carpet, arms and legs extended like a pinwheel, Dix not only allowed my animals to lap at his face but licked them back. I wondered if he were really one of those boy orphans raised by wolves.

"Come here," he said, pulling me toward him on the floor. "I've always gone for women who were out of my league."

"I'm confused." I jerked away after he kissed my mouth, jabbing his tongue inside. "Aren't you gay?"

"Why would you think that?"

"The business with the lipstick and the thong."

"You seem too smart to be so narrow-minded. You think only a guy who swings his dick and acts like a stiff and plays football can be straight? It only means he's afraid of being queer. Classic gay-basher mentality."

Dix had a point. I knew firsthand how false appearances could be and the extent to which a person might go to cover up the truth. Wasn't it possible for a man to desire women while winking at sexual stereotypes? It could be a sign of true security with his masculinity, which, in that case, was very sexy. Then again, it could indicate my Sonia Rykiel knitwear was in jeopardy because a cross-dressing trainer was planning to squeeze into it.

I reminded myself that Sam Walton started out in Kingfisher, Oklahoma, as a JCPenney management trainee, eventually building the largest retail empire in the world. He drove to work, wearing a baseball cap, in a Ford pickup with his dog, Ol' Roy, riding shotgun. Who was to say Virgil "Dix" Philpott of Ridgeway, Virginia, couldn't market his name and become the next Body by Jake?

I knew I should rely on a romantic surge protector for my heart. Although Dix didn't drink or drug, he knew all about recovery because of his father. Veterans of Twelve Step programs consistently warned that early sobriety was a vulnerable time and to avoid "Thirteen Stepping," or being seduced by a senior member. Abstinence was also an opportunity for me to put into practice the lessons I'd learned since becoming single.

"I'm not going to sleep with you tonight," I announced. "I always get attached when I do that. Let's wait to—"

"Don't spoil the moment," he silenced, covering my mouth with his.

Shit. Appealing to my sense of spontaneity. Nice move.

"Well, then, there's something else you should know," I hedged. "Ten days ago, I had an operation, a small benign tumor removed from my breast. I still look pretty beaten up."

"Can I see it?" Dix requested.

Can you see it?

Four years earlier, I'd had a lumpectomy, which was also negative. After the surgery, I begged Charlie to look because I was too scared to see the damage. Unable to stomach the gore, he fled the room. Now Dix, a guy I didn't even know, was actually *requesting* a viewing.

"At your own risk," I exhaled, unbuttoning my blouse, removing my bra, and peeling off a fresh gauze bandage, which I'd taped on just before leaving the gym. Although the Ace bandage served its purpose during my workout, keeping my parts where the surgeon originally placed them, I shut my eyes, held my breath, and waited for Dix to request a Dramamine.

"To me, there's nothing sexier than a woman with scars," he said, planting a half-moon of tiny kisses along the edge of my nipple, one for each of the ugly black stitches.

CHAPTER 14

*I*T WAS A SATURDAY AFTERNOON in December. Dix had taken me to a Jivamukti class followed by a wheatgrass at a juice bar to wash down blue-green algae capsules. Returning to my apartment, he candled my ears before we enacted the Sanskrit meaning of *yoga* as "union." I assumed a Downward Facing Dog pose while he did me doggy-style.

Dix decided my buildup of bodily toxins could never be released without his version of a colonic: a good ass fucking. As I lay facedown on my bed, he kneeled behind me. Spreading apart my cheeks, he took his time scrutinizing my puckered orifice, stretching the skin between his fingers. I felt entirely exposed and tried to constrict the muscle in protest. He split my buttocks even wider, letting a teardrop of spit fall from his mouth and run to my crack, creating a slick trail from butt to pussy hole. Reaching around, I grabbed his cock, lifting my hips to back into it. This was a maneuver Dix called "stump training," the same as when a horse breeder foals a mare by coaxing her hindquarters into a stallion.

Never an overeager stud, Dix had a remarkable ability to allow his prick to soften ever so slightly so that a woman could accept its infiltration. Exhaling, I relaxed my sphincter, allowing him to penetrate a millimeter at a time. I gasped sharply when he hit a point of resistance. Plying on, he felt like a hot lance cutting through me. To ease the pain, he slid his hand under my pubic mound, frigging my cunt and strumming my clit. My bottom started to gyrate.

Bracing my shoulders against the bed, Dix fissured my rectum with the entire length of his cock, his thrusts punctuated by a succulent sound, the smacking of his balls against the slimy opening of my pussy. I was at his mercy, my trust never so great. If he had reamed too hard, he would have pushed me over the edge to agony. Instead he used his cock like a matchstick, sparking my nerve endings without quite setting them aflame, magically holding me at the brink of ecstasy. Reaching between my legs, I ground his hand into my pussy. The mauling felt divine.

With one heartless stroke, he burrowed into my bowels. I let out an animal cry, clamping my cheeks together, locking his member in my viscera, the final pollution of pleasure. Timing his climax to mine, Dix deposited a rich paste, the salve for my soreness soon to set in. I sank facedown into the mattress, quivers threading over my skin as he rolled off my back onto his, a trickle of nicotine-tinged warmth discharging from me. Soiled and smelly, we lay like that for a long while.

"Where is this headed?" I asked, basking in whatever brain chemicals make a female seek postbuggery proclamations of love.

"Where is what headed?"

"This. Us."

"I don't know what you mean by *headed*. Are we going somewhere?"

"Stop fucking with me."

"You just said you didn't want me to ever stop fucking you."

"Why are you reducing what I'm saying to a joke? We've been together two months."

"Chill out, okay? We took HIV tests together and have unprotected sex. What does that tell you? I'm here now, aren't I? I can't give you more of a commitment than that."

Forget the long term; even the short term was impossible to plan with Dix. He was now working independently, having quit his job at Reebok. From six AM to ten PM, seven days a week, he was booked back-to-back with private clients. After his last session, he sometimes dropped by my apartment. By then, Dash was fast asleep, and if it weren't for *Law and Order* reruns I would have been, too.

"This is not a real relationship," I continued. "During the week, we can't spend the night together because Dash is here and on weekends, you're catatonic. I want to get dressed up and go out with my boyfriend. It was like this with Charlie. You're unavailable but you're not even my husband. Why am I doing this?"

"I need a woman who is going to be supportive, not have a JAP attack just because everything doesn't happen her way. I stand on my feet fourteen hours a day, making other people feel good, dealing with demanding women. *Dix, I'm not seeing a difference,*" he mimicked, his voice pinched and whiny. "*Dix, do I need lipo?* After putting up with them, there's you."

"You make it sound like I'm a punishment."

"I want to start my own business. You have no clue the pressure I'm under."

"You want me to behave like a wife and stand by you. What do I get out of it?"

"What you want is a man to take care of you. I'm not that guy. It's not in my programming. Even though you talk feminist shit, you expect a husband to pay for you. And you already have that."

Dix hit the bull's-eye: my ongoing financial dependence on Charlie. His divorce rumblings had quieted down for now. I had no idea why but wasn't about to ask, knowing better than to look a gift horse in the mouth. Although I was still officially on leave from MoMA, I did occasional gallery lectures, gigs that earned me so little—seventy-five dollars—the paychecks barely amounted to more than my Chase Manhattan monthly banking fees.

Working part-time allowed me to remain on call for Dash, a

damn good reason to continue benefiting from Charlie's largesse. But Dix's attitude made me question whether I wasn't really looking for an excuse for my lack of career advancement. Was I afraid of taking a leap forward because I might never get anywhere?

"Positive thinking creates positive results," he said. "Jesus said, 'If ye have faith as a grain of mustard seed, ye shall move mountains.'"

"I don't even know what that means," I sulked.

"If you want success, you can't think about failure. Only people who believe they're going to make money end up making money. Look at me."

Dix had no modesty when it came to announcing his yearly earnings: a six-figure income that included plenty of cash. Whenever he reached into his pockets, the bills went flying. There was no need for ATM withdrawals because he kept his green hidden around his apartment—in photo albums and freezer containers. If I hadn't witnessed with my own eyes the perfectly legal contents of his gym bag, I would have suspected my boyfriend was a Cali cartel member.

Dix had no interest in spending his cash on me, however. After leaving Reebok, he immediately incorporated himself as a business. In addition to IRAs, a 401(k), and money market funds, he'd picked up plenty of financial tips from his clients over the years, investing in mutual funds, stocks, and real estate ventures. In truth, he cared more about the S&P 500 Index increasing than he did about anyone's body mass index decreasing.

"Why is it so important I make money?" I said in a small voice. "You're always bragging you earn more than a lot of doctors and lawyers, so what's the big deal about supporting me?"

"I can't afford you," he said. "Make something of yourself first and then we'll talk."

"Make something of myself?" I bristled. "What do you call four years of graduate school, working at MoMA, being a wife, a mother, a teacher, an art critic, running a home, and recovering from a drug addiction? I've done a lot with my life. Are you saying I'm nothing?"

"No. I'm saying become someone. Then you'll know what you want. And maybe it won't be me."

• • •

My MoMA boss was badgering me. When she had agreed to my leave, it was on condition that I complete a teacher slide set about modern art and images of war before the end of the year. I was procrastinating. Although I had done similar things before, this time was different. Now I was drug-free.

"I don't know how to do it," I complained to Susan, my former co-critic and dear friend from grad school, who had recently landed a job as an art magazine editor in Los Angeles. "Now that I'm off coke, I'm terrified if I sit down and try to write, nothing will come out because it was only the blow talking."

"I have an idea," she said. "Why don't you write a review for me? I think you'd be a fantastic person to cover Paul McCarthy's show."

McCarthy was a performance and installation artist whose raunchy, scatological humor found full expression in hot dogs, fudge, and Miracle Whip.

"Since we're friends, the pressure won't be so great," she counseled. "You'll write one sentence at a time and take a break to stretch your legs. Call whenever you need me."

It was a writer-on-a-walker approach to recovery. Every time I reached the end of a paragraph, it felt like a rehab milestone. Upon completion of the victory lap, I phoned Susan to announce I'd crossed the five-hundred-word finish line.

"I knew you had it in you!" she cheered after I read my piece aloud. "You did a great job. You brought a lot of energy and humor to it. I'm so happy you've turned yourself around."

I had to admit I enjoyed doing the review, my voice gaining an unexpected timbre of directness and sarcasm now that Charlie was no longer my literary model.

As a litigator, he was trained to win with words. Trying to emulate him, I wanted to sound as smart, to be logical and analytical. For papers in college and graduate school, I had relied on him for editing. Now, without him around, I couldn't count on his red pen. I realized all my years of turning to him for help had gradually eroded my self-confidence. The assignment from Susan had been my chance to start over, to prove I could write solo and sober.

Since I'd never been a nine-to-five type anyway, I made a decision. The minute I finished the MoMA slide set, I would forfeit my laminated ID card. The next time I entered the museum, it would be as a visitor.

Yes, I wanted to be a real writer. I'd always been accused of self-absorption, and the craft was a productive way to get lost in my own thoughts, translating flights of fancy into the tangible and comprehensible. But making writing a full-time job meant I needed not only an assembly line of ideas but also a Rolodex of contacts.

"Luck is where preparation meets opportunity," Dix advised. "Get your name out there and it will happen."

A dealer friend of mine said *The New York Observer* was looking for a contemporary art critic, a countervoice to their conservative columnist Hilton Kramer.

"We'll give you a try on spec," said the newspaper's managing editor.

"What's *speck*?"

"You don't know what *on spec* is? It means you cover five gallery shows in fifteen hundred words without agreeing to a fee in advance. Hand in the copy and I'll let you know."

She never even bothered to send a rejection letter for my pieces.

Next, I contacted *Vogue*.

"Hi, this is Elizabeth Hayt and I'm calling to pitch a story about a young generation of female political artists," I said, running off half a dozen up-and-coming names. I was hoping if I didn't stop to take a breath, the features editor—one of Anna Wintour's caddies—wouldn't hang up on me.

"E-liz-a-beth," he said, enunciating each syllable, pronouncing with a sibilant hiss the *z* in my name, as he did any word with an *s*. "An-na hates po-li-ti-cal art."

"Maybe if I wrote up a proposal and you showed it to her she—"

"Did you hear me? *No.*"

Guess what appeared in the magazine three months later? An article about young women artists creating personal art with a political message written by none other than that snake editor.

With each rejection, I took to my bed, clutching my little dogs. What was I thinking, starting a writing career when professionals ten years younger already held staff positions and six-figure book deals? Why would an editor take a chance on me?

Ordering a subscription to the *American Kennel Club Gazette,* I was contemplating a different direction entirely—dachshund breeding—when an out-of-the-blue phone call proved my pessimism was premature.

"Hi, I'm Mitch Owens, a reporter for the Home Section of *The New York Times*," my caller said. "I got your name from an art gallery. They said you knew something about a salad plate by the artist Damien Hirst. It's supposed to look like an ashtray. I'd like to run an item about it and was wondering if you'd mind helping me out."

"Sure. Last spring, I wrote about the plate for *Elle Decor* but they never ran it. The piece is dead now so you can use whatever you want. It's short. I can just read it to you over the phone."

By the end, he was laughing. "Have you ever thought of writing for us?"

It was my turn to laugh.

"You should," he said. "You're good. Do you have any ideas?"

• • •

Earlier that autumn, Dix and I had spent a weekend in York Harbor, Maine. He had reserved a suite in a majestic colonial inn overlooking the rocky coast. Because he rarely took time off from work, I was hoping for an airbrushed getaway: windy seaside strolls in bulky sweaters, steaming bowls of fish chowder, and lots of lazing in an antique brass bed.

Dix had a very different plan: a visit to Sentry Hill Quilts. I hated quilts, which reminded me of grody bed-and-breakfasts where spiders crawled across your pillow and innkeepers straight out of *The Shining* served homemade scones with suspicious cheer.

But I wanted to be a part of Dix's life, to understand and support his passion. Before his mother ran away, she worked at Pannill Knitting as a "linthead," one of the female employees who sewed sweatpants, for which she was paid by the piece. After her shift, she made stuffed animals out of cast-off factory scraps and cut-up, worn-out clothes. She sold the toys in the basement of her church after Sunday-morning services to help raise funds.

It pained Dix that he had no keepsake of her handiwork, which led to his fetish for quilts. An avid collector, he crowded them into his apartment, a six-hundred-square-foot fifth-floor Chelsea walk-up. Engineering a system of wall-mounted rods affixed with giant metal clips, he hung the coverlets from the ceiling like rows of Oriental carpets. His bed had to fight for space between the kitchen stove and sink.

Our first stop in York Harbor was a mustard farmhouse graced with an American flag. At the sound of tires crunching the gravel driveway, Betsey Oates—middle-aged, broad in the back, and very bosomy—threw open the front door.

"What are we dreaming about today, Dix?"

She led us to a timber-frame barn, a Bed Bath & Beyond of

quilts stacked floor-to-ceiling. "Log Cabins?" she gestured. "Pineapple Patterns? Flying Geese? I've been hiding this one especially for you. An heirloom from a Hancock descendant. Stowed in a trunk. Never been put up for sale. Have you ever seen such crewelwork? Plaid wool! Calico center medallion! Twenty-one-step dyeing process! I'll give it to you for fifty percent off: nineteen hundred dollars."

Wasn't it P. T. Barnum who said, "There's a sucker born every minute"?

Three hours later, the sun was setting, I was starving, and on the floor were three piles of quilts: "definites," "maybes," and "rejects."

Dix's inability to commit to a relationship was part of a bigger problem: an inability to commit to anything at all.

"So what do you think?" Dix asked me, his pupils dilated and white sediment encrusting the corners of his lips.

"I think the same thing now that I did an hour ago. Take the Double Wedding Ring quilt with the Prairie Point edging, as well as the Mariner's Compass."

I can't believe I've been here so long, I actually know the names of these fucking rags.

"Why?"

"I told you why. Or you told me. The workmanship."

"But what about the Victorian Crazy Quilt made of men's ascots? It's got a lot of gold. My favorite color."

"Okay, that one, too."

"That's a lot of coin. And I still won't have any fine whiteworks that show off the quality of the quilter's needlework."

"So forget the Mariner's Compass."

"Forget the Mariner's Compass? Don't you appreciate the precision of its curved forms and fine tips? I can't let that go."

"I don't know what to tell you anymore," I moaned. "I don't know. I don't know-oh-oh-oh."

This must be how Team Delta military interrogators get detainees to crack.

Goddamn Betsey wasn't weakening at all.

"You can spend as long as you want," she reassured. "Once you have me, you have me."

Like genital herpes.

"I'm going to sleep on it and come back tomorrow," Dix decided.

And that was how my boyfriend and I spent our romantic weekend: playing three-card monte with bales of used bedspreads, looking for an ace of spades of stitchery. Our Sunday flight was not until evening. By that morning, I was begging to leave early.

"You can take a taxi to the airport because I'm not going," he said. "I told you I was coming here to buy quilts and you wanted to come along. If it were up to me, we'd be at the Days Inn, not a three-hundred-fifty-dollar-a-night room, which I only agreed to to keep your pampered ass happy."

I could never anticipate what Dix had the wallet for. He tipped taxi drivers ten dollars but fired his housekeeper, who had been cleaning his place twice monthly for years, after she upped her forty-five-dollar fee by five dollars. He surprised me with a Miele Silver Moon canister vacuum that must have cost a grand yet pitched a fit at Le Colonial when the dinner bill came to $160.

"I'm sorry for behaving like a brat," I said, regretting I was so spoiled. "I'm a little tired, that's all. I know choosing the right quilt is important to you."

Sympathizing with a captor? It's called the Stockholm syndrome. How long before I wear a beret, hold up a bank, and rename myself Tania?

En route to the airport, Dix made a final stop at Betsey's just in case there was an item he'd overlooked. Of course, the only thing he missed was our plane. A dozen quilts and fifty G's later, he wound up with the entire lot. And I, after a three-hour standby wait at the terminal, was left with a new perspective on the Lord's work.

• • •

"What do you think of a story about quilts as collectibles?" I asked Mitch, the *Times* reporter. "There's a woman in Maine who has four hundred in a barn. Some are pretty valuable. More than twenty thousand dollars. They tell American history. Slave quilts, pioneer quilts, political quilts."

"I love quilts. Write up a pitch and I'll pass it on to my editor."

A week later, no answer. A month later, still no answer. Another month? Nope. Did I wait and play it cool? Of course not. Every Monday for two months straight, I called, leaving the same voice mail: "Hi, this is Elizabeth Hayt. I'm following up on a story idea I submitted . . ."

"Did you 'Mitchell' today?" Dix asked, now referring to my hounding of the man as a verb.

Eventually, I gave up, assuming my proposal was rejected, and instead offered it to *Art & Auction,* for which they would pay a thousand dollars. I happily signed a contract, knowing beggars couldn't be choosers.

Or could they?

"Is this Elizabeth Hayatt?" asked a female voice when I answered my phone. "I'm the editor of the Home Section. I hear you're writing a story for us about quilts. We need it by next week? Fifteen hundred words for five hundred dollars, okay?"

The editor of the Home Section? What about Art & Auction? *I can't afford to make enemies. But I also can't afford to turn down* The New York Times. *Five hundred bucks less but worth a fortune.*

"Uh, of course, no problem, next week, fifteen hundred words."

After I explained my predicament to *Art & Auction*, they were remarkably forgiving. In fact, they wished me well, leaving the door open. "Anytime you have another idea for us . . ."

"You see?" Dix said, when I called to tell him the news. "I told you it would happen if you kept your faith. 'Go thy way; and as thou has believed, so be it done unto thee.' Now aren't you sorry you gave me shit about the quilts? Thanks to me, you're writing for *The New York Times*."

I was silent, not wanting to give him the satisfaction. However, later, when enough hours had passed and he arrived at my apartment after work, I, like vassal to liege, expressed my thanks, going so far as to credit Dix's faith in me for my lucky break.

In the end, though, my story never ran. I should have taken it as a sign. Just because you're kissing someone's ass doesn't mean you have to kiss his ring, too.

CHAPTER 15

I REFUSED TO THROW IN THE TOWEL. Despite not getting a hit, my chance to play in the big leagues spurred me to try harder. I was a natural reporter. Neither a snoop nor a people person at heart—key attributes for a newsperson—I did possess excessive candor. Though derided by some (Charlie) as a character deficit, and others (American Psychiatric Association) as symptomatic of a histrionic personality, the trait turned out to be a great asset for an interviewer. Granted, my subjects weren't national security risks, but I had an instinct for the right questions, ones that cut to the bone, never shying away from the personal. The result was colorful "human interest" stories, journalistic semantics for invasions of privacy with high entertainment value.

On a Friday night in early March 1997, my skill revealed itself at a Sabbath dinner in Flatbush at the home of Orthodox wig makers whose wares—made of human, rather than synthetic, hair—were advertised as the Rolls-Royces of head coverings. When my second breast lump appeared and I worried about the prospect of chemo, I befriended the family after purchasing one of their designs (another overreaction since the tumor was again benign).

The Sabbath table—formally set with a white Battenberg lace cloth, five lighted silver candelabra, and an Old World chalice—was a banquet of yellow foods: challah bread, gefilte fish, chicken soup,

roast chicken, potato kugel, and kasha varnishkes. If Dean Ornish
had been invited, the flagrant absence of high-fiber foods would
have caused his arteries to collapse on the spot.

Ashamed of my Judaic ignorance, I wished for an excuse more
ennobling than Americanization. Thankfully, out of the 613
mitzvahs—or commandments the Torah says Jews are obligated to
observe—one is to herd strays of my sort back to the flock, leading us out of biblical illiteracy.

When the table talk turned to the family's work in the weeks
ahead, I asked why the wig trade was shifting to high gear.

"It's the season," explained Claire, the Hungarian-born sixty-
something family matriarch in rhinestone-rimmed glasses, glitter
nail polish, and a Zsa Zsa blond wig. "Everyone wants a new wig
for Passover."

"How come?"

"Tradition. Just like you buy new clothes for spring, you buy a
new wig."

"Or wigs," chimed Chaya, one of her daughters. "Some people
buy more than one. We have a customer who has three on order."

"Why does she need three?"

"She doesn't *need* three. She *wants* three. They're all the same
color but different styles."

Shalom, Cher?

"How much was the most expensive wig you ever sold?" I
asked, knowing Claire's did not come cheap.

"Four thousand dollars," answered Chaya. "It was thirty-six
inches long. The length determines the price. And then, of course,
there's the cost of the cut on top of that. Some of our customers
go to famous hairdressers who charge several hundred dollars, like
Oribe."

Oribe? I'm sorry, but the words Orthodox wigs *and* Oribe—*a one-
name hair wonder with full-sleeve tattoos who was J.Lo's mane mascot—
do not belong in the same sentence.*

"Are you ever allowed to take it off?" I pressed.

"For your husband."

"Do . . . you . . . shave . . . your . . . heads?" I asked, fearful the question was taboo.

"Nah, that's for the Hasidim." Claire waved her hand as if swatting a gnat. "They're a different sect with different customs."

By the end of the meal, I knew I had a story. My sources would talk, the subject was fresh, and the topic timely. Now all I had to do was psych myself up and sell the idea.

In AA, they tell you to "act as if"—behave as if you're sober—to overcome any skepticism about the program and your ability to recover. The rationale is that in time, the act becomes reality. It was a method I adopted for *The New York Times:* pretend I was already one of them to get another assignment.

"Hi, I'm Elizabeth Hayt and I'm a contributor to the Home Section," I said, rehearsing my lines for Dix. "I have a proposal for the Sunday Styles Section. Orthodox Jewish women primping for Passover who buy expensive new wigs and go to celebrity hairdressers to cut them."

It was a go. On April 27, 1997, the Sunday before the beginning of a Jewish holiday celebrating freedom, and almost fifteen months after my marital separation, I played in The Show.

• • •

Having never taken a journalism course, I fudged my familiarity with editorial lingo—the "nut graf," "TK," the "lede," the "kicker." Not owning a computer, only an electric typewriter, I called my wig piece into the *Times*'s "recording room"—a service predating the Internet used by correspondents without telecommunications linkups to file stories. Reading mine over the phone into a tape machine, which would later be transcribed, I felt as outmoded as a World War II newsman. By my third assignment, I got up to speed and went modem.

It still astonishes me that a *Times* reporter could ever get away with fabricating stories, so closely were mine scrutinized. Perhaps because I was a freelancer rather than staff writer, no less than three different editors read over my work. And the copy desk did more than dot every *i* and cross every *t*. They were vicars of linguistic veracity, the pontiffs of what ultimately made it to print. Once, one staffer called me to fact-check a quote, challenging whether I really meant to use a comma instead of a period.

As a cub reporter, my lifetime of intellectual insecurity finally paid off. The last thing I wanted was to get caught with my pants down. To cover my ass, I cast the widest net possible, following leads that led me nowhere and hunting down sources of my sources.

It made no difference that my beat didn't reach the top of the news pyramid—war, politics, business, and crime. I took equal pride in exploring softer strata—arts, entertainment, personalities, and lifestyles—even if my pages wound up as birdcage liners. Overcoming my sense of being a nobody, I was building a future independent of a husband's. My life and work became one and the same. Everything I did, everywhere I went, and everyone I met now assumed new meaning: a potential story.

No matter how many times my byline appeared, it was always as exciting as that first Sunday morning when I heard the thud of the *Times* dropping outside my front door and I knew my name was in it. *"Extra! Extra! Hayt's in print!"*

Dix was just as enthused. He kept track of where and when my articles ran. On the street, I occasionally bumped into one of his clients, who reported that Dix constantly talked about my work. Whenever I was dry of ideas or disheartened because one of my pieces had been killed, he reminded me how far I'd come in such a short time.

While my drug cravings didn't die completely, every story renewed my strength to stay away from cocaine. Writing became my emotional chiropractor, keeping me adjusted. That, combined with convincing myself that God had a blacklist for certain members of the press and my name would appear on it in indelible ink if I ever used again, helped me to remain straight.

Sometimes the exposure of being a reporter got me into trouble. The flip side of my excessive frankness was a lack of self-restraint and a tendency to commit social bloopers.

"You're unintimidated," said Charlie in one of our infrequent conversations about something other than Dash. "Whether out of ignorance or audacity, you are initially unimpressed by social status and fame, which makes you willing to walk up to your sources and say something that might be insulting or makes you sound like an idiot."

One Saturday night, I was reporting on a story about Stella McCartney, daughter of Sir Paul, the Beatle, and, at that time, the fashion designer for Chloe. She and I met at Pastis, where we were ushered to a diesel power corner: Puff Daddy, Minnie Driver, Jerry Seinfeld, and Calvin Klein were all seated there, caught up in cross-table conversations.

The chumminess of the crowd was contagious. A renowned architect and Pritzker winner—one of the most important honors in the field—arrived, his distinctive shock of white hair making him immediately recognizable. Although we had never actually met, I took it upon myself to join the others in offering effusive greetings.

"Hi, I'm Elizabeth Hayt," I said proudly. "I write for *The New York Times.* I called you a couple of months ago to interview you about museum shows you were interested in seeing this fall. That was a great quote you gave me about Duchamp and Picasso."

Blank look.

"I just have to tell you that I went to Spain last month and visited Bilbao, where your museum changed my life," I gushed. "It was more transcendental than seeing the Sistine ceiling. You. Are. A. Genius."

"That's true, miss. But you're thinking of the other guy."

"You mean you're not Frank Gehry?"

No, he was Richard Meier. Gehry was his archrival.

I spent the rest of the night trying to crawl my way out of the grave that I'd dug for myself. My only consolation came from my imagined epitaph: ANYTHING FOR FASHION. My story about Stella qualified as that.

Although my love for clothing was hardly a secret, I was unable to overcome my early-childhood indoctrination that caring about fashion was for the featherbrained. As a girl doodling ball gowns in the margins of a notebook, I shielded them with a hand so my parents and teachers wouldn't discover my forbidden desire. Thinking about garments was escapist, the cipher for my fictional transformation into a demoiselle more blithe than the suburban snot nose I was.

Attempting to put my mind to good use didn't get me very far, however. As an art history graduate student, I tried to dedicate myself to lofty interpretations of high culture, but it was toggery that kept my attention. In the library, I tucked *Vogue* between the pages of *Artforum* so I could surreptitiously study the latest looks on the Aspen slopes (not that I skied). It took more time for me to decide what to wear for an exam about Post-Impressionism (something low-cut, flouncy, black stockings, very Moulin Rouge) than to study for it.

To me, personal style was not only a form of self-expression and self-discipline but also a divine pursuit. Stepping into black fishnets and wrapping pearls around my neck were rituals of faith, testaments to believing a night on the town held miraculous promise.

While Charlie would leave the room rather than discuss raiment, Dix understood my enchantment. For him, dressing was an art of distinction, his taste leaning toward that of a psychedelic dandy. When he wasn't training in a flame-retardant bodysuit, he might be sporting a vintage swallowtail frock coat, dragon-print vest, colorful cravat, and jewel-toned velvet bell-bottoms. A top hat was the finishing touch.

Once I became a style writer, I was finally free to own up to the truth—how I looked was as important to me as what I was looking at. My afternoons of retail therapy could now be considered hands-on research. When Donna Karan happened to be in her

Madison Avenue boutique the day I strolled inside and she ordered me, unaware I was a member of the press, to put on a black bustier dress, personally dropping to her knees to pin the hem, my purchase was a reason to write about her salesmanship.

My true liberation occurred during a fall 1998 trip to Europe to interview a designer for the *Times*. At the Guy Laroche showroom on the Rue de la Tremoille, I met the creative director, Alber Elbaz, and marveled at the details of a hibiscus-red dress. It was printed with a large flower, the stem actually a trompe l'oeil construction out of a seam. That someone could care so much about something so small as a stitch brought tears to my eyes.

That was the moment I knew I was right where I belonged—Paris, the capital of haute couture, in an atelier surrounded by radiant frocks. I called my mother at once to announce I was ending my double life. All these years I'd been a lover of frippery trying to pose as an intellectual. It was time to burst out of the closet.

"Maybe you'd like to take up sewing?" She laughed.

• • •

Stephen King has said that every novelist has a single ideal reader in mind, a person for whom a story is written. For King, his wife, Tabitha, is that reader. Mine turned out to be my Styles Section editor, the first heterosexual male with whom I had an entirely professional relationship.

Resembling a boyish Marlboro Man, his looks were unexpectedly pleasing, his voice gravelly and measured. Though not without a sense of humor, he was a total cynic, as well as the least flirtatious, most buttoned-up family man you could ever meet.

Fair, honest, and even-tempered, he accepted stories only on the basis of merit. Because he avoided mind games and power trips, he gave me an opportunity to compete with more seasoned writers, though I produced little that seemed to impress him. My lack of experience made him skeptical of my skills and wary of my ideas. To grant me an assignment, he required convincing—examples, studies, polls, percentages, proof. No matter how many times he agreed to a pitch, the next one was never any easier. However, he was willing to offer guidance and approval, though the latter was always backhanded: "For someone who never took Journalism 101, you might have the makings of an ace reporter."

On April 18, 1999, just shy of two years to the day after my wig article ran, I wrote a piece for the Sunday Styles Section about a new generation of glamour-puss artists. By then, I had accumulated a stack of press clips, but this one landed on the top, "above the fold." The lead story. My first.

My mother temporarily lost the power of speech. Andrew offered a simple "Nice job," and Warren called from Florida (where he and his family were living) to inform me of his new celebrity-hood as my brother. When my father phoned, he told me some of his colleagues had asked if he was related to the "Hayt" who wrote for the *Times.*

"You've worked very hard," he added. "I'm proud of you."

Holy smoke, did he just use the P word?

I didn't think it was possible for things to get any better until I turned on my computer and the e-mail flag popped up. "You've come a long way, baby. From the wigs of Williamsburg to the sirens of SoHo. Congratulations."

I read the lines over and over in a vain attempt to find the scorn between them. The sender was my editor.

The following year, he put me on contract to write ten features. Between that and other freelance assignments, I was able to edge my individual income above the national average. It didn't qualify me as rich but at least I could support myself.

Well, in any city but Manhattan.

• • •

Scheduling my reporting and interviews from nine to five, I wrote after Dash went to bed when there were no calls, deliveries, and barking dogs to interrupt me. I was a nocturnal creature now, and my diurnal rhythm became synchronized to Dix's. Late at

night, after we were both done working, we unwound through
meaningless phone conversation.

"Is one of your feet bigger than the other?" he asked at four AM.

"Yes."

"Which one?"

"The left," I answered.

"Commonly the right is bigger. That's why they give you the
right foot first when you buy shoes."

"Which of yours is bigger?" I asked.

"My left most of the time but I've had the experience where
my right is bigger than my left."

"What do you think that means?"

"It leads me to believe I'm having a shift in foot size."

"And?"

"It's a phenomenon," he concluded.

The inanity of our communication expressed a mutual appreciation for the absurd, a sort of private language, like one shared by
dolphins. No other man besides Dix could understand the hours I
spent in my closet, trying on and creating outfits I'd never wear.
Other than me, in whom could he confide his worry that his eyebrows were thinning? He, a Confederate cracker, and I, a Long Island JAP, were a match, though admittedly a rather clumsy one.

As an enfant terrible, Dix had another ally in Dash, the two
sharing an equal appreciation for toilet humor.

"Did you just take a blowout dump?" the former asked the latter after he emerged from the bathroom.

"What's a blowout dump?" My son was laughing even before
hearing the answer.

"The kind that's preceded by a fart so vicious, you have to
check the bowl afterward to make sure there are no cracks."

Although Dix was hardly a model of maturity, I had no worries
about his negative influence on my son. Not only did they spend
minimal time together, I never referred to Dix as my "boyfriend"
or even held his hand in front of Dash. Why cause him Oedipal

anxiety when my future with Dix wasn't heading toward marriage? Better to limit their competition—to burping contests.

Still, Dash became an unintentional victim of my relationship with Dix, or rather our nightsomniac yakkety-yakking, which resulted in my keeping vampire hours. By the time I conked out, it was near dawn. When the clock struck seven AM, I behaved like Count Dracula, dead in his coffin, recoiling from the morning light. It fell on my young Renfield (who turned on the coffeemaker in advance) to summon me forth in order to escort him to school, which I did in a trance.

As the day progressed, the blurring of work and home provided another source of conflict. In the afternoon, Dash was greeted not by a mother offering milk and cookies, but one wearing a headset, scribbling furiously on a notepad. Unwilling to break my train of thought, I ignored his banging on my bedroom door. When he burst inside like a firefighter storming a burning building, it took all my self-restraint to merely keep my back turned, silently waving my son away.

"Why can't you cover the mouthpiece to say hello to me?" he complained later, after I hung up.

"Because the person might be in the middle of a really good quote and if I interrupt, I'll lose the flow. If you knock and I don't answer, just know I'll be out to talk to you as soon as I can. I won't forget you."

"Well, what about instead of looking at me as if you want to kill me, you say, *Sorry. Wait one minute.*"

"I'll try," I said.

"Don't try. Do it. For me."

At least I couldn't be accused of raising a kid afraid to speak his mind.

For Parents' Night at school, Dash wrote and illustrated a storybook called *Miles of Montauk* about a summer trip with his father. It included scenes and descriptions of the sand, ocean, starry night sky, and a walk they took on the beach. Flipping through the pages,

I realized I was not in any of them. But at the end, when I read my son's inscription, my throat grew so tight, I couldn't swallow:

> *This book is dedicated to my mom*
> *Who taught me one of the tools in*
> *Education, is writing and my mom*
> *Made a career out of writing*
> *And that's why I dedicat this book*
> *To my mom Elizebeth Hayt.*

CHAPTER 16

March 9, '99

Dear Dix—

I'm in Paris on assignment for Vogue. It's show week, fall collections. At Chloe, Camilla Parker Bowles and Paul McCartney seated opposite sides of the runway. Playing in the background was his song "Maybe I'm Amazed"—Anna Wintour smiled at me, or maybe it was my coat—dyed-green astrakhan fur by Gucci.

Here with retailer Jeffrey Kalinsky whose blue Hermès Birkin—check-in suitcase size—dwarfs his Crunch-buff body. We're staying in Place Vendôme at the Hotel Ritz (his dime). "You have to know how wealthy women live in order to buy for them," he said. Who was I to argue?

For now, I'm his trainee, traveling with him to showrooms in a chauffeur-driven black Mercedes. In a few days, I'll be ready to report on my story: being a buyer for a day, choosing a collection for his new store, which will open in the Meatpacking District this summer. Between runways, rolling racks, and the Ritz, I've found nirvana.

Wish you were with me—
E

I TORE IT UP. DIX AND I were incommunicado—not because of the Atlantic divide but due to his oceans of rage, which had wreaked havoc on my home front.

In my building, I lived on the same floor as two members of the co-op board, whose apartments bracketed mine. Once Charlie moved out, their harassment started. I wasn't sure why; maybe someone wanted to buy my place and the torture—threatening notices, accusations of phony infractions, arbitrary fines, and prank doorbell ringing—was intended to force me to sell. In particular, my playful hounds were targeted for persecution. It left me scratching my head. Even Hitler liked dogs.

It seemed in my best interest to maintain a low profile on my premises. Why create additional headaches when I could rely on my neighbors for them? What I hadn't counted on, however, was a boyfriend with an anger management problem.

At the end of February, Dix had spent a weekend at my place. He was trying out a new image—Ted Kaczynski inspired—anorak with fox-fur-trimmed hood, Merrell Wilderness boots, long disheveled hair, and straggly beard. As outcast styles went, I wasn't into the Unabomber, but Dix had his own ideas about fashion.

Leaving my apartment on Sunday night, he opened the front door and my dogs darted underfoot, chasing after him. I had no time to grab them before one of the co-op board witches simultaneously entered the hallway. Probably on her way out to dinner, she was working a 1980s look, too un-ironic to succeed as retro, making it merely passé: an emerald-green Escada suit with carbon-dated shoulder pads, standard-issue Fred the Furrier black mink, and Lady Dior handbag with gold letter charms, an accessory that had died along with its most famed carrier, the Princess of Wales.

"Get those dogs out of here!" my neighbor squealed. "They urinate all over the carpeting! It stinks here because of your dogs! Have you smelled the carpeting? Get down and smell it!"

"Sorry, sorry," I said, corralling them inside.

"What did you just say?" Dix confronted my neighbor, her attack triggering his inner Mr. Hyde. "Did you just order my girlfriend to 'smell the carpeting'? Who the fuck are you, bitch? Why don't *you* smell the fucking carpeting?"

"Calm down and let her go down the elevator alone, Dix," I ordered.

"What are you, some sort of drug dealer?" She eyeballed him. "I don't like how you look. Your kind doesn't belong in this building."

"Ignore it," I begged, knowing her low-life slur would have the same effect as pulling a pin from a grenade.

Immediately draining of blood, Dix's face became cadaver pale, the underlying skeletal structure and blue veins visible beneath his taut skin. Curling back his lips to reveal his snaggle teeth, he clenched and unclenched his fists, pumping up the wiry muscles now springing in his neck. Growling expletives and spraying saliva, he thrust out his chest, inching his feet closer and closer toward her.

"Oh, and what *kind* is that, you motherfucking cunt?" He glowered. "You have a problem with me? Get out of my fucking face, otherwise you'll wish you hadn't messed with me."

"How dare you threaten me! I'm calling the police!"

Crouching on the floor behind my front door, I took cover, dreading the next charge.

Assault? Battery? Manslaughter?

The fighting didn't last long; how or why it ended, I couldn't say. Perhaps one of them escaped into the stairwell, or the elevator arrived and they both got inside. If so, I was certain that when the doors snapped open, out would stride Dix, cool as Hannibal Lecter, while blood seeped from the roof's safety hatch.

At a CA meeting, I once heard a speaker confess there was no orifice of his body in which he hadn't put drugs, either to hide them or to get high. His habit drove him to the most lethal neighborhoods of the city, but by far the most treacherous was "right here," he said, tapping his own head.

Obviously, he hadn't been inside Dix's.

It always amazed me my boyfriend was able to keep his fury within the bounds of the law. Escalating hostilities to the point of brinksmanship, he retained enough control to back off before bones started breaking and teeth flying. He never hit anyone (myself included), though once, on the beach in the Hamptons, he picked up and swung a massive piece of driftwood, nearly clubbing a jogger who thought it was funny to lunge at my little dogs.

"You're a reversal of three million years of human evolution, Dix." I had stormed off in disgust.

"I'm sorry I reacted so aggressively," he mumbled, bowing his head. "At that moment, my protective instincts kicked in."

Remorse, shame, fear, self-hatred, these were the emotions that typically followed his Caligula tirades, which ultimately culminated in a deep depression. When his workday ended, he would collapse on the hardwood floor of his apartment, staring up at the rows of quilts, unable to move to his bed. He would pass the night in a fitful sleep, without a pillow or blanket, waking to head- and body aches. The discomfort and deprivation were his punishment. For days, even weeks, he would talk of having no reason to live, wishing the end would come.

"To be committed is my only hope for serenity," he concluded.

I found him shrinks who invariably prescribed mood stabilizers, which Dix always rejected. He wanted to remain himself, in touch with his true feelings, even if they were psychotic.

Still, I maintained faith. His postludes of regret were evidence he had a conscience. Perhaps with enough reassurance, support, and commitment, I could bring out his softer side, helping to stabilize him. Life might be his cross to bear but I—newly healed from my addiction—had the capacity to share Dix's burden.

Aw, shit, who am I kidding?

I liked the fucking drama. The conflicts and traumas were an emotional roller coaster, a razzle-dazzle ride of gravity-defying highs and stomach-flipping lows. My history of rakish boys and substance abuse were proof of my self-destructive extremism. Dix was like a drug and, when my life got routine, I mainlined him for a jolt.

But his face-off with my neighbor was too dangerous, even for me. A few days later, when he called to apologize, I let him have it:

"What the fuck is wrong with you? The co-op board wants to ban you. The management company told Charlie I date derelicts. Now he's worried about Dash's safety."

"That bitch got in my face," Dix retorted. "Why are you taking her side? What I did was self-defense."

"Self-defense? Was my neighbor about to smite you with her Dior bag? Don't you get it? This is where I live. This is where my son lives. I'm out. Done."

Parting words before I left for France.

• • •

I am not a great grudge keeper. My anger is immediate, sharp, and relatively short-lived. By the end of my trip to Paris, my troubles at home seemed far away and, in between, I'd had lots of comic relief.

At the Alain Tondowski shoe showroom, Jeffrey did a swan dive on top of a pair of black pony stilettos. After four hours at Place Vendôme's Commes des Garçons, a stark space filled with riotous designs in glen plaid, gold, and sequins, he ordered his driver to go across the street to the Ritz and bring him back a hamburger deluxe, a door-to-door delivery I could only imagine a first for the French. In another showroom, I acted as a fit model, trying on the clothes. When Jeffrey glimpsed me undressed, he blanched, not out of modesty, but rather horror: How dare I wear white Hanro underpants when Gucci made a sheer black G-string with rhinestones studding the butt strap?

On my fifth day, I went to the Martine Sitbon showroom to do my "buy," retailer parlance for placing an order. "Any last-minute advice?" I asked Jeffrey.

"It's all about the feel of the clothes. That's the cha-ching factor."

"Cha-ching?"

"The cash register, darling. Now, go!"

Ruby once told me black, brown, navy, and beige are the only shades that sell but it's the splashes of color that seduce a customer. Concentrating on neutrals, I spiked my buy with personal temptations—a tangerine tulle party dress and slouchy cardigan in nubby salmon-pink wool. After three hours rifling through the clothes, flipping through sketchbooks, and studying swatches, I had shopping mouth and was maxed out on spending Jeffrey's money. There were so many factors in making a selection. Do women who live in warm climates also dress according to seasonal colors? What cuts are most flattering on a size 12? The only thing I knew for sure was what would look good on me in Manhattan. Buying for the masses was guesswork.

In the end, Jeffrey canceled my three-page order.

"You were only thinking of yourself," he said, wagging a finger. "That's the most fatal mistake a buyer can make."

It was Saturday night, my last at the Ritz, and I lay sprawled across my peach satin bed, too beat to even bother with room service. Upon my arrival, I had a scratchy throat. After a week of secondary cigarette smoke, I had progressed to rattling lungs and coughing spasms.

Feeling lonely and sorry for myself, I debated whether to pick up the phone.

Dix was definitely off the hinges but maybe I had been too hard on him. After all, my neighbor did provoke him. In New York, it was now three AM. He'd still be awake.

Dialing his cell, I could barely hear him pick up. There was a lot of background noise: clapping, chanting, fiddle playing, and tambourines. It sounded like a Gypsy hoedown.

"What did you say?" I yelled.

"I'm out."

"Where?"

"At Casa Romana."

"What's that?"

"A dinner and dance club in Queens."

Dancing is "a perpendicular expression of a horizontal desire." Re-member?

"Are you by yourself?" I asked.

"No. I'm with a friend."

But you have no friends.

"Which friend?"

"You've never met."

"Who is it?"

I'm getting short of breath.

"Adina."

Here comes the sweat.

"Who the fuck is Adina?"

• • •

I hated them. Like canker sores, there was no way to stop them: Alexis, Beth, Caryn, Danielle, Eileen, Georgette, Heidi, Ilene, Jackie, Katie, Libette, Moriko, Nina, Olivia, Penelope, Rachel, Sara, Taina, Vanessa, Wendy, Xaviera, Yolanda, Zoe.

The women heard about Dix through magazines, TV, and word of mouth. His cell never stopped ringing. Actually, he had two: one for celebrities and another for everyone else, each with a distinct jingle, enabling him to prioritize his calls.

He'd finally scored his own studio, not quite the town house on which he'd planned, but a step in the right direction: eight hundred square feet on Madison Avenue. The buzzer simply said DIX.

At first, he encouraged me to visit. It didn't take long before I couldn't stomach the sight of him massaging his female clients' shoulders, telling them how great their arms looked. The women slid hundred-dollar bills inside his stretch-pants pockets, their fingers lingering the way men's do when tucking money into a stripper's garter. One lady got overheated in her sweatpants and top so she removed them, exercising in only her thong and bra. At Christmas, he received cards that read: "No one works my body the way you do."

It was not enough that they showered him with Prada, Armani, and Louis Vuitton. In exchange for a training session, a dermatologist gave Dix a full-body skin check—in the buff, of course. An Aston Patterning practitioner used her touch to release the tension he was "holding" in his soft tissues. Which ones, I didn't ask.

"How come you introduce me as 'my girlfriend, Elizabeth,' to your older, married clients but only as 'Elizabeth' to the ones who are young, pretty, and single?" I asked Dix.

"I have no idea what you're talking about. You're imagining things. You shouldn't be so jealous."

"Oh, no? What was going on in the restaurant last night between you and that Italian waitress?"

"I can't help it if women think I'm hot."

"Why did you tell her to drop by for a complimentary workout?"

"It's good for business. She's a cute girl and if someone asks how she stays in shape, it could bring me a new client."

"I thought you don't have time for new clients."

He sure couldn't fit me in anymore. Managing my own muscle tone, I had gone back to Tae Kwon Do. Although men had always complimented my figure, my boyfriend was another story. "You could use some more work on your obliques," he commented after sex. "Your butt cheeks will also wind up looking like pancakes if you don't do daily pelvic lifts."

If it wasn't bad enough that Dix felt free to criticize my body, he never held back about complimenting others—right in front of me.

"If you weren't hot for that waitress last night, then why did you tell me she had 'killer' legs after she took our order?" I pressed on.

"Because she did. Why are you worried? I'm not going to fuck her. I'm not that way. You know I'm not a very sexual person. Unlike you, I don't have to get laid all the time."

That was for damn sure. After our first night together, when he made the initial moves, I discovered his sex drive rarely shifted to high gear, despite my attempts to take the lead.

"The man has to be the one to go after a woman," he complained.

"Says who?"

"Nature. The law of the jungle. Women shouldn't be the aggressors. It's a turn-off. Besides, every woman wants to be dominated."

Is that a hint, Tarzan?

Inviting him over, I had offered myself up as Jane, wearing a brown faux suede jagged-edge miniskirt and halter top. Too bad I didn't own one of those sex swings, otherwise I would have sailed into my bedroom with a bush cry. At least I had a selection of Christopher Street specials given to me by various boyfriends as novelties: a bunny vibrator whose ears doubled as clitoral stimulators, double-header dildo for dual orifice penetration, black leather collar with stainless O-ring, wrist and ankle shackles, basic metal police cuffs, feather tickler, and jelly latex ball gag.

When Dix arrived, I assumed my setups would prompt him to get into character. Instead, he pulled a camera from his black nylon Prada backpack (a gift from a satisfied customer, naturally).

"This would make a great photo shoot," he said, looking through the lens.

Oh, I get it. I'll play a novice porn model and you the horny photographer.

I reclined on my bed, allowing him to arrange the props and direct my poses. "Stroke your nipples with the feather tickler." He clicked the shutter. "Put the vibrator in your pussy." Click. "Now in your mouth." Click. "I want to strap your arms and legs to the bedposts." Click. "Bite on the ball and I'll muzzle you." Click. "When I release you, flip over so I can manacle your wrists behind your back and see how this double-header dildo works." Click. "The collar really looks fabulous. I'll free your hands so you straighten your arms and lift up your torso. Keep your hips down and arch your back as far as you can go." Click. "You *are* really flexible. Can you bend your knees and touch the back of your head with the soles of your feet?" Click. "Let's see what will happen if I put the shackles around your ankles and cinch them to the collar ring. Wow. An advanced Cobra pose." Click. "Hold that longer." Click. "A little longer." Click. "You're doing great." Click.

No, I wasn't. The pull from my ankles on the back of the collar was slowly strangulating me. When I tried to bend my elbows in order to release the tension, my shoulders dropped, lowering the angle of my spine, which caused the tourniquet around my neck to tighten.

"Enough," I gasped.

Click. Click. Click. Click. Click. Click. Click. Click. Click. Click. Click. Click. Click.

"Let me go."

Click. Click. Click. Click. Click. Click. Click. Click. Click. Click. Click. Click. Click.

"Please."

Click. Click. Click. Click. Click. Click. Click. Click. Click. Click. Click. Click. Click.

Safe-word? Signal to stop? Why didn't we agree on one beforehand?

The room appeared to be tilting, the periphery of my vision breaking up. There were pulsars of white light and exploding yellow novas. Pressure was building behind my eyeballs. My heartbeat raced, ricocheting against my ribs. I attempted sucking in air but my tongue felt like a waterlogged sponge. Sputtering sounds escaped from the back of my throat—the last thing I remembered.

"Are you okay?" Dix asked, unclasping the collar. "I was looking through the viewfinder and saw you fall over."

"Where . . . am . . . I?" I gulped for oxygen, trying to orient myself. "How long was I out?"

"I'm not sure. I called your name but you didn't respond. I knew something was wrong. I untied you immediately."

Hugging myself, I started crying. My neck was sore and my body damp with sweat. What happened? Did Dix try to kill me? Was his sadism for real? Was it my fault for starting the whole thing? At what point did the role-playing turn into Russian roulette?

"You scare me," I whispered.

"Please, don't say that." His eyes moistened as I winced from his embrace. "I never meant to. I thought it was what you wanted. You seemed so into it. To tell the truth, it scared me, too. Kinky shit is just not my thing. I'm traditional when it comes to sex. I've never done anything like this before. I really care so much for you."

I threw on a bathrobe, frantically gathering up all the X-rated paraphernalia. Running outside my apartment to the incinerator, I dropped the toys down the hatch, burning the evidence of a Jezebel fantasy gone wrong.

Dix promised nothing like that would ever happen again. And from then on, I allowed him to be the one to initiate sex, finding satisfaction in the arrangement. His knowledge of the female body was as complete as *Gray's Anatomy*. He was able to turn me into an orgasmatron as easily as screwing in a lightbulb.

In fact, he approached the task with the same diligence and dis-passion as an electrician. Foreplay was minimal and talking out of the question. Emitting not a moan or grunt and barely an exhale, he merely stiffened his toes before ejaculating. When I expressed a wish for him to be more responsive, he scrunched up his face in revulsion. My pleasure was his objective, not because he enjoyed making me feel good per se but rather because it fed his ego as a lady slayer.

Outside the bedroom was a different story. At the beginning of our relationship, before I restarted my career, I was happy to run an errand or two for him—dropping off his laundry at the dry cleaners or getting his film developed. But after my writing took off and the demands of work added to my responsibilities at home, my Girl Friday hours came to an end. Dix was none too happy to go back to licking his own stamps.

One day, he was sick with a stomach virus and wanted me to come over to take care of him. I asked Franci, Dash's babysitter, to stay late and give him dinner. Before heading over to my boyfriend's apartment, I had to walk my dogs, as well as finish a writing assignment. By the time I climbed to his fifth-floor walk-up, weighted with a bag of groceries—the stuff my mother used to supply when we kids were sick—it was three o'clock in the afternoon.

"What took so long?" he fumed, watching me unpack the provisions. "Who were you gabbing on the phone with, your mother or Ruby? Why did you buy me canned chicken soup with sodium? You should know by now that salt and sugar lower my immune system."

A recent e-mail popped into my head:

```
Subj: A Fairy Tale for the Assertive Woman
From: Ruby@hotmail.com
To: Elizabeth@aol.com
```

```
Once upon a time, in a land far away, a beauti-
ful, independent, self-assured princess happened
upon a frog as she sat contemplating ecological
issues on the shores of an unpolluted pond in a
verdant meadow near her castle. The frog hopped
into the princess's lap and said, "Elegant lady,
I was once a handsome prince until an evil witch
cast a spell on me. One kiss from you, however,
and I will turn back into the dapper young prince
that I am and then, my sweet, we can marry and
set up housekeeping in your castle with my mother
where you can prepare my meals, clean my clothes,
```

bear my children, and forever feel grateful and
happy doing so."

That night, dining on a repast of lightly
sautéed frog's legs seasoned in a white wine and
onion cream sauce, the princess chuckled to herself and thought: "I don't fucking think so."

"Would you like to eat what's on this tray or wear it?" I said,
serving Dix in bed.

"You know, you're a real bitch. Not a nurturer. I need a woman
who gives me alcohol baths when I'm sick. Who squeezes the
blackheads on my back. I want a woman who is happy to have me
crawl into bed at any hour. I can't be on your timetable."

"That's because you want a woman who has no timetable. She
should be a round-the-clock caretaker, nanny, nurse, secretary,
maid, and ass-wiper all in one. But guess what? They only work in
shifts and charge by the hour."

"A real woman can do it all. My mother worked in a factory,
raised me, and nursed my sick father."

"Aren't you forgetting? She also ran away."

When I landed my *Vogue* story to go to Paris as a buyer, my path
appeared very clear. I *was* a real writer, a working writer. My
mother was so excited, she called every day to find out what I was
working on. People recognized my byline, and a prominent literary agent took me to lunch at the Four Seasons' Grill Room.
When Ruby asked what I would do differently if I won the Lotto,
I said, "Absolutely nothing." This was the jackpot. Doing what I
was doing.

As my winnings grew, my availability to Dix decreased and I
could no longer fill his needs. They became a black hole in my life,
a nothingness devouring all surrounding matter and light. When
he asked me to accompany him to the Outsider Art Fair and I had
to decline because of a deadline, he reminded me how easy it
would be for him to outsource my position.

"You're trying to manipulate me to sacrifice my work for you," I said. "But writing is my priority. At the beginning, you told me to become someone. Now I am someone, but maybe you were only attracted to me because I was a loser and it made you feel better about yourself."

"You're lucky to have me."

"*I'm* lucky to have *you*? And why is that?"

"Who else would want you? You're still a married woman. It's been three years. You and Charlie can't let go of each other. You'll never get divorced."

CHAPTER 17

MY RAPPROCHEMENT WITH CHARLIE HAD begun in July 1999, six weeks after I went to the Hamptons and found a summer rental for Dix and me. We had been dating for nearly three years at that point.

The house was a sweet little Cape Cod cottage with a wraparound porch, as well as indoor and outdoor fireplaces. It should have been a lovers' hideaway. Instead it was a Gaza Strip, the site of our constant clashing. Although I was earning some money by then, it wasn't enough to foot the rent, so Dix covered the damage. We drove out in separate cars. I left Manhattan early on Fridays and set up house before he showed. Deferring his departure to avoid the weekend traffic, he arrived anywhere between three AM and dawn. When the door creaked open, it unleashed a barking barrage from my dogs, detonating me out of sleep.

"Since I paid for this place, you can't tell me when I can come and go," he snapped at my objection to being so violently awakened.

Passing through a room, Dix was a walking cyclone. In addition to scattered newspapers and empty Evian bottles, there were "as-yougo" piles—wet towels and swimsuits, to be picked up "as you go." Since *you* meant "me," I spent the entire summer one scullery task away from a nervous breakdown.

One weekend, I didn't have my Jeep because Charlie was using it. I had no choice but to commute to the country with Dix. By the time he left his workout studio, went home to his apartment, got his things, retrieved his car, returned to the studio where he'd left his camera, stopped for something to eat, filled his gas tank, picked me up, and drove the ninety-mile distance on the Long Island Expressway, we didn't pull into the driveway of our house until sunrise on Saturday.

Highly fatigued, I knew my fuse was bound to blow. We had little more than twenty-four hours before an about-face back to the city. Late Sunday afternoon, as I began the process of closing up—emptying the dryer, locking the windows shut—Dix was reclining on a lounge chair in the yard. "Please carry the garbage bags outside to the cans," I called from a back screen door.

He was eating wedges of papaya, dropping the rinds on the grass, allowing my dogs to chew them. I told him to stop because they would get sick. Instead, he picked up the fruit skins, hand-feeding them to the pooches. Again, I asked him to stop and help me with the trash. Again, he ignored me. So I marched outside, grabbed the papaya, and mashed it into his bare chest.

"You're lucky I don't turn your face into pulp," he rasped, flicking off the fruit before hightailing to his car, screeching out of the driveway, and leaving me stranded.

Ours was an "anger-habituated relationship," according to psych-speak, a union in which aggression creates both emotional connection and division. When Dix and I first met, we each believed we'd found the "one," the other half completing our stunted selves. We took turns needing to rescue and be rescued. Over time, unable to fulfill each other's demands and failing each other's fantasies, we replaced them by rage, a mutual reaction to our competing claims of betrayal.

"I have a problem," I said, calling Charlie on his cell, tracking him down in Montauk where he was staying for the weekend. "My ride back to the city fell through and I'm stuck here in East

Quogue. I can't take my dogs on the Jitney. Would you mind driving me home?"

Thankfully, he didn't ask why they puked orange slime the whole trip, or who was paying for the summer house. Charlie and I kept our romantic lives private, which helped to keep any potential ill will between us at bay.

Traveling with him was pleasant enough, the conversation light and familiar. Dash, now eleven, was away at a sleepaway camp in the Berkshires. In his last postcard, he reported that he'd bleached his hair platinum like Eminem's.

"He wants to be cool," I said. "To distinguish himself from the other boys."

"I'm always in favor of hair as a form of self-expression," Charlie concurred. "Maybe Tipper Gore will even slap a parental advisory label on him."

Charlie and I were working well together in handling our son. "You know what's good for Dash and I know what *he* thinks is good for him," Charlie summed up after we'd received our son's below-average reading scores earlier that spring. I announced that the time had come for tutoring and private school, to which Dash protested with slamming doors until his father exercised his powers of persuasion.

"I'm better at seeing the world from his perspective," Charlie said. "You say he has to do shit that he doesn't like and I get him to do it and make him feel good about it."

The team playing worked. Over the years, Dash had become more flexible. Around age nine, he allowed blue to bump aside green as his favorite color. Chef Boyardee, tuna salad, and chocolate pudding packs were no longer his only staples. In fact, by ten, he wanted his own *Zagat*, checking off restaurants to which he'd been and highlighting those he hoped to try. His epicureanism became so serious, I had to travel to Sullivan Street to Joe's Dairy for their renowned fresh buffalo mozzarella.

"Not exactly a prepubescent stereotype, is he?" I said to Charlie.

"Some parents have to worry about their kids sneaking into the bathroom to smoke a cigarette or stealing from the liquor cabinet. When ours does something to excess, it's with grated cheese."

By twelve, Dash had not only adapted to living under two roofs but also found the humor in it. For a school assignment titled "How My House Represents Me," he wrote:

Unlike most people, I have two houses that represent me. My mother's house shows the intellectual side of me while my dad's house shows the fun and cool side of me. My two houses are my split personalities. At my mother's house, I am William the polite, sophisticated man who knows all about Wall Street and the fine arts. While at my dad's house, I am Randy, the wild, rambunctious party animal.

At my mom's house, my room has a fancy bed with fancy pillows that match. While at my dad's house, my room has a bunk bed with sheets that don't match but are really comfortable. At my mom's house, I have a desk with pencils and a bulletin board. While at my dad's house, I have a desk that has trophies on top.

Even though these two houses are very different, there is one thing at both of my houses that represents me. I love baseball! At my mother's, I have many photographs of famous baseball players all around my room. At my father's, there is a ton of baseball memorabilia and a gigantic collection of baseball cards.

These houses may be different, but they both represent my personality—or is it personalities?

The Sunday Charlie rescued me in the Hamptons, our trip took an unexpected turn when he dropped me off in front of my building. "This was really fun," he said nonchalantly, depositing my bags and dachshunds on the sidewalk. "Do you want to have dinner sometime?"

Dinner? As in a . . . date?

"Ah . . . well . . . sure . . . let's . . . yes . . . definitely . . . dinner," I answered, too stunned to realize my dogs' leashes were tangling around my ankles until I took a step toward my building and my feet flew out from under me, Cosmo-Kramer-style.

Later in the week, Charlie and I met at Island, an upper Madison Avenue restaurant and our old haunt.

"I had a really good time driving with you last weekend," he said.

"Why? What was so special about it?"

"It was the most casual of conversations but I felt you've changed. You seemed interested in me. You were really listening."

"It's true. I have changed."

Of course, regressing to food fighting is hardly a change for the better . . .

"Have *you* changed?" I asked.

"I'd need to spend the rest of my life in therapy to change. But one lesson you've taught me is that being open and honest really works."

"Then there's something you should know."

I told him about my coke wipeout, confessing my fear he'd take Dash from me. I reassured Charlie I'd gotten help and, for the past three years, had been clean and sober. I no longer went to meetings, however, because I didn't want to become a lifer at Twelve Step programs.

"I don't want to think of you as weak," he responded. "For a person of so much strength and energy, a drug addiction is so pedestrian and uninteresting. I don't think any less of you."

How could a successful Jewish lawyer with a forgiving heart and track record of commitment still be eligible in Manhattan? Answer: JDate hadn't launched yet.

"I've dated, had a few relationships," he responded when I asked had he had a girlfriend since we'd split. "I've enjoyed the freshness of messing around with women. The problem is, after I begin sleeping with one, I lose interest. I have trouble seeing myself in another relationship equal to ours."

Me, too. I couldn't imagine being married to anyone other than Charlie. But more profoundly, I couldn't see myself in a marriage at all. The minute I tried to picture it, a familiar claustrophobia took hold. In fact, just being around conventionally married couples—the type that got permission from each other before making plans and went to bed together at the same time—convinced me I'd be more at home in a lunar colony.

Once or twice yearly, I went to California to visit my girlfriends, Susan, now a mother of two daughters who'd given up art criticism to become a mystery writer, and Cathy, a multimillionaire who left her career to be a stay-at-home mom with four kids. Our reunions had the spirit of spring break in Daytona—until my friends' husbands arrived. They were both great guys but their presence caused an involuntary female reaction: We reined in our looseness, and the surrounding space seemed to shrink accordingly.

I was happy to return alone to my hotel room. Nearly two decades earlier, both of these women had been my bridesmaids, and now were again standing at the opposite end of the aisle from me. My perspective had radically changed: Marriage wasn't called wed-"lock" for nothing.

By early 2001, headlines were ablaze with women choosing to stay single rather than settle down. Tina Brown, editor of *Talk* magazine, assigned me to report on the trend—but *not* as it applied to the unwed. A generation of wives—baby boomers with earning power and emptying nests—were suddenly flying the marriage coop.

"I see it all around me," Tina briefed. "They realize they're self-sufficient and independent. Their kids are growing up and the women are at a point in their lives when they're hitting their stride. Having a husband has sort of become a drag."

Ruby was a perfect example. After her divorce was finalized, she moved to the Flatiron District in Manhattan, buying and renovating a loft with her half of the marital assets. She received additional income from Keds, royalties for a baseball sneaker that she'd designed.

"I feel like my whole personality has changed," she said. "The key was getting my own home and making it beautiful. This is my haven. Finally, I've got money. Being a single woman is like living off the land, like monks who survive on tomatoes and olives. You need companionship and conversation but that's what girlfriends and gay friends are for. You need sex but you don't need to be married. My new boyfriend, Tom, waits till I come first. What more could I want from a man?"

• • •

I had come to love living alone, looking forward to weekends when Dash was at his father's. As a writer, I felt free without being directionless, working whenever and for as long as I wanted. The stillness of my apartment was rapturous. Often, I wrote throughout the night, words alighting like fireflies in my head.

Dix and I got together less frequently. We either were in one of our breakups or had an unspoken agreement that it would be more profitable to invest the time in our respective careers than into a dead-end romance. That left Marilyn, Joe, and Jackie as my constant and only bedmates. Although hairier than the average guy, at least they didn't snore.

It was only after my family's get-togethers, enveloped in our clannish cocoon, that I seriously questioned being single. My brothers' marriages seemed pretty stable, and my parents' had not only endured but had actually improved over the decades. They were now intrepid travelers, drawn to countries on the State Department's Immunization and/or Travel Warning List. I felt left out, not being part of a twosome or sharing adventures with a partner. Although I was currently content putting out a place setting for one, would I feel that way in the future? Was I putting momentary gratification before long-term security? Was it like using saccharine instead of sugar to remain svelte in the present only to cause cancer later? And if that happened, wouldn't I want a husband by my side? Someone who loved me through thick and thin, especially if my hair really *did* fall out?

For the first few years of my separation from Charlie, the only occasions we spent together were child-related: parent–teacher conferences, school performances, and sports events. Missing his humor, I wanted to hang out with him afterward and tried baiting him with questions about politics, appealing to his appetite for punditry. It was an exercise in futility. The minute I let up, he took off.

None of the men I'd met to date could equal his wit, brainpower, and humanity. Some were richer, sexier, and more eye-catching but only he could walk through a department store, pass a garment bursting with plumes, and offhandedly quote Emily Dickinson, "Hope is a thing with feathers."

Did the fact that I had yet to give up my married name express my true attachment? During my honeymoon, when hoteliers first referred to me as *Mrs.*, I thought it was funny that everyone was pretending I was a grown-up. Then I started to notice people treated me differently—with greater respectfulness and deference—if I used my husband's last name.

Although I never officially changed my last name, I adopted his in practice. It was so much easier opening charge accounts and getting the building repairmen to fix something in my apartment when I identified myself as *Mrs.* Occasionally, I hyphenated my maiden and married names, telegraphing to the world I was still my own person yet hadn't been condemned to spinsterhood. Even after Charlie moved out, I left everything—household utilities, bank accounts, medical records, and my driver's license—as it was, in his name. I told myself I didn't want to bother with the hassle. It was only as a writer, for my byline, that I returned to my given name: Elizabeth Hayt.

The back-and-forth between Charlie's and my matrimonial lawyers had died down. Without any impetus for divorce—no custody problems or second marriages on the horizon (once he started making more money, he had the opposite reaction of most men in his position and became *more* generous)—we got lazy about legally terminating our marriage. Our dependence on each other grew.

"I feel responsible for you," he said, intervening when I received a co-op warning letter. "I made promises, both explicitly and implicitly, that I would never let any harm come to you."

One morning in April 2000, I woke up to discover my breasts were lopsided. While the right remained a full B, the left had withered to an A. No, I hadn't taken a hit in the chest in Tae Kwon Do or been crushed by an inflatable dashboard airbag. According to the FDA, the three-year complication rate for saline-filled implant leakage and deflation was 3 percent. My tit was simply a deviant statistic.

The replacement surgery was no big deal, but when I emerged from the IV sedation, my reaction, though not uncommon, was a first for me. Shivering, scared, and crying, I called out—not for my mother, who was scheduled to pick me up, or Dix, technically my shag partner, but for Charlie. A nurse tracked him down at his office and the next time I opened my eyes, he was there by my side.

Soon after, he started suffering acute anxiety attacks before court appearances. He became lethargic, irritable, and unable to sleep. After pushing himself to make partner, he had reached a level at which putting in long hours and winning cases were no longer enough. He had to become a rainmaker, bringing business to his firm. The pressure was immense and his lifestyle joyless. *What's it all for?* he asked himself.

We hashed over career alternatives, rejecting them for more immediate changes: Work at home whenever possible, hire a trainer, splurge on a sports car, and take a first-class Caribbean vacation. "You were terrific," he told me after getting himself back on track. "You were tolerant of my rambling. You're the only person who gets me and doesn't judge me."

Our relationship evolved into a real-life Ross-and-Rachel romance. Like the *Friends* TV couple, Charlie and I had separate apartments, shared a child, relied on each other for companionship, and avoided sex at all costs. For that, I had Dix on the side. Mine seemed the best of both worlds: not quite single, yet still solo.

For several years, the arrangement worked. Charlie and I were riding parallel escalators, one always going up while the other was heading down. The moment we crossed was tantalizing, yet transitory. Neither of us had the courage to reach across the railing and grab on.

Summer after summer, we drove together to the Berkshires to see Dash at camp. The night before visiting day, Charlie and I shared a hotel room. We took turns changing in the bathroom and slept in separate beds. Had we not remained tied as parents, our connection would have already unraveled. But for me, Dash was living proof that the last time Charlie and I got it on, we ended up getting it right.

Just before my son entered seventh grade, he and I were having dinner, talking about one of his friends, a child of divorce, who no longer saw his father because he was remarried and had another family. I asked Dash how he thought he might react to a stepparent.

"I would throw a fit," he said, pushing his plate away. "I wouldn't allow it to happen. If stepparents enter the picture, then we three won't be a family anymore. If you married other people, it would ruin my bliss."

Ruin his bliss? Married couples staying together for the kid's sake is a classic, but staying separated and *married for the kid's sake, now there's a modern twist.*

"It was just an abstract question," I reassured him. "It's not about to happen. And even if one of us wanted to get remarried, it would take a long time since we're still not divorced."

"You're not divorced?" he gasped, his eyes round and shiny. "All these years, I thought you were and you hid the papers from me. Now, I have even more hope."

"More hope?"

"Late at night, after I turn off the TV, before I go to sleep, I think that you and Dad will realize you shouldn't get old alone because you were meant to be together."

With those words, my contented coil of solitude started to loosen and I began to wonder: What would it take for Charlie and me to go beyond our goodwill and guardianship in order to make Dash's fantasy come true?

CHAPTER 18

THE SIGHT OF MY CHILD was startling. Now in eighth grade, he was half a foot taller than me, with linebacker shoulders and narrow hips. His hair was the color of espresso, his jaw squared off, lips full, his eyes green and sultry. Girls checked him out.

"Today, a high school student talked to me," Dash said, walking through the front door in a red Phat Farm hoodie. "I was a little scared when he stopped me. He said, 'Where'd you get that sweatshirt?' I thought he was going to diss me but instead he said, 'That's pretty cool.' I was so psyched about my outfit, I wanted you to be home to see it. Will you take me shopping again?"

Dash asked about my day before disappearing into his bedroom to do his homework. I went back into mine to continue writing. That was our routine. Reconvening a couple of hours later for dinner, we ate takeout with the TV on, a double violation of The Rules of Good Parenting. It was the first season of *The Bachelor*, starring Aaron Buerge. Since the start of the show, I had been rooting for Helene Eksterowicz, the slim-figured brunette.

"How can you watch this?" Dash shook his head. "No true love can come from it. It makes romance a blood sport."

"How did you get to be so wise?"

"I listen to the Beatles."

A car commercial interrupted, one of its selling points being air-conditioning.

"Isn't that like saying it comes with an engine?" Dash quipped. "Why not throw in the steering wheel, too?"

After dinner, I wiped down the table and he carried the dirty plates into the kitchen where, upon opening the dishwasher, I overheard him say to himself in a perfect Sean Connery imitation, "Down the hatch."

From Jim Carrey's Ace Ventura to Christopher Walken's The Continental, Dash was a great mimic. His drama teacher at school said my son was the first student in ten years with *Saturday Night Live* potential. I wasn't so sure. Comics are stereotypically head cases, which mine definitely wasn't. Self-assured and outgoing, he was a poster pubescent for normalcy. He got himself to school on time, played intramural sports, and, to the best of my knowledge, said no to street drugs, illegal file sharing, and turnstile jumping.

Still, I wasn't going to do anything rash like shelve my *Diagnostic and Statistical Manual of Psychiatric Disorders*. The average age of onset for schizophrenia in males is eighteen. That meant I had several more years to clear before I could stop worrying about Dash hearing voices and talking to himself at coffee shop counters.

It took me the first decade of his life to forgive myself for not experiencing nurturing as my second nature and devoting myself to all aspects of his upbringing. Once I survived those years and my boy actually thrived, I overcame a fear that the only alternative to a Disneyfied version of maternal self-sacrifice—Bambi's mother— was a postpartum psychotic, like Andrea Yates, who drowned her five children in a bathtub.

When Dash was a toddler and I complained to my mother that I would have better luck domesticating feral animals than taming the beast that I'd borne, she reassured, "You grow with your child." Little did she know her advice was consistent with evolutionary theories confirming that adult human females are innately neither maternal nor selfless. They traditionally learn to care for their young over time, relying on other females for help. Parenting was indeed a process, and I depended on a roster of babysitters for assistance. It was not until Dash became a preteen that I hit my stride as his mother. Was it because he was more independent or I was?

Although I had no interest in sports, I became a roundball fan once I started attending Dash's after-school games. Caught up in the quick pace and nonstop action, I stood on the bleachers, cheering his name whether he scored a basket, intercepted a pass, or committed a foul. I assumed the ref's whistling could only mean my son had made a perfect play.

One Friday night, Dash made an unprecedented request. Ordinarily, he went to his father's, but this time he wanted to stay with me.

"Sure," I said. "But is something wrong?"

"No, I just changed my mind."

"How come?"

"The dogs," he said, averting his eyes.

"You see them all the time. Is there anything else?"

"I can talk to you. I don't have to hold back my feelings. With Dad, I don't want to show my emotions. Sometimes it's hard because you're a mother and I'm a son. But I like that you're feminine."

"How did you get to be so self-aware?" I asked.

"I don't think it has to do with you. I get the best of both you and Dad but I think I have a weird gene that has made me who I am."

Scratch low self-esteem from Mom's worry list of latent neuroses.

Of course, our rapport was not always so lovey-dovey. When writing, I barked at Dash if he used his bedroom as a handball court or had an outburst of video-game rage. Strict about my own work habits, I was equally hard on him about his.

"Kill that goddamn TV!" I blasted, walking into his room, busting him while doing his homework.

"You do this all the time," Dash hit back. "I'm a good student but you make me feel like I disappoint you. You're never satisfied."

Packing up his computer, he slammed the front door behind him. Sometimes the grass was greener at Dad's, after all.

• • •

On the morning of September 11, 2001, right after the South Tower collapsed, Charlie abandoned his office, picked up Dash at school, and rushed over to my place, where we holed up, listening to the sirens and helicopters outside. In the afternoon, we walked to Lenox Hill Hospital because Charlie wanted to donate blood. Yom Kippur was still two weeks away but, back at my apartment, we said a prayer and lit a memorial candle early.

Two days later, school reopened, and Dash returned home with unexpected news.

"I want to be bar mitzvahed."

For years, I had been bugging him to go to Hebrew school, which he'd absolutely refused. Suddenly my very secular son was reaching out to find his holy roots.

"I don't just want to do it in English," he continued. "I want to learn Hebrew. I don't want people to think that I'm having a bar mitzvah for the gifts or the money or the party. I feel as if I've been missing something."

Denying the terrorist attacks had anything to do with his spiritual awakening, Dash credited his buddies, many of whom would be celebrating their bar mitzvahs over the coming year.

"You'll feel pumped, man," he repeated one of them saying. "Confident."

Levitating with happiness, I envisioned myself like the Great Neck mothers of my youth: overdressed, blotting away tears, listening to her son reading aloud from the Torah, already planning his future as a brain surgeon.

But the figment didn't last long. Unlike most Jewish boys who study for years to prepare for a bar mitzvah, which occurs at age thirteen, Dash only had four months. His birthday was in December. We didn't even belong to a synagogue. How the hell was I going to produce my son's coming of age?

I immediately called Temple Emanu-El, a Reformed congregation on Fifth Avenue.

"You want to do *what*?" the receptionist squawked. "Your son is *how* old? He wants to start *now*? You've gotta be kidding!"

"But wasn't Henny Youngman seventy-three?" I said.

"He wasn't bar mitzvahed here." She hung up.

Whose commitment is God testing? Dash's or mine?

It took a few more weeks before I found Rabbi Joel, a twenty-eight-year-old Hebrew teacher, living in downtown Manhattan. As a congregant at East 14th Street's Town and Village Synagogue, he pulled a few strings to get Charlie, Dash, and me a family membership, as well as secured a date for my son's bar mitzvah.

On Saturday, November 2, 2002, a little more than a year after he expressed his wish and six weeks shy of his fourteenth birthday, the big event occurred. The ceremony was called for four PM, beginning during the *mincha*, or afternoon prayer, continuing into *havdalah*, a sunset service. Between the mysticism and sensuousness of the rituals, which included wine, chanting, and burning incense, the theater of worship was bewitching. With dusk falling and candle flames twitching, my son's face glowed in chiaroscuro, its mysterious luminance redolent of a Rembrandt portrait.

Nothing in my life had prepared me for the experience. When Dash was small, time passed so slowly, but now that his childhood was over, the years leading up to it seemed no more than a few footsteps preceding a spontaneous, giant leap.

Wearing a dark pin-striped suit and aftershave, he was nearly a young man, his baby fat gone and body hair sprouting. Had it really been *that* long since I had to lace his shoes for him? When did he learn how to knot his own necktie? It was hard to believe we had come this far.

Now I didn't want him to be so close to adulthood. It was too soon. We were at a new beginning, getting to know each other.

The fun was just starting—yet in only four and a half years, he'd be going to college. The time we had left together amounted to less than a third of what we'd already shared.

Standing at a lectern with the Torah parchment scrolls open before him, Dash cantillated the story of adversarial twin brothers, Jacob and Esau. During a couple of practice runs, I'd sat in the back of the sanctuary, coaching him to project his voice. Dropping a few octaves over the last year, it now resonated strong and buoyant.

The kid was pulling through, reading Hebrew—not an English transliteration, but the real thing. At the end, he gave a speech about what his bar mitzvah meant to him, comparing the challenge of his preparation to Jacob's long-suffering journey, which ended in an affirmation of his faith. From the confidence of my boy's countenance, I knew his friends were right. Charlie and I clasped hands. Dash was not the only one feeling pumped.

Afterward, we threw a blowout for 125 at the Essex House where the ballroom's baroque resplendence was a perfect setting for Jews Gone Wild. The room was rocking and I was rolling, shimmying, shaking, swinging, kicking, clapping, snapping, and boogying my fucking ass off. My dress—a Carolina Herrera number in Chinese red silk—had big bell sleeves with accordion pleats. Whenever I raised my arms, they looked like wings. *Perfect.* That night I was flying.

Andee created the party's feature entertainment: an iMovie with soundtrack chronicling Dash's childhood. Images of birthday parties, Halloween costumes, family gatherings, and sports highlights slid across a giant video monitor. Accompanied by Stevie Wonder's "You Are the Sunshine of My Life," there were several shots of my son and me: he, as a baby, and I napping on a picnic blanket; as a toddler splashing me in the Caribbean waters of Aruba; as a kindergartner tossing apples to me from a tree at Masker Orchards; as a six-year-old roasting marshmallows over a beach bonfire with my brothers; a seven-year-old hiking up Bear Mountain with our puppies; and a nine-year-old hugging me after I passed my black-belt test.

Sliding from one to another, the pictorial transitions were too quick. I wanted to freeze-frame each scene, climb inside, and relive the moments with Kodachrome clarity. By comparison, my memories were so distant and vague. Had I known Dash would be my only child, I would have done things differently: milked every mundane moment—feeding, bathing, dressing—instead of hurrying to move on. In hindsight, I realized how much I'd missed, as well as what I'd denied him.

I had a new appreciation for my parents' greatest gift to me—my brothers. As boys, they had been as annoying as bees buzzing around my head but, as men, they were among my best friends, the regulars in my life to whom I spoke on the phone and on whom I could count to always be there for me. Dash would never have that security—the indivisible bond of blood, fortified by child-hood memories—or the luxury of collective commiseration about wacky parents and how they were getting on.

Had I not had the abortion back in 1993, I now would have a second child who was eight and a half. Yes, all these years, I'd been keeping count. Even though it was the right decision at the time, I often thought about what I had given up, especially when I studied the faces of my brothers' girls, my young nieces. What would a daughter of mine look like?

"It stays with you every single day," my mother confirmed when I confessed my persistent feelings. "Even now, I still feel sad, especially when I see you three kids all together."

Lately, I found myself smiling at little ones in their strollers. If a woman appeared over thirty-five, I wondered whether getting pregnant had been a problem. Was her child adopted? Spotting a Chinese baby girl, I might ask her Caucasian parents which agency they used. At forty-one, my chances were running out.

What kind of mother would I be a second time around? I certainly wasn't the same as when I'd given birth to Dash. Did I have a greater capacity for patience and tolerance, which early child rearing demanded? But what about the energy for all that heavy lifting?

At the end of the party, when the houselights flipped on, Charlie and I slumped into a pair of banquet chairs.

"This is all because of you," he said.

"Making a party isn't such a big deal."

"I wasn't referring to the party. I meant our son."

"But you're the one he worships."

"I ride on your coattails. You're a natural. For a person who is rather self-absorbed, you have drawn a line. On one side is your space and work and on the other side is him. Your identity is not bound up with him. You've not linked your self-esteem to him. It's so unbelievably healthy."

So the verdict was in. I hadn't repeated my mother's mistake; I'd spared my child the ultimate burden—me. Maybe I wasn't as selfish or ambivalent as I thought. Maybe I'd only been honest, admitting to the hard parts of raising a child, as well as my self-doubts. My goal as a mother had never been to make Dash like me, but to let him know there was always someone in charge so that he would feel safe and cared for. I wanted to give him the security and self-confidence to be able to lead his own life when the time was right, a time getting closer and closer.

"I've been thinking recently," I said to Charlie. "This whole experience has made me want to do it again."

"*What? Now you* want to have a bat mitzvah?"

"No, another child."

CHAPTER 19

On Sunday, July 4, 2004—Independence Day—I turned forty-three. It was a jubilee event. I was celebrating my recent book contract and, after eight years of separation, was reuniting with Charlie. Not that it was official. We hadn't told Dash. But with him away at summer camp, his father and I were spending weekends together in Southampton in a turn-of-the-twentieth-century shingle-style bungalow with a swimming pool—a rental in hedgerow heaven.

All my life, I'd hated my birthday because it fell on a national holiday. My friends were always away, restaurants either crowded or closed, and stores shut tight. If I wanted to throw a party, it had to be well in advance. By the time the real date rolled around, it was anticlimactic.

But this year made up for all the previous busts. Charlie and I were entertaining a houseful of guests: Andee and her spouse equivalent, Mick; Ruby, her son, Joey, and her boyfriend, Tom; Mathilde, my mate from MoMA, and her honey, the spanking sergeant.

That morning, we awoke to glorious skies. Breakfasting outdoors, everyone sat around a patio table crammed with bagels, coffee, and *The New York Times*. The water of the pool was sun-dappled, its surface glimmering like a bed of opals. Joey, now a college student, played a recording of Rod Stewart's "Forever Young" as my birthday anthem. Charlie gave a pyrotechnic recitation of "The Declaration of Independence."

Later, he took my dogs and me for a spin on Old Montauk Highway in his convertible, a cream-colored vintage Mercedes with caramel leather seats. Wearing Oliver Peoples shades and a purple-striped Etro shirt (my picks), he was smoking a Cohiba, talking about volunteering for the Democratic National Committee for the upcoming presidential election. His seat belt accentuated the softening of his middle, and the afternoon light glinted off his silver-flecked hair. The man I married never looked better to me.

After my odyssey of lust and twisted romance, I had returned home. Kansas seemed pretty wonderful compared with the other side of the rainbow, where there really were men without hearts, brains, or courage. Although my adventures had led me back to my origins, I was no longer the same as when I first set out. I'd been hurt but had learned how to heal myself. I'd gotten lost but had found my bearings by charting a new road.

It had been almost a year since Dix and I broke up. By the time we did, our relationship had worn down to nothing more than a stump—but still, it staggered me when I heard his new girlfriend was twenty years my junior. In reaction, I called in the artillery.

"Weren't you just here a month ago?" asked Dr. Patricia Wexler, a dermatologist with whom I made an emergency appointment for a blitz of wrinkle-filler injections.

"Yes, but I think I'm looking a little droopy around the mouth. Or maybe it's the eyes. Do you think my jawline is starting to soften?"

Wheeling over a standing exam lamp, she studied my face under the bright bulb before inspecting my skin with a magnifying lens and penlight. Nodding, she pulled out a prescription pad and wrote:

Powder—Shiseido
Eyebrow Wand—Bobbi Brown, "Rich Brown"
Cream Eye Shadow—Stila, "Lily"
Powder Blush—Stila, "Tint"
Lips—Stila, "Grapefruit" gloss and "Ava" lipstick

"Take this to the cosmetics department at Barneys," she said, handing me the slip of paper. "If you're still finding flaws, try upping your Zoloft."

I got the message. Enough with the Botox. Time to bury myself in my book. Other than my son's company during the week, I made virtually no contact with the outside world during the winter months. The hibernation was insufferable. My only breaks were occasional trysts with my contractor (his girlfriend had cut him off when he refused to leave his wife). Although our encounters temporarily revived my ability to whistle while I wrote, by spring I was ready to sing a different tune, one that would rise to the symphonic.

The overture began when my dog Joe had an epileptic seizure. Rushing him to an animal hospital, I asked Charlie, who was particularly empathetic since he suffered from the same neurological condition, to meet me there.

Although we still hadn't made any headway in our Ross–Rachel stalemate or discussed having another child after I'd expressed my desire at Dash's bar mitzvah, I had recently consulted a fertility specialist. At my age, I wanted to know whether or not my eggs had expired.

"I got the results from my blood test," I blurted to Charlie while we were waiting for the vet in an examining room. "Everything's normal. My FSH is 5.5."

"What are you talking about? What's FSH?"

"It's the hormone that stimulates the ovaries to produce eggs. Mine is in the ideal range but—"

"You're fertile?" he interrupted, smiling.

Instead of explaining that I'd still need artificial additives to get my eggs to hatch, I threw my arms around his shoulders. His response was unprecedented: He kissed me. And kissed. And kissed. A heart-pounding, thirst-quenching, teenage, wartime, fifteen-years-of-no-kissing kiss. Had the animal environment spurred Charlie's loss of inhibitions? And how far would he have gone if the vet hadn't caught us canoodling?

"Why did you smile when I told you about my fertility?" I asked Charlie, resuming our make-out session in the back of a cab, heading home after my dog was treated.

"Because it's something we're good at."

"Are you saying you want to?"

"There are a lot of steps that have to come first. We don't even live together."

I immediately contacted the divorce lawyer to whom I had paid a retainer long before. I'd kept her on retainer for the past eight years in anticipation of the dreaded time when I would need her services; now I decided it was finally safe to reclaim my money. I added it to the first installment of my book advance in order to pay for the Southampton summer rental. Owned by well-known authors, the house had good karma, a perfect place to finish my manuscript and begin anew with Charlie.

It was the first time I'd had the financial wherewithal to help fund our lifestyle. I wasn't just paying for my hair or clothes but rather something both of us would share. In truth, I was initially stung that he didn't tell me to put my pennies away. Wasn't it demeaning for him to allow me—a girl who earned a tenth of what he did—to crack open her piggy bank?

"It's weird," he said. "But I kind of like it."

I guess I liked it, too. My financial contribution made me feel responsible and capable, giving me a new sense of power. More than "adding a woman's touch to the home," I was bringing some bacon to it.

On my birthday, when Charlie and I returned to our house after the drive along Old Montauk Highway, my friends were preparing a Fourth of July feast. Dining alfresco on the patio now twinkling with tea-light candles, we ate steamed lobsters and corn-on-the-cob. Once the night air grew chilly and mosquitoes started to bite, the party moved inside. Standing around the kitchen, my girlfriends bestowed their gifts and Charlie presented a lemon coconut cake. Elated to end the festivities on a frosting high, I couldn't have imagined a greater rush still to come.

"Excuse me," he said, ducking from the room.

"I've never seen Charlie so completely happy," Andee whispered.

"You're really yourself with him." Mathilde sighed. "It's so nice to see someone love and appreciate you for who you are."

A few seconds later, he reappeared, prompting a collective gasp.

"Happy birthday," he said softly, handing me a shopping bag emblazoned CARTIER.

For as long as I could remember, presents had been a sore spot between us. Perhaps it had been my early disappointment at receiving ill-chosen items, like an electric lumbar massager or a silk teddy fit for a zeppelin-size Anna Nicole Smith, which had convinced Charlie I was a woman impossible to please. Whatever the inciting cause, he gave up trying.

But the extravagance he now tendered more than compensated for his history of empty-handedness. Inside the bag was a sizable jewelry box covered in Cartier's iconic red leather edged with gold garlands. When I popped the case, I couldn't believe my eyes. Stuck to the center of a plush white satin lining was a mini yellow Post-it inscribed with a handwritten note: "Whatever watch you want—Love, Charlie."

• • •

The first thing I did when I returned to the city after the holiday weekend was to try on every timepiece at Cartier. Stainless steel? Too sporty. Diamonds? Too flashy. Gold? Gold was good. It had weight, value, and durability, as well as a bright luster, which would soften over time, becoming more beautiful with age. Rejecting battery-operated quartz, I chose an automatic because it was everlasting. I'd found the bling equivalent to my relationship with Charlie.

Although I was excited to wear the watch, I didn't press him for it. It took a month before he actually gave it to me. Preoccupied with a corporate looting litigation, he couldn't get to the store to make the purchase for ten days. He then offered to drop it off with my doorman, but I wanted Charlie to present it in person. Because he had to travel out of town for his case, he missed a couple of weekends with me at the summer house. The next occasion we were together was in the Berkshires at our son's camp visiting day but Dash's father forgot to bring the bullion. Finally, in early August, we returned to Southampton for a three-day weekend where I awaited the bestowal with a loudly ticking heart.

Friday passed. Saturday came and went. By Sunday afternoon, still no watch. Had Charlie changed his mind? If so, he didn't show any signs. It was business as usual: He got up early in the morning to work; I wrote late into the night; we swam in the pool with my dogs; we drove around in his convertible.

Fearing he'd think me greedy, I didn't dare ask about the gift. It wasn't as if I'd expected or requested the watch in the first place. It was a gesture of love. Which made his withholding all the more confusing. Had I done something wrong?

"It's about control," Ruby analyzed when I sneaked a call to her after Charlie went out to run an errand. "He knows once he gives you the watch, he'll have to have sex with you."

It was true. Charlie and I hadn't had sex. Although we'd kissed, held hands, and groped a bit, we still hadn't done *it*. In fact, we'd been sleeping in separate bedrooms since the start of the summer.

We were taking it slowly, rediscovering each other after years of living apart, trying to avoid old patterns. I knew my sexual aggression turned him off so I was keeping it in check. Waiting for him to come to me, I was also protecting myself from rejection. A lot was riding on what would happen between the sheets. But then again, more was riding on what *wouldn't* happen between the sheets.

By Sunday night, it looked as if the only thing I'd be riding would be the remote control as I cable surfed for HBO.

"Two minutes to showtime," I called out to Charlie at eight fifty-eight from the living room couch where my dogs and I were cozily installed under a throw blanket.

"Have you forgotten this?" he asked, entering the room with another Cartier bag.

"Oh . . . wow . . . um . . . now?" I stammered, confused why he'd chosen the moment when *Six Feet Under* was about to start to finally give me the gift. "I thought we were planning to watch TV together. I don't want to miss the beginning or rush through opening my present. Do you mind if I wait till after?"

"Whatever." He swallowed, looking away.

"Come sit here," I said, patting the cushion beside me.

Two hours later, I was rubbing my hands together, warming them up for the feature presentation. Savoring every second, I carefully unwrapped the box, peeking under the lid. There it gleamed, the golden watch.

"Do you think it's time?" I suggested, checking out the chunk of Mr. T on my wrist.

"Time? For what?"

"Let's go upstairs and turn out the lights and get under the covers and have sex. Maybe we can find some whiskey around this place and you can take a shot and I'll pop a Xanax and then we won't be so nervous."

"I think we need to spend more time together so it comes more naturally, if you'll pardon the expression."

For an instant, I felt relieved, but then I was overwhelmed by disappointment. Why didn't he want to do it? Was I to blame? Did my glib remark about self-medicating hurt him? Oh, why hadn't I turned off the stupid TV?

Back in the city, I continued to anguish. After all my years with Charlie and all my screwing around, I was through with setups, booty calls, and swapping matchbooks with phone numbers scribbled inside. My only chance for a successful marriage would come from being totally devoted to it, a commitment I'd finally made, though I hadn't spelled it out to my husband. Since he was really and truly now the only guy in my life and I was "saving" myself for him, our state of "celibating" was leaving me sex-starved.

"Wake up, Charlie!" I cried into his answering machine at one in the morning, his prime time for sleep and mine to write. "I want to come over to your place and get into bed with you. I neeeeeeeeeeed you!"

Zzzzzzzzzzzzzzzzzzzzzzzzzzzzzzzzzzzzzzzzzzzzzzzzzzzzzzzzzzzzzzzzzzzz was his response.

The next day, when I logged onto my computer, the e-mail flag popped up:

```
Subj: Ode to My Assailant
Date: 8/4/2004 9:14:46 AM Eastern Standard Time
From: Charlie@aol.com
To: Elizabeth@aol.com
```

My mind was tormented this dawn by the rantings of a stalker on my message machine. It was not 'til the cock crowed that I heard her pleas as I was abed last night with my second love—the goddess of sleep. As was said by my cousin, the Danish prince: to sleep, perchance to dream, but alas, not to be jumped. Ay, there's the rub. This too shall be avenged.

Until then, dear mistress, I remain forever, your devoted (though somnolent) servant.

Who knew I'd married a troubadour? Instead of singing lyric poetry beneath my balcony, Charlie started wooing me through text messages. From my bedchamber, I replied with smutty quatrains delivered by high-speed modem.

Our supercharged verse was causing my chastity belt to tighten. I assumed my courtier's codpiece was swelling with a similar discomfort. Surely, our next rendezvous would climax in a release of the mounting tension.

But it didn't because there was no next rendezvous. At the last minute, Charlie begged off meeting me in Southampton, fearing he was catching a cold. I spent the weekend in the country alone with my dogs.

One week later, Dash came home. Taller, trimmer, and suntanned, he was quite the heartthrob. No wonder he'd landed a starring role as Danny Zuko in the camp production of *Grease*. Rumor had it that he was also a leading man in real life during his weeks away. Now back, he seemed lovelorn and blue. I was entirely sympathetic.

Much as I hated to admit it, my child's homecoming was bittersweet. Sure, I had missed Dash, but I no longer had Charlie to myself. One of the paradoxes of our marriage was that our son existed as both the welding and the wedge between us. Keeping our footless romance from him, Charlie and I didn't want to get his hopes up until things were settled between us. Now that Dash had returned, I knew my chances for intimacy with his father would go from slim to none.

In fact, it was only a matter of days before the two of them took off for Washington, DC, to visit one of Charlie's best friends and attend a streetball game. After that, they spent a week in Montauk, rollicking at an oceanfront resort for their annual end-of-August vacation.

Meanwhile, I was holed up in Southampton, trying to finish my book. Although the bulk of it was completed, the conclusion left me stumped. Sketching different versions, I couldn't settle on one. I began doubling back, rewriting earlier chapters and rearranging sentences. Spinning my wheels, I was making motion but without any forward movement; I was getting nowhere.

With fall around the corner, my manuscript deadline was closing in. I started to spiral into a serious panic. Working in an office in the house, I was too afraid of not completing my book to leave my computer. Because I didn't have a real-life ending, I couldn't finish the story. Staring at the cursor flashing against the blank screen, I sat there frozen, indifferent to the time of day, oblivious to whether the sun or moon was up. Although I felt hungry, I was too nauseous to eat. Despite being exhausted, I couldn't sleep. My eyes were burning, my head was aching, but time was running out. *Write, Elizabeth, write.*

Once I made a mental list of people I knew in the Hamptons who might be able to hook me up with some coke, I realized I'd better summon my personal EMS unit.

"I can't finish my book," I sobbed to Charlie, calling him in Montauk.

"You need to take a break," he comforted. "How about we come and visit?"

He and Dash drove to Southampton, where they spent Labor Day weekend with me. It turned into a three-day party after my son invited a couple of his camp friends to stay, too. They were upright teens, the kind who wouldn't swipe the car keys for a midnight joyride. When I caught them spying on a young woman next door who was sunbathing topless, it was a relief. At least they weren't total dweebs.

"This is the best," I said to Charlie, reclining beside me on a chaise, watching the boys barbecue burgers and dogs. "It feels great to have a full house. Do you think we can buy an apartment in the city that will be big enough for you, me, Dash, *and* all his friends?"

"We'd definitely need a lot of room," he answered. "Space is the key."

At the end of the weekend, our last at the house, we packed up and piled into my Jeep for the drive home. After dropping each of the boys off, as well as our son who was staying at his father's apartment that night, Charlie double-parked in front of my building.

"I already miss you," I said, my eyes misting. "I can't face my book. I don't know how to fix it or to end it."

"Maybe I can help. You're just too close to it. Do you want me to read it?"

Exhaling, I handed over my work.

• • •

The following week, on Monday afternoon, September 13, Charlie announced he was ready to finalize our divorce.

"Finalize our divorce?" I shrieked in disbelief. "What happened to our reconciliation?"

We were seated in a Sutton Place psychiatrist's office belonging to Dr. Alan Manevitz, a family therapist with whom Charlie and I had met before the summer to help with our marriage. We had been scheduled to see the doctor again after Labor Day, an appointment that turned out to be more urgent than I anticipated.

"I don't want a future together," Charlie said in the doctor's office.

"Why not?" I gurgled, feeling as if I'd been wading in a calm ocean when, out of nowhere, a tidal wave had swelled, knocking me into churning waters.

"The money, the fancy lifestyle. You want me to be someone I'm not."

"Why would you say that? I've told you over and over how incredible you are."

"It's not so much what you say, but the way you say it. You can be so hurtful."

"When? How? Whatever I did wrong, I can work on it. I love you. You're my best friend. My life. My everything. I wouldn't be who I am today without you. I'm not going to give up on us now. Not after all we've been through."

"It's precisely because of all we've been through that I don't want to do it anymore. You're my best friend, too, and I love you, but over the summer I realized that whatever was toxic about our relationship in the past is still there for me."

"Toxic? Why didn't you tell me this then? Why the watch and the e-mails? Why the talk about another child?"

"I had hopes. I wanted it to work out. The truth of the matter is, I should have ended it a long time ago but I didn't have the confidence, so I stayed with you since I'd already won you over, to a point. To make it work would require a hell of an effort but it seemed easier than starting fresh. It just wasn't sufficient to create physical intimacy."

"Are you saying you're not attracted to me?"

"You're a goddess, but what turns me on is someone who adores me. Someone who loves me for who I am. You can't give me that."

The wave hurled me to the shore, where I now lay, coughing and gasping.

"What I'm gathering," Dr. Manevitz interjected, "is that, Elizabeth, you always had one foot out the door in the relationship but now you've finally got both feet in it. You're prepared to take on the constructive criticism of Charlie and make the changes you need in order to be a couple but he's no longer willing to do that. Charlie, while half of you thought you wanted to get back together, in the process of trying, you changed. You're ready to move on."

How was it possible that I had come to the conclusion we were meant to be together, and he just the opposite? It was consummate proof that, although I'd known Charlie for nearly a quarter of a century, we'd never been on the same page. It didn't matter how much we loved each other; there had always been a gap between us, a rift in communication, imperceptible thorns preventing us from getting close.

Marriage wasn't the answer. Although it had bonded us as a family and given us our child, being husband and wife hadn't guaranteed that Charlie and I would grow together. We had evolved as individuals but not as a couple.

This was not the ending I wanted. In fact, I hadn't even allowed myself to envision it, yet I now had to ask myself: Was mine the hand that had ultimately let the curtain fall?

I had given Charlie my book. Sooner or later, he would have to read it. I needed to come clean. In order for our relationship to work, we would have to be honest and open. I wanted him to know what I'd done, who I'd been, and how I'd overcome my past. If he could forgive, accept, and love me after facing that truth, our future would be secure. Of course, what I—in all my self-absorption and idealization of Charlie as my Rock of Gibraltar—failed to consider was his transformation, too.

Just as writing about our relationship had forced me to relive both our lives and reappraise myself, perhaps his reading of it compelled him to do the same. Did my depiction provoke him to question how he'd lived his life and the decisions he'd made? Was it a catalyst for his rejection of me?

I hated to think I'd sabotaged my own happily-ever-after ending. But by accepting Charlie's offer to act as my editor, I invested him with a measure of creative control. No longer a passive character, he could exercise his will. He became a collaborator in authoring the completion of my story.

For the first time, Charlie didn't rewrite my words. He didn't have to—he altered the script by simply refusing to follow it. He asserted his independence when he turned down the role in which I'd cast him: my hero, the last man standing. In effect, he stole my ending, replacing it with his own, a revision rendering me, the protagonist, powerless.

But was the real me powerless, too?

After Charlie and I separated, I had lived out my adventures in the name of independence. But how authentic was my autonomy if I was able to tempt danger and toy with my own destruction, knowing there was no real risk because Charlie would still protect me? Even though we were no longer living together and he might have a girlfriend and not want to take me back, I believed he'd never turn his back. Not on me.

I was the mother of his child. More significantly, I had convinced myself that Charlie's love was eternal, an immutable truth on which I could always rely to keep me anchored. It steadied my insides when everything else went topsy-turvy. My faith in his commitment enabled me to brave a new world after we split up. I remained secure that he would never let my life go wrong.

Now Charlie was severing his ties to me, which meant he was also cutting my cords of dependency on him. He was setting me free and I had no choice but to fly solo, staying aloft on my own. In the end, returning to my hero hadn't proved I'd grown up and found my inner strength. But surviving without him would.

When Charlie and I left the shrink's office, it was dusk. He flagged a cab for me but I told him to take it, wherever he was going. Although it was only early September, the air had a slight snap, a hint of seasonal change. The freshness felt good against my face, which was sticky from crying, and helped clear my stuffy nose. Without any forethought, I followed my instincts, walking the mile and a half home.

I stopped before entering my building. It wasn't much to look at, the white brick facade unremarkable and dingy, but overall the place had been good to me. I associated it with more beginnings than endings. When Charlie and I first bought our apartment, we did so with the promise of a new life—our son. After my husband left, it was the place where I began my career as a writer, my bedroom doubling as my office. Now, once again, I was returning to start over.

The following day was Dash's first of tenth grade. There probably wasn't much for me to do but still, I felt I needed to get him settled. My dogs were surely hungry, whimpering in the kitchen, waiting to be fed. My mother was expecting me to call: The next saga of our endless conversation would be my divorce. By the time

I sat down to work on my book, the hour would be late and the night long. A lot lay ahead of me.

Crossing the lobby of my building, heading toward the elevator, I smiled out of habit at the doorman.

"Good evening, Mrs. . . . ," he greeted as always.

Normally, I paid no attention, but this time I stopped dead in my tracks, pivoting to face him.

"Instead of calling me *Mrs.*, would you please use my real name? Maybe you don't know it, but it's Elizabeth Hayt. H.A.Y.T. From now on, that's the only name I want to go by."